Melanie Klein and Critical Social Theory

C. Fred Alford

Melanie Klein and Critical Social Theory

An Account of Politics, Art, and Reason
Based on Her Psychoanalytic Theory

Yale University Press *New Haven and London*

Designed by James J. Johnson
and set in Melior Roman type by
dnh typesetting, inc., Cambridge, Massachusetts.
Printed in the United States of America by
BookCrafters, Inc., Chelsea, Michigan.

Library of Congress Cataloging-in-Publication Data

Alford, C. Fred.
    Melanie Klein and critical social theory: an account of politics, art, and reason
based on her psychoanalytic theory / C. Fred Alford.
        p.   cm.
    Bibliography: p.
    Includes index.
    ISBN 0–300–04506–9 (alk. paper)
    1. Psychoanalysis and culture. 2. Klein, Melanie. 3. Reparation (Psychoanalysis)—
Social aspects. 4. Civilization, Modern—20th century—Psychological aspects.
5. Social psychology. I. Title.
BF175.4.C84A4   1989
150.19′5′092—dc20   89–8903
                                                                             CIP

The paper in this book meets the guidelines for
permanence and durability of the Committee on
Production Guidelines for Book Longevity of the
Council on Library Resources.

10   9   8   7   6   5   4   3   2   1

Contents

Preface

My first reaction to Melanie Klein was that I could not imagine a psychoanalyst whose work is less relevant to social theory. This is not only because she, unlike Freud, never developed the social implications of her teachings beyond a few brief, scattered remarks. It is also because her categories are about a private, internal world, far removed from the public world we normally inhabit. Gradually it came to me, however, that this is really the strength of her theory. My task, as I see it, has been not to make her categories more social and relational (enough object relations theorists, as they are called, have done this already) but rather to show how the inner world she describes helps to make the outer world we all live in.

"Reparation and Civilization" was my working title for this book, but my editor tells me, correctly, I am sure, that this is insufficiently descriptive. I mention it here because the working title captures the spirit with which I began the project: to write a Kleinian version of Herbert Marcuse's *Eros and Civilization,* which is Marcuse's radical reworking of Freud's *Civilizatioh and Its Discontents.* As the book developed, however, I began to find this approach somewhat confining, and the current title actually better reflects my interests. Nevertheless, my original way of looking at Klein has remained a guiding principle: to show how her work might answer some of the questions with which the Frankfurt School of Critical Theory was concerned, questions they could not adequately answer, owing in part to the limitations of Freudian psychoanalysis. Many of my answers, it will become apparent, are not those that members of the Frankfurt School would have found very attractive, and I do not claim to have been true to the spirit of their work in this regard. Yet I do think I have been true to the spirit of their approach to psychoanalysis, which always appreciated that it was the most private, personal, and apparently least social aspects of individual psychology that were actually the most important in explaining both individual and group life.

A Senior Fulbright Research Fellowship to the Federal Republic of Germany provided me with the freedom and change of pace necessary to write parts of this book. Professor Hans Albert at the Universitaet Mannheim was once again my gracious host, and Herr Dr. Volker Stittgen's seminar on "Kunst und Erkenntnis" helped me organize my thoughts on chapter 4, "Art and Reparation." To walk directly from this seminar to the Kunsthalle Mannheim, which has a nice collection of nineteenth- and twentieth-century art, was a treat.

My colleague Jim Glass remains an inspiration. Another colleague, Steve Elkin, read an earlier version of the manuscript (all but the art chapter). He is a tough customer and made a number of helpful suggestions, especially regarding the relationship between my concerns and the more usual concerns of political theory. Thomas Cimonnetti continues to render assistance. Elaine Feder Alford, my wife, helped me with the material on role theory in chapter 3. And the students in my spring 1988 graduate seminar in group psychology helped me write the book.

CHAPTER ONE

Melanie Klein as a Social Theorist?

The implications of a single question guide this book: What would be the consequences for social theory and philosophy if the psychoanalytic theory of Melanie Klein is correct? Often I address this guiding question by means of a slightly more precise one: What would a Kleinian version of Herbert Marcuse's *Eros and Civilization* look like? Would her psychoanalytic theory allow us to address the same social, political, aesthetic, and philosophical issues that Marcuse addresses using Freud's? Would her theory allow us to make progress on these issues? I answer yes to both questions. To take Klein seriously is not necessarily to take her literally. At several points I differ with her position in decisive respects. Taking Klein seriously means developing the implications of her thought as consistently and thoroughly as possible, even when these implications are troubling. In other words, I have tried not to flinch.

Quite unlike Freud, Melanie Klein failed to develop the social and philosophical implications of her psychoanalytic theory beyond a few brief, scattered remarks. Some Kleinian analysts, such as R. E. Money-Kyrle and Elliott Jaques, have made a start on such a theory, and Dorothy Dinnerstein has drawn upon Klein to explain "sexual arrangements and the human malaise." At various points I consider these and the relatively few other authors who have used Klein to better understand large groups. Much of my work is necessarily foundational, however, demonstrating that Kleinian psychoanalysis does indeed have social and philosophical implications. One reason Klein's work has not been drawn upon more freely by social theorists is probably that her categories seem so private, internal, and personal. Unlike those object relations theorists whose work has found a greater resonance among social theorists, such as W. R. D. Fairbairn, Harry Guntrip, and D. W. Winnicott, Klein set up categories that are not obviously and immediately social and relational.

I do not seek to overthrow this impression of Klein. Quite the contrary. Theodor Adorno was correct when he stated that psychology is most valuable when it focuses on the psychic sources of individual distress. "The further it departs from this area, the more tyrannically it has to proceed and the more it has to drag what belongs to the dimension of outer reality into the shades of psychic immanence."[1] Rather than argue that Klein's categories are already social and relational, I contend that they have social and philosophical implications. This is something different from attempting to transform her psychoanalytic categories into social ones from the very beginning. It is the difference between psychology and sociology.

Klein and the Frankfurt School of Critical Theory

Historically there was no contact at all between Klein and the Frankfurt School of Critical Theory, whose leading members were Theodor Adorno, Max Horkheimer, and Herbert Marcuse. This is so even as their dates overlap. Klein was a contemporary of Anna Freud and, like the Freuds, left Germany for England prior to the outbreak of World War II (Klein's father was a student of the Talmud, her mother the daughter of a rabbi). For a number of years during and immediately after the war, Klein was the leading intellectual force in the British Psycho-Analytical Society, at that time the most influential psychoanalytic society in the world.[2] Her seminal paper "A Contribution to the Psychogenesis of Manic-Depressive States" appeared in 1935, twenty years prior to Marcuse's publication of *Eros and Civilization.*[3]

Yet, the Frankfurt School, deeply interested in psychoanalysis, showed no awareness of her work. The reasons are complex, but the most important is surely that in America, where most of the members of the Frankfurt School found haven, psychoanalysis had taken a different turn than in England. American psychoanalysts such as Karen Horney and H. S. Sullivan had abandoned much of Freudian instinct theory, particularly the *Todestrieb* (death instinct), for an approach that instead stressed the virtues of maturity and social integration. At the same time in England, however, Klein and her followers, such as Joan Riviere and Susan Isaacs, were applying developments in Freud's late metapsychology (precisely those developments that Marcuse turns to in *Eros and Civilization*, such as Freud's speculations about life and death "beyond the pleasure principle") in a clinical setting, using this experience to develop Freud's theory further. It was as though two ships of émigrés had passed in the night.

It probably would not be fruitful to speculate about what might have happened had the Frankfurt School learned of the work of Klein and her followers. One suspects, however, that they would have found her work difficult to integrate with their theories.[4] Both Klein and Freud are antiutopians; but because Klein's categories are more descriptive and less philosophical than Freud's, the Frankfurt School would have considered them more difficult to "sublate" into the ground of utopia. Yet, while the Frankfurt School might have had difficulty integrating her work with theirs, this is no reason not to make the attempt. One reason is because Klein's categories are really those of the Frankfurt School as well. Though Marcuse in particular writes of a desublimated Freudian eros as the alternative to instrumental reason, he is actually concerned with a much more complex and subtle set of alternatives than eros versus technological logos—alternatives that are also reflected in Klein's account.

Juergen Habermas, a second-generation member of the Frankfurt School, has characterized the project of the school as an attempt to speak for those who cannot speak for themselves: victims of injustice and oppression who have suffered and died.[5] It is to this theme, not to eros, that Marcuse turns at the conclusion of *Eros and Civilization*, arguing that suffering, premature death, "the unredeemable guilt of mankind" (who so often could have caused it to be otherwise), the remembrance of those who suffered, and even their redemption are the fundamental concerns of critical social theory. *Eros and Civilization* concludes with these lines: "But even the ultimate advent of freedom cannot redeem those who died in pain. It is the remembrance of them, and the accumulated guilt of mankind against its victims, that darken the prospect of a civilization without repression."[6]

These are the themes—greed, hatred, aggression, the guilt that these ugly passions evoke, and the attempt to make reparation for the damage they cause—that guide Klein's work. And they are the same themes that recur in the Frankfurt School's attempt to reformulate humanity's relationship to nature, as well as the concept of reason on which this relationship is based. Klein and the Frankfurt School speak the same language, even if they did not speak it to each other.

Eros or Love?

Why does Marcuse not just come out and say it: the goal is a society in which love triumphs over hate, and for love to do so it must gain pleasure from the welfare of others, sometimes even sacrifice for them? Instead, Marcuse tries to derive these ideals from eros. The answer has to do in part with the role of eros in founding a biological basis for socialism, as Marcuse calls it, and in part with a reductive tradition within psychoanalysis, in which eros comes to include every relationship of care, concern, esteem, and affection. There are not qualitatively different types of love, only degrees of inhibition of original aim. Freud, and presumably Marcuse, sees such a comprehensive view of love as an advantage: "As for the 'stretching' of the concept of sexuality . . . anyone who looks down with contempt upon psychoanalysis from a superior vantage point should remember how closely the enlarged sexuality of psychoanalysis coincides with the Eros of the divine Plato."[7]

But this is precisely the problem. Plato addressed in a systematic and literary manner an insight that most Greeks were quite at home with (Hesiod, *Theogony*, lines 115–125; Euripides, *Hippolytos*, lines 1–64; Sophocles, *Antigone*, lines 782–797): namely, that eros is single-minded and often greedy in its pursuit of pleasure. Even in praising eros, Plato has Socrates stress the way in which eros wants not merely to experience beauty but to own, possess, and control it, now and forever (*Symposium*, 203b–e). Socrates goes on to employ an interesting personification. The father and mother of Eros, he says, are Contrivance and Poverty. For this reason, Eros is always poor and, far from being sensitive and beautiful, is hard, weather-beaten, shoeless, and homeless, like his mother. As his father's son, however, he schemes to get what is beautiful. He is bold, always devising tricks, a lover of wisdom, a magician, a true sophist

(203b–e). Eros, it appears, is so intensely needy that he can never be satisfied, and so desperate that he will scheme and deceive to get all he can, and more. Too much is never enough. Plato's *Phaedrus*, his other great dialogue on eros, is really no different, only more subtle. As Charles Griswold points out, the Socratic lover loves another in order to realize his own perfection, wholeness, and beauty most fully. The value placed by the lover on the unique individuality of the beloved is secondary (*Phaedrus*, 250b–257b).[8]

Eros, it appears, is not truly concerned with the object—the person—in itself, but only with the object as it is, or may become, a source of satisfaction to human needs and desires. If this is so, how in the world can the project of the Frankfurt School, a project based upon concern for those who cannot meet or defend their own legitimate needs, be successfully grounded in eros? The psychoanalyst Donald Meltzer compares the Freudian view of love with a capital investment aimed at profit making. You do not invest your libido unless you hope to get back more than you give. "You cannot exactly think of yourself as a benefactor of mankind when, by loving, you set up a factory, as it were, rather than endowing a charity."[9] Since it is often the case that those who suffer cannot give back anything (and those who have died never will), why bother investing in them? To feel better about oneself, one might argue in reply. But there are so many more pleasant ways of accomplishing that than confronting suffering and guilt, and eros is an expert in finding every one of them.

Posing the problem confronted by the Frankfurt School in terms of the selfishness of eros does not imply an alien perspective, one that creates a problem only by drawing upon a different theoretical perspective. To the contrary, the Frankfurt School was very much aware of the limits of Freudian libidinal hydraulics. They simply did not have an alternative, because any alternative seemed to require abandonment of what they found so fruitful in Freud: depth psychology, by which they meant the instinct theory. (Although in his later works Freud developed a different model of love, based on identification, we shall see that identification suits the program of the Frankfurt School even less well than eros.) Although she never admits it, Klein in effect abandons Freudian instinct theory. Does this make her a revisionist? Not really, for it is not instinct theory per se that the Frankfurt School found so valuable but rather the insight that humans are motivated by passions so profound that they will never be thoroughly socialized or co-opted. Klein only strengthens this view.

The Truth of Freud . . . and That of Klein

The Frankfurt School's attraction to Freudian instinct theory should not, as suggested above, be interpreted as implying that they simply believed it to be true. Their view of the truth of Freud's theories was more complex than this. As Max Horkheimer put it in a letter to Leo Lowenthal, in an attempt to characterize the Frankfurt School's "official" position on Freud, "Even when we do not agree with Freud's interpretation and use of them [the drives], we find their objective intention is deeply right and that they betray Freud's great flair for the situation."[10] Horkheimer found it "deeply right" because Freud's drive theory expressed the unalterable opposition between actual human needs and a historical world that demands suppression of these needs as the apparent price of survival.

The greatness of Freud, stated Adorno in "Die revidierte Psychoanalyse," consisted in his letting such contradictions as that between human nature and society's needs remain unresolved. He refused "to pretend a systematic harmony when the subject itself is rent."[11] Unlike Horkheimer and Adorno, Marcuse seeks to transcend this unalterable opposition between man and world, as is well known. This should require no compromise with the instincts, however; rather, the world would itself be utterly transformed, so as to meet every human need. In sum, the position of the Frankfurt School seems to have been that if one interprets Freud's drive theory as an account of human nature that stands outside history (Marcuse suggests that Freud need not be interpreted in such a fashion[12]), then it is literally false. Nevertheless, Freud's theory serves a progressive purpose, calling attention to the intense, socially oppositional character of eros, as well as the repressiveness of modern society that makes even the most successful life seem to want to terminate in death (the apparent result of the *Todestrieb*). As usual, Adorno put it most succinctly, arguing against Erich Fromm that "in the age of the concentration camp, castration is more characteristic of social reality than competitiveness."[13]

My approach to the truth of Kleinian theory is somewhat different. The Frankfurt School seems to regard Freud as factually mistaken in fundamental respects but nevertheless correct in the *tendenz* (ideological tendency) he gives to social theory. I regard Klein's fundamental principles as factually correct but many of the details (whereas a strict Kleinian might not regard these as mere "details" at all) as unnecessarily specific—indeed, misleading in their specificity. Somewhat vague as an abstract declaration, this point should become clearer in chapter 2, in which I examine Klein's theory in detail. Thus, when I employ phrases such as "Kleinian social theory," one might more accurately read "Kleinian-inspired social theory," the degree of inspiration varying according to the particular issue being discussed. Though I disagree with several aspects of Dinnerstein's interpretation of Klein in *The Mermaid and the Minotaur*, her fundamental approach seems correct. One can regard certain details, such as Klein's elaborate account of the phantasies of the nursing infant, as metaphorical without abandoning Kleinian theory per se. In a justly famous remark, Adorno states that "in psychoanalysis nothing is true except the exaggerations."[14] Klein's "exaggerations" are found not in her account of the world of internal object relations (these are just details) but in her thesis that we make the world by projecting our love and hate into it.

David Pope has what I consider the most productive approach to Klein, arguing that one can frequently ignore the nouns and adjectives; the real action is with the verbs.[15] By this he means that the actual content of the child's phantasies, to which Klein devotes an enormous amount of detailed attention, is not central. For example, Klein devotes a great deal of attention to the "good breast" and the "bad breast." She sometimes seems to mean the actual breast, sometimes something more abstract, like the infant's emotional attitude toward the mother at a particular moment, which is represented by the idea of the good breast. Klein, however, does not always distinguish the two, tending to identify an emotional state with the content of the phantasy that it presumably evokes. In telling us to focus on the verbs, Pope is telling us to focus on the emotional action that is occurring at the particular moment—for example, "The child loves the mother now, but when he is frustrated he hates her." Those reading Klein for the first time are commonly put off by the detailed phantasy world she describes—possibly because she has captured an important truth, and confronting it makes us uncomfortable. But surely it is not this simple. Sometimes Klein seems to be reducing emotional experience itself to the content of particular phantasies and in so doing loses the global character of the original emotional experience.

I pay attention to the verbs by focusing on the passions with which Klein is concerned. Love and hate are the preeminent passions. The other powerful emotions, such as envy, gratitude, guilt, grief, and mourning, may be seen as versions and combinations of the two master passions. It is these passions, and the fear and conflict that these overpowering feelings may evoke, that impel individuals to employ the psychological defense mechanisms with which Klein is concerned, such as splitting, projective identification, idealization, and manic denial. To see the passions in this light suggests an important point. They are in many respects functionally similar to the drives, both in the way they produce experience and in the way they evoke defenses against the conflicts they generate.

Freud writes of the drives as making a demand upon the mind for work.[16] Similarly, the *Oxford English Dictionary* defines the experience of passion as one in which an external force, an overpowering emotion, makes a demand upon the mind. We "suffer" passions, in the original sense of the term, because passions so often seem to make demands that throw us into conflict (for example, the hate we may feel for someone we love), just as the drives do. It is on this aspect of Klein's account that I focus, an aspect that connects her work to that part of Freud's that the Frankfurt School found so valuable: the demanding, not readily civilized nature of the drives. Does this mean that I too ultimately choose Klein for the *tendenz* she gives social theory? No, for while the Frankfurt School did not accept the truth of the drives, I embrace the truth of the passions. It is they that make the world go around.

Taking Klein seriously is not the same thing as taking her literally or accepting everything she has to say as true. Taking her seriously means distinguishing between what is valuable and what is not, and being very clear about what one is accepting and what one is rejecting. At several points, particularly in my discussion of Kleinian (that is, Kleinian-inspired) aesthetic theory, I shall argue that the Kleinian account is fundamentally mistaken about a particular issue. I shall then attempt to correct it. This shows more respect for an

original thinker than does the hagiography that sometimes characterizes attempts to apply the psychoanalytic ideas of famous analysts. In the last part of chapter 6 the issue of psychoanalytic revisionism is addressed. At this point it will become clear, if it is not
already, that the dangers of revisionism stem not from the explicit
rejection of aspects of a psychoanalytic theory but rather from the
attempt to conceal fundamental differences, as though a psychoanalytic account were compatible with virtually any conclusion.

The Four Rs

The social theory inspired by Melanie Klein addresses four issues
with which the Frankfurt School was especially concerned: (1) to
make *reparation* for millions (no, billions) of human lives shattered
by greed, aggression, and fear; (2) to *remember* and memorialize the
suffering of those who cannot be made whole again; (3) to *reform
reason,* in order to make it less instrumental and domineering; and
(4) to *reconcile* with nature in recompense for its domination by
men and women. I shall call these the four Rs. Each R, it is apparent,
deals with the costs of human hatred and aggression. Yet, while
Klein addresses the key concerns of the Frankfurt School, she does
so from the perspective of love and concern rather than of eros.
While much of the next chapter will be devoted to explaining what
Klein means by love, and contrasting love with eros, it may be helpful here to offer a preliminary definition.

The concept of love and reparation developed by Klein is captured well by the term *caritas,* a term that Klein herself does not use.
Defined as affection, love, or esteem, the term connotes the value of
the object loved rather than the intensity of desire. Thus, a Latin
dictionary will usually give the first definition of *caritas* as dearness
or high price. *Amor* may be used of animals, whereas *caritas* applies
only to human relations. While the Greek *eros* may be rendered by
the Latin *amor, caritas* has a richer set of connotations than the
Greek *philia.* The Greek *agape* comes closer but carries so many
additional connotations that it is best avoided.

Klein's focus on love rather than eros is not without costs—costs
that the Frankfurt School, especially Marcuse, might not have been
willing to pay. Eros is a source of opposition to and transcendence of
the prevailing order, a bulwark of the "Great Refusal." It is these

attributes of eros that led the Frankfurt School to embrace Freud, even when they considered him literally mistaken. Love, in the Kleinian tradition, is less oppositional than eros (though it is also less liable to corruption, what Marcuse called "repressive desublimation") and more inclined to come to terms with imperfect people and an imperfect world. Yet, if this is so, why turn to love, especially if one takes the concerns of the Frankfurt School seriously? Because many of these concerns are not adequately addressed by eros, no matter how sublimated. Love can solve certain theoretical problems—certain aporias—in critical theory that cannot be solved by eros. Eros, as the Frankfurt School was quite aware, is fundamentally selfish. This makes it a powerful source of opposition. It does not make it a very good vehicle by which to address the four Rs. Yet, the four Rs are at least as central to the program of the Frankfurt School as are opposition and transcendence, to which they are closely related in any case.

Whether the gains of a Kleinian approach are worth the costs (and there are other costs yet to be reckoned with) only the reader can decide. While neither a society based upon Kleinian ideals nor one based upon Marcuse's seems likely to be realized soon (if ever), a society based upon *caritas* is one I find more attractive than one based upon eros. This, though, is not the primary reason I have chosen Klein. It is rather because I believe that her fundamental psychological assumptions are correct. The Frankfurt School was aware of the limits of eros but lacked the theoretical resources in psychoanalytic theory to construct an alternative. Klein provides this alternative, while avoiding the "Neo-Freudian revisionism" the Frankfurt School so carefully sought to avoid. For example, of all the psychoanalysts to follow Freud, none took the *Todestrieb*—and aggression generally—more seriously than Klein. Not only does Klein value even harsh truths over utopian ideals of harmonious integration of individual and society, but she also constructs a theory whose implications are essentially tragic, especially for the group.

Klein's account is tragic in three senses of the term:

1. Martha Nussbaum argues that the *katharsis* of pity and fear, part of Aristotle's definition of tragedy, refers not to emotional purging but to a *clarification* of these emotions.[17] Pity and fear are also the key Kleinian categories. Pity, for Klein, is expressed by making

reparation for the harm we have caused others. And fear is ultimately fear of our own aggression and hatred, which threaten to destroy those we love. Klein clarifies these emotions, showing how they motivate almost all human conduct and in so doing create a world. I seek to show how these emotions, and the world they make, may be used to clarify the conduct of groups as well.

2. The Kleinian account is tragic in the sense that it reveals a greater discrepancy between individual and group morality than one sees in Freud. Kleinian theory reveals that individuals have a greater potential to care unselfishly and to sacrifice for others than Freud thought possible. At the same time, Kleinian group theory is at least as harsh and pessimistic as Freud's. It is this greater discrepancy between individual potential and group realization that is tragic.

3. From a Kleinian perspective, morality has to do with the victory of love over hate. Even in mature and well-integrated individuals, however, this balance is always fragile and temporary, liable to be tilted toward hatred by stress and loss. It is the fragility of this balance, its vulnerability to external events, that is tragic.

These three senses of the tragic in the Kleinian viewpoint are present in each chapter. They are addressed most thematically, however, in chapter 4, which deals with Kleinian aesthetic theory.

Possible Preliminary Objections

Freud refers to the "overdetermination" of symptoms, in which different desires, conflicts, and beliefs may be expressed in the same symptom.[18] The possibility that some of these desires, conflicts, and beliefs, particularly as they pertain to the group, are better explained by other, nonpsychoanalytic accounts cannot be excluded in advance. However, a common misunderstanding exists regarding this issue that can now be corrected. It is mistaken to assume that a psychoanalytic account is necessarily in competition with more institutionally oriented accounts of group life, so that only one can be correct. For instance, everything Max Weber says about bureaucracy may be true. Yet, this does not mean that a psychoanalytic account, which sees bureaucracy as a defense against threats to the self posed by the group, is false. Both are true; the psychoanalytic function (defense) works through the institutional function (the coordination

of action). One might call this the 100% + 100% solution, as opposed to the intuitive (and false) belief that these accounts are competitive—that is, if an institutional account explains 80 percent of
what is going on, then a psychoanalytic account can explain no
more than 20 percent.

My goal, in any case, is not to show that Klein's is the only
plausible account of group conduct. Rather, it is to demonstrate that
a Kleinian account reveals aspects of group conduct that are not
adequately attended to by other accounts but which upon consideration seem important and in need of explanation. By group conduct
I include the cultural products of groups, such as art and philosophy. Showing that a Kleinian account can solve some problems
that the Frankfurt School could not, primarily because the school
remained too bound to a Freudian account of eros, is one way of
demonstrating this.

One of the most difficult objections to address is that Klein's
account (or the precepts of psychoanalysis generally), in the words
of her critics, "just doesn't seem plausible to me"; or that these ideas
"all seem so farfetched." This is such a difficult objection in part
because in spite of the efforts of Adolf Grünbaum and a few others, it
is almost impossible to corroborate or disprove the findings of
psychoanalysis.[19] In addition, the critic is often talking not about
a specific psychoanalytic claim but about the larger psychoanalytic worldview, which he or she presumably finds wanting vis-à-vis
another—be it Marxism, game theory, structural-functionalism,
or whatever. Against such total criticism, which must be taken seriously, albeit not too seriously—that is, it should not stop the holder
of the psychoanalytic worldview in his tracks—I offer these observations.

First, even comprehensive criticism must be what Germans call
wohlwollend, or well-meaning, if it is to be worth responding to.
This means that the criticism must see some point in the project,
some possibility that the assumptions are correct, or correctable.
The psychoanalytic approach, more than most others, seems to generate a large number of especially intransigent critics (a phenomenon for which the analyst always has a ready explanation!). To
those who find the concept of a dynamic unconscious with its own
laws—laws that powerfully impinge upon every aspect of life—so
improbable as to be not worth considering, there is little to say.

For those critics who are *wohlwollend*, but unconvinced, I

employ two argumentative strategies. First, I demonstrate that the approach of the Frankfurt School, which builds its psychoanalytic social theory on Freudian eros, is incoherent, given their goals. Klein's account, on the other hand, is not incoherent but fits their goals. If she is correct, she would successfully address problems the Frankfurt School took seriously but could not solve. Second, I interpret Klein's theory as an account of the passions, so as to show how the conflict of love and hate makes a world. Such an account transcends psychoanalysis, in so far as most great art and literature concern the same topic. Klein is thus connected, in my approach, to nonpsychoanalytic accounts of subjectivity that many find compelling. Another way to convince well-meaning critics is to show how the concepts of psychoanalysis illuminate the traditional concerns of social theory. It is to this demonstration that I now turn, showing how the currently influential critique of liberal individualism makes a number of tacit assumptions about the self, assumptions that psychoanalysis addresses explicitly and critically.

The Socially Constituted Self?

Since the Frankfurt School first turned to Freud, psychoanalytic social theory has developed in several different directions. One seeks to redefine the nature of the individual and in so doing to challenge liberalism. On the Continent, and in literary circles in the United States, this path has emphasized the deconstruction of the myth of autonomous individuality. Jacques Lacan's psychoanalytic theory is a key source for this project. Among social theorists in England and the United States, this path has taken a somewhat different direction. The focus has been upon using psychoanalysis to reconstitute (rather than to abandon as mythic) the idea of individuality, showing the individual to be essentially social or relational in nature, so that his very self depends upon the selves of others. This view is employed to criticize liberalism, understood as a philosophy that places highest emphasis on the rights of autonomous, generally competitive, acquisitive individuals. This criticism has a long history, reaching back to Plato's attempt (*Republic*, 462b–466d) to give his guardians a socially constituted self and thereby to overcome the effects of individualism, greed, and faction that seemed to be destroying Athens. Recently, however, this program has been given impetus by Michael Sandel's *Liberalism and the Limits of Justice*.

Sandel argues that John Rawls' *A Theory of Justice*, the single most influential work of liberal social theory in many decades, postulates a view of the self so pale, vague, and insubstantial that its rights are hardly worth protecting. Sandel contends that such a view "makes the individual inviolable only by making him invisible."[20] For Rawls, the individual appears to have no personality, no tastes, no attributes, no passions: he is little more than a shade. In fact, says Sandel, Rawls covertly—and inconsistently—holds to a more substantial view of the individual, in which one's attributes (such as skills, talents, and abilities) are sometimes seen as an essential part of his being, even as these attributes also belong to the community. The reason this substantial view of the self is obscured, suggests Sandel, is because it is a view in which the self is in key respects merged with others, so that "the relevant description of the self may embrace more than a single empirically-individuated human being."[21] Put simply, if we regard an individual's attributes as something to be shared with the community, and then reject the official Rawlsian position that attributes are separate from the self, then the self becomes something to be shared with the community as well.

To be sure, Sandel recognizes the risks of making the boundaries of the self too permeable, a risk that may lead to what he euphemistically calls the "radically situated subject." Nevertheless, Sandel sees the socially constituted self as the solution to the problem of liberal individualism. The problem, to put it succinctly, is a competitive individualism that sees others primarily as means, leading to a society in which egoism, greed, faction, alienation, and withdrawal from public life predominate. The solution is that the individual define himself in terms of his membership in a community, a solution that—if it is to be as thoroughgoing as Sandel intends— seems to require extending the boundaries of the self to include others.

Sandel's book has generated considerable debate (including the charge that it is an invitation to fascism) that does not need to be considered here. Only one issue is relevant: While the concept of the socially constituted self is central to Sandel's project, his book contains virtually no analysis of what this term might mean. Not only does Sandel not turn to psychoanalysis or psychology, neither does he turn to what is politely called philosophical anthropology: speculation cum anthropological or historical research regarding human nature. Nor does he turn to art or literature. Sandel treats the concept of the socially constituted self as if it were a strictly formal assumption, a postulate necessary for the solution of a theoretical problem in social theory, but having no existence outside this particular context. The self becomes an arbitrary constant: whatever it takes to derive a community from separate individuals. Others have seen this gap in Sandel's account—or they have seen it in the critique of liberalism generally, which amounts to the same thing—and have sought to fill it in. Indeed, this is the concern of most psychoanalytic social theory today. The title of a recent essay by Nancy Chodorow, "Toward a Relational Individualism: The Mediation of Self Through Psychoanalysis," captures perfectly the spirit of this project.[22] Another even more programmatic attempt to fill in this gap is criticized below, that of Jeffrey Abramson in *Liberation and Its Limits: The Moral and Political Thought of Freud*, an attempt that transforms Freud into a theorist of love and community. First, however, the relationship between my use of Klein and the project of founding a socially constituted self should be discussed.

My approach to psychoanalysis is less instrumental than that of Chodorow or Abramson. Rather than use Klein to fill in the gaps in a particular social theory, I ask how a Kleinian account might explain the empirical conduct of groups. That is, I derive an account of group life from Klein, rather than use her account to fill in another. I do this by developing her concept of the individual, paying particular attention to assumptions about the individual that might influence how he interacts with others. I then derive (in a thoroughly informal fashion) a Kleinian group theory from these assumptions, taking pains to see if it seems to explain the reality of life in large groups. Since several psychoanalysts influenced by Klein have written about group life, these derivations are subject to correction. Because my primary theoretical concern is not the critique of liberalism, but problems in the Frankfurt School's use of Freud (of course, the Frankfurt School was also critical of liberalism; yet they extended their criticism to include Western thought generally, and it is this that I focus on), the issue of the socially constituted self is not systematically addressed. After developing the Kleinian account as fully as possible, however, I do, in the final chapter, address the implications of her thought for this issue in two ways. First, I reinterpret Rawls' *Theory of Justice* from a Kleinian perspective, arguing that what Rawls calls the original position can fruitfully be interpreted in terms of what Klein calls the paranoid-schizoid position.

While undoubtedly one-sided, Rawls' view of the individual is nonetheless more substantial than Sandel's view, as Rawls appreciates the intensity of our fear and greed as well as the way in which these emotions threaten to remake the world in their image. It is the purpose of his solution to the problem of justice to prevent this from happening. Second, I address the problem of the socially constituted self to develop a critique of what I call "object relations revisionism." In order to render the self more social and less acquisitive and individualistic, authors such as Nancy Chodorow and Jessica Benjamin have turned to a largely British school of psychoanalysis called Object Relations Theory, founded by Melanie Klein; but their approach to this school risks transforming psychoanalysis into social psychology. The title of this section is intended to evoke the epilogue of Marcuse's *Eros and Civilization*, entitled "Critique of Neo-Freudian Revisionism." Unlike Marcuse's, however, my concern is not so much that these authors end up sacrificing liberation for adaptation, but that they treat psychoanalysis as a means to a new order whose insights need not be adhered to in the theoretical construction of the new order itself. Such criticism would, of course, also apply to Marcuse.

Liberation and the Limits of Freudian Psychoanalysis

No one has seen the gap in Sandel's account of the self more clearly, nor sought to fill it in more programmatically, than Jeffrey Abramson in *Liberation and Its Limits*, a title evidently intended to evoke Sandel's book.[23] I address Abramson's book here because it fosters a misunderstanding of the relationship between individual psychoanalysis and group psychology, a misunderstanding that must be corrected before one can even begin to construct an adequate psychoanalytic social theory. Abramson begins his book by thanking Sandel, who supported Abramson's insight that "Freud's vision of human liberation must be distinguished from the pale individualism dominant in our culture."[24] About this Abramson is surely correct. There is nothing pale about Freud's view of the individual or individualism. Freud's individual is wracked by desire, guilt, hatred, fear, and aggression, which threaten to tear him and the groups to which he belongs apart. Furthermore, Abramson recognizes that in Freud's later works particularly these emotions came to be defined in terms of how they enable the individual to relate to others. Instinctual desires reflect not merely tension within the organism that seeks an outlet but serve to establish relations with others. In the jargon of psychoanalysis, these emotions are object-related from the very beginning of life. Identification, the most primitive expression of eros, is a good example. Identification makes no conceptual sense unless it is understood in relational terms—one individual identifying with a particular other. Similarly, Freud redefined sexuality. Rather than see it as an urge to use the other to reduce the level of tension within oneself, Freud came to define eros as the drive for unification with another, in which pleasure is experienced even from the effort of extending oneself toward another.[25]

These changes in Freud's thought are important in understanding Melanie Klein, whose work is indeed founded on a relational view of the drives and emotions. One could even argue that these aspects of Freud's thought allow one to see psychoanalysis as a moral science, in so far as psychoanalysis transcends a strictly instrumental view of human relationships, one in which others are little more than objects by means one reduces tensions. What these changes do not do is establish a basis for genuine community. Abramson's key argument is that identification is "an augury of more liberating sorts of human attachment," based upon what people share, rather than what they can get from each other, as in liberal communities.[26] Freud would, of course, agree that identification may be the basis of community, an argument he advances in *Group Psychology and the Analysis of the Ego*. The question is, What kind of community? According to Freud it is a community in which the individual's "liability to affect becomes extraordinarily intensified, while his intellectual ability is markedly reduced, both processes being evidently in the direction of an approximation to the other individuals in the group."[27]

Abramson's response to Freud's assessment is straightforward and gives the game away: "But to find that our personal identity is politically movable and indeed comes to 'approximate' the character of the community in which we live is not necessarily to experience the kind of deindividuation that Freud feared."[28] Either Abramson is prepared to trade off individual identity for community, or he has found sources of support for individual identity within communities that he has not told us about. For nothing in his analysis tells us why it is not necessary to experience in groups the kind of deindividuation that Freud feared. Aristotle's views on political friendship, to which Abramson refers, are not counterevidence.

Donald Meltzer points out that Freud, though rather ambiguous on the subject, actually uses identification in two ways in *Group Psychology and the Analysis of the Ego*. The first is "introjective identification," in which aggressiveness against the father is turned against the self (or that part of the self that identifies with the father). This process is the foundation of civilization, with all the harshness that it implies. The second form of identification is "primary identification" or symbiosis, in which love of another is inseparable from wanting to be like the other.[29] While such love may enrich romantic relationships (*Symposium*, 192c–193a), it is hardly a decent basis for political friendship, since it is based on a tendency to deny the separateness and autonomy of the other. The object is "simply not recognized as separate," says Meltzer.[30] Though Aristotle stresses that genuine friends (that is, in virtue of their goodness) must have much in common, he says this not to encourage their identification but because he appreciates all that divides them. For Aristotle it is *because* so much divides individuals that truly caring for each other's welfare is noble. Absolutely nothing in Aristotle's discussion of political friendship supports Abramson's implication that it involves or requires primary identification (N. *Ethics*, 1155a–1160a30).

Abramson also distinguishes types of identification, arguing that "horizontal identification" (apparently equivalent to Meltzer's primary identification; if Abramson has a more differentiated concept, he never develops it) avoids the problems associated with Freud's "hierarchical account of group psychology."[31] This is, in fact, the case. Primary identification, however, involves risks of its own (which Abramson does not seem to fully appreciate), risks associated with failure to respect the autonomy of others. To equate primary identification with Aristotle's robust concept of political friendship seems quite misleading.

Abramson's reasoning seems to be that the transference, in which the patient comes to see the analyst as mother or father figure and to love (and hate) the analyst as mother or father, is a form of identification, presumably a mixture of the projective and primary types. As such, the transference (in which two people are engaged in what is, after all, also an economic transaction) might become a model for the identification that binds groups and nations. To be sure, there is a hierarchical aspect to the transference relationship, but it ideally reflects a liberating authority in that the analyst ultimately seeks to help the analysand free himself from the transference, in which every relationship comes to mirror the hierarchical relationship with parents. With these considerations as a basis, Abramson concludes that "if such liberating authority and human association are available in therapy, they are *in principle* available in politics."[32]

Abramson never goes any further. This remains an assertion, not unlike Juergen Habermas' belief that psychoanalytic discourse can serve as a model for the ideal speech community, but without any of Habermas' effort to develop the institutional links between psychoanalysis, discourse, and society. But what reason is there to assume that what is available in intimate relationships, such as care, concern, understanding, and love, is automatically— "in principle"—available in politics? In fact, my book argues precisely the opposite. A Kleinian account of the group is valuable because it explains why the love and concern available in individual relationships is not available to the large group. Indeed, this is my thesis.

"Moral Man and Immoral Society"

Abramson's account, like so much psychoanalytic social theory, assumes that the theorist's task is completed when he has shown that human nature contains within it the potential to establish loving, sharing connections with others. It is this potential that presumably provides the psychological content and support to the ideal of the socially constituted self. In fact, the demonstration of such a potential only makes the theorist's task more difficult. For he must then explain why this so rarely occurs on a large scale, a seemingly obvious point that so many theorists ignore, or downplay, perhaps because it is they who ultimately define political life in terms of intimate, rather than public, relationships. Against such an account, mine seeks to explain why the love and concern seen in intimate relations are so rarely found in the group. This argument has nothing to do with a group mind; nor does it invoke the methodological doctrine of emergence. Rather, the argument is, in part, that we purchase harmony in our private relations by investing our aggression in the group.

My argument is complex and occasionally speculative. What is not speculation, but fact, is that large groups often behave in ways that would shock the consciences of individual members were the same acts undertaken by individuals qua individuals, not group members. The conduct of soldiers during wartime is an obvious example. In *Moral Man and Immoral Society*, Reinhold Niebuhr argues that individual egoism is magnified in the group. Generally eschewing psychological explanations, Niebuhr argues that because the group frequently lives in a more hostile environment than the individual, the group must press its demands selfishly in order to survive. If a group member were to treat the members of *other* groups unselfishly, he might well be betraying the legitimate interests of his own group. To be moral, one must often be immoral.[33]

Very little of my argument overlaps with Niebuhr's. Nevertheless, his realism about group life, about how harsh, cynical, and selfish large groups generally are (and perhaps sometimes have to be), remains a valuable insight as well as a lesson in intellectual forthrightness. As far as group psychology is concerned, to take this lesson seriously means not devoting all one's attention to devising various possibility theorems, showing that this or that ideal social arrangement is possible, because under some circumstances (such as the psychoanalytic transference!) human nature displays attributes that would support such an ideal. To take Niebuhr's insight seriously requires that we also try to explain why groups often behave so badly, especially since the individuals in the group are frequently quite decent. Such contradictory behavior is the most obvious fact about group life, one all too easily ignored by a focus on the abstract potential of human nature. This criticism, of course, fits Marcuse just as well as Abramson. In addressing the concerns of the Frankfurt School, I try to be faithful to their intent. No attempt is made to reproduce their solutions via a Kleinian account.

Plan of the Book

Chapter 2 examines the psychoanalytic theory of Melanie Klein in some detail, in particular the way in which the theoretical concerns of Klein match those of the Frankfurt School. Despite the fact that Klein never developed a group psychology, I discuss why her account is nonetheless a suitable foundation for group psychology. The justification of my treatment of the passions as primary is also developed. This is necessary, as it involves a revision in Klein's account.

Chapter 3 develops a Kleinian-inspired group psychology. It is the longest and most important chapter, and much that follows depends on it. The emphasis is on the theoretical and empirical issues that a group psychology must address (with little attention paid to the concerns of the Frankfurt School per se). Among the issues dealt with in this chapter is the relationship between individual and group. Hence, the philosophical problems of methodological individualism, emergence, and the so-called "group mind" are examined. Whereas Freud saw the group as modeled on the authoritarian love of the family, a Kleinian perspective sees the group as defending against primitive anxiety. The problem with groups is that they are so good at defending against this anxiety that they forestall the emotional conflicts that lead to moral learning. Here is the source of one of the tragedies revealed by the Kleinian perspective. Individuals are frequently able to love and care for others out of genuine concern for their welfare. Group morality, on the other hand, rarely transcends *lex talionis*. Chapter 3 concludes with an extended case study, which shows that a Kleinian account can explain a puzzling phenomenon, one that at first might not seem to lend itself to a Kleinian analysis: the great appeal of Ronald Reagan.

Chapter 4 explores Kleinian aesthetic theory, which sees art as a symbolic act of reparation. Yet, while such an account is useful, it is only half the story. Like Kleinian psychoanalysis, Kleinian aesthetics places too much emphasis on internal reality, too little on its external counterpart. Art is also about coming to terms with the real world, particularly its unresponsive givenness. After developing an alternative psychoanalytic account of art, an account only loosely based on Kleinian aesthetics, I show that my account better addresses the concerns of the Frankfurt School than the implicit Freudian view (art is sublimated eros) they so frequently turn to. The chapter includes an extended analysis of one of Klein's few studies of a work of art, Aeschylus' *Oresteia* trilogy. Just as Horkheimer and Adorno's study of Homer's *Odyssey* served as a motto for their critique of

Dialectic of Enlightenment, so Klein's study of the *Oresteia* serves as a motto for a Kleinian version of the critique of instrumental reason, a theme of the fifth chapter.

Chapter 5 argues that what the Frankfurt School calls instrumental reason can fruitfully be interpreted, from a Kleinian perspective, as an expression of primitive anxiety and greed. Unlike the Frankfurt School's alternative to instrumental reason, however, the Kleinian alternative—what I call reparative reason—does not deny aggression but rather seeks to integrate it, recognizing that humanity must impose its categories on nature in order to survive and prosper. Though reparative reason is concerned with the welfare of the object, it is defined in this chapter primarily in terms of its loose and flexible symbolic structure. This definition allows reparative reason to be expressed in terms of recent developments in the philosophy of science. I further explore the flexible symbolic structure of reparative reason by contrasting the attempts of Juergen Habermas and Carol Gilligan to reformulate Lawrence Kohlberg's stages of moral development. It is argued that Gilligan's reformulation comes much closer than Habermas' to capturing the spirit of reparative reason. Chapter 5 also develops a Kleinian interpretation of the Frankfurt School's most prized and utopian goal: reconciliation with nature, an interpretation that recognizes the validity of their concerns, if not their solutions.

Most of this book concerns what the Kleinian account can do. Chapter 6 pays some attention to what it cannot do, arguing for the obvious point that it cannot replace moral theory. It is in this context that I criticize Richard Wollheim's interpretation of Kleinian morality for failing to appreciate what is unique to her account: its discovery of the other-directed character of reparative love. The other two sections of this chapter, on Rawls and "object relations revisionism," have already been discussed.

Imagining how the Frankfurt School could have drawn upon Klein is an organizing principle of this book. I do not, however, adhere to it slavishly. The concerns of the Frankfurt School, if not their solutions, are the proper concerns of any ambitious social theory. Showing that a Kleinian-inspired social theory can address these concerns is a way of showing that it is to be taken seriously. When this is best shown in ways that do not require reference to the Frankfurt School, I do not refer to it.

CHAPTER TWO

Psychoanalyst of the Passions

Passion is the essential force of man energetically bent on its object.
—Marx, *Economic and Philosophic Manuscripts of 1844*

In 1925 Klein was invited by Ernest Jones to give a series of lectures on child analysis in England. Two years later she emigrated there, where she remained for the rest of her life. Klein was the first psychoanalyst to practice genuine analysis, as opposed to educative techniques, with young children.[1] At the time child analysis was believed to be an especially appropriate (that is, less demanding) specialty for women.[2] Klein provided the child with small toys, interpreting his or her play in terms of how it expressed phantasies of love and hate. Prior to Klein's work it was generally felt that psychoanalysis could not be successful with young children because of their inability to develop a genuine transference. For this reason Sigmund Freud did not analyze "Little Hans" ("Phobia of a Five Year Old Boy") but instead advised Hans' father how to do so. Anna Freud continued this tradition, urging a supportive and educational approach with young children. Against this position Klein argued that Anna Freud's educational approach simply split the transference, driving the negative transference (that is, feelings of anger, rage, and resentment against the analyst) deeper into the unconscious. The failure to develop a genuine analytic situation with the child was, said Klein, the result of Anna Freud's methods, not a justification for them.[3]

Continuities and Discontinuities with Freud

At first Klein's work was in harmony with that of the British Psycho-Analytical Society. For some time a number of psychoanalysts had felt, despite the objections of Anna Freud, that genuine analysis of young children was possible, and Klein's work struck a responsive chord. On the publication of Klein's *The Psycho-Analysis of Children* in 1932, the president of the society, Edward Glover, wrote an especially positive review, treating the book as a breakthrough in the development of psychoanalysis.[4] In 1935 this harmony began to dissolve with the publication of Klein's "A Contribution to the Psychogenesis of Manic-Depressive States," her first major theoretical paper. In this and following papers Klein began to challenge key Freudian theoretical assumptions, all the while arguing that she was only elaborating upon them. For example, whereas Freud saw the superego as arising during the resolution of the Oedipal phase at the end of early childhood, Klein pushed back the beginning of the Oedipal stage, and with it the emergence of the superego, to the first year of life.

In fact, framing the issue as a question about the age at which the Oedipus complex emerges, as both Klein and her critics did, only intensified the conflict between them, while disguising even more fundamental disagreements. For by the term "Oedipal" Klein meant not a sexual interest in mother but a pregenital desire to possess and control the riches and goodness of mother's body, a desire that frequently expresses itself in phantasies of oral incorporation. And by superego Klein meant not the internalization of father's authority but the young child's innate sense of guilt at its own greed and aggression toward mother.[5] While trying to establish her theoretical continuity with Freud, and in so doing managing to transform Freud's theory, Klein was in fact developing quite a different psychoanalytic theory, in which the key developmental events are pre-Oedipal, centering not so much on eros as aggression. For Freud, it is the male child's emerging genitality that makes the Oedipal conflict possible and repression necessary. Does it actually make any sense to state, as Klein does, that the "early stages of the Oedipus conflict are . . . largely dominated by pregenital stages of development?"[6] Rather than contributing to the continuity of psychoanalysis, the designation of every positive and possessive attitude toward mother as "Oedipal" only makes the contributions of Klein's own system more obscure.

Yet, there are genuine continuities between Klein and Freud. In *Beyond the Pleasure Principle* (1920), Freud revised his instinct theory, introducing the concept of the death instinct. Prior to this

Freud argued that there were two sets of instincts: the sexual instincts and the self-preservative or ego instincts. In his 1914 paper "On Narcissism," however, Freud conceptualized narcissism as the "libidinal component of the egoism of the instinct of self-preservation."[7] By viewing narcissism as the coming together of egoism and libido (that is, self-love), Freud in effect abandoned the duality of eros and ego, as he was soon to recognize. It was not until *Beyond the Pleasure Principle*, however, that Freud restored the duality of the instincts, combining self-preservation and libido into eros, the instinct to preserve and extend life, and setting this instinct against what he would later call Thanatos, the death instinct. Klein is one of the very few psychoanalysts to take the *Todestrieb* seriously. Indeed, she transformed Freud's most ambitious metaphysical speculations about an innate destructive impulse into a clinical hypothesis. Her critics questioned her pointedly on this, arguing that Freud never intended his metaphysical speculations as an explanation of aggression in very young children. Yet, once again this disagreement concealed more than it revealed. For in transforming the *Todestrieb* into a clinical hypothesis (as an explanation for young children's anger and hatred), Klein transformed the concept itself. Indeed, she transformed the very meaning of the drives.

For Freud, the drives originate as tensions within the body. This physical tension affects the mind, whose basic function is to meet the needs of the body by eliminating drive tensions and preserving a state of equilibrium. Libido and aggression produce experience by means of the bodily sensations to which they give rise. But for Klein, on the other hand, libido and aggression are always contained within, and always refer to, relationships with others, either real or imaginary, as Greenberg and Mitchell point out in *Object Relations in Psychoanalytic Theory*.[8] For Klein the body is not so much the source of the drives as it is the means of their expression. In a word, the drives for Klein are emotions—passions—directed towards others, real or imaginary, from the very beginning of life. Rather than referring to directionless, objectless psychic energy, which only later becomes attached to objects as love or hate, the drives for Klein refer to patterns of feelings toward real and imaginary others, patterns that Klein suggested were sometimes innate and sometimes merely universal. The body, rather than being the instigator of the drives, is rather the universal medium through which they are expressed. In the case of the aggressive drives, it is not a pretty picture.

> Loose motions, flatus and urine are all felt to be burning, corroding and poisoning agents. Not only the excretory but all other physical functions are pressed into the service of the need for aggressive (sadistic) discharge and projection in phantasy. Limbs shall trample, kick and hit; lips, fingers and hands shall suck, twist, pinch; teeth shall bite, gnaw, mangle and cut; mouth shall devour, swallow and kill (annihilate); eyes kill by a look, pierce and penetrate.[9]

Klein never confronts the difference between her view and Freud's on the drives. The closest she comes, as Greenberg and Mitchell point out, is in her discussion of the nature of a psychological object (a person, or a part thereof, as well as images in unconscious phantasy). For Freud, she notes, the object is always "the object of an instinctual aim," whereas her own view is that it represents "in addition to this, an object-relation involving the infant's emotions, phantasies, anxieties and defenses."[10] It is this object relation that *is* the drives in Klein's system. As Greenberg and Mitchell put it, "Drives, for Klein, are relationships."[11] An important consequence is that Freud's distinction between id and the ego (that is, between energy and structure) becomes redundant. "The central conflict in human experience, for Klein, is between love and hate, between the caring preservation and the malicious destruction of others."[12] However, since love and hate are already object-seeking, they already have a structured relationship to reality, internal as well as external, a relationship that does not require either ego or id to give it direction or coherence. In Klein's system, for example, it is not so much the ego or superego that constrains aggression, but love. Later it will be argued that this relative absence of psychic structure in Klein's system makes it an especially appropriate foundation for group psychology.

Klein sees aggression as the infant's natural psychological response to frustration, a response so total and undifferentiated that it is experienced by the infant as threatening his own annihilation. Thus, the infant projects the aggression outwards, where it is eventually experienced in paranoid fashion—as an attack on the infant from outside. There is, in this play of projection and introjection, no place for a longing for the cessation of stimulation, the Nirvana principle, that Freud sees as the telos of the *Todestrieb*. However, like Freud in *Civilization and Its Discontents*, Klein sees guilt as primarily a consequence of aggressive (rather than sexual) phantasies and desires. As Freud put it there, "I am convinced that many processes will admit of a simpler and clearer explanation if the findings of psycho-analysis with regard to the derivation of the sense of guilt are restricted to the aggressive instincts."[13] Indeed, Klein interprets the infant's paranoid fear of attack by what is in reality his own aggression as a manifestation of guilt, albeit an especially primitive one, governed at this stage not by love but by fear: the principle of *lex talionis*. The Kleinian infant is motivated by neither the pursuit of pleasure, nor even the cessation of stimulation, but by an inherent destructiveness. The child's dominant aim at this stage—which she soon came to call the paranoid-schizoid position—"is to possess himself of the contents of the mother's body and to destroy her by means of every weapon which sadism can command."[14] As the long quotation on how the child uses its body to express its drives suggests, the child has no shortage of imaginary weapons.

There are still other continuities with Freud. Freud first believed that repression causes anxiety. This stemmed from Freud's libidinal hydraulics, in which anxiety was seen as a biological conversion of libido that is frustrated or blocked in the process of repression. As Hannah Segal observes, Freud imagined anxiety to bear the same relationship to repression as vinegar bears to wine.[15] However, in "Inhibitions, Symptoms and Anxiety" (1926), Freud reversed the process, seeing anxiety as the cause of repression. He also elaborated on four basic sources of anxiety, each belonging to a different stage of development: loss of the object (mother); castration fear; superego anxiety; and the loss of love. In the case of the loss of the object, Freud understood the anxiety as stemming from the intensity of instinctual demands, which emerge from the life and death instincts but have no coherent mode of discharge.[16] Klein's discussion of the origin of infantile anxiety in the disintegrative effects of rage on the nascent ego seems to be based on similar considerations. A connection between Freud's later thought and Klein's can hardly be denied, a connection that goes some way toward supporting Klein's claim that she was merely developing Freud's later insights, whereas her critics remained bound to Freud's earlier work. At the same time, we have seen that the story is not this simple either.

Klein also agrees with some of Freud's last observations, in "Splitting of the Ego in the Process of Defense" (1938) and in "An Outline of Psycho-Analysis" (1940): namely, that ego splitting is a key mechanism of defense, that all defense mechanisms involve ego splitting to some degree, and that an excessive use of defenses will always weaken the ego.[17] In fact, much of Klein's project can be interpreted as an elaboration of the Freudian mechanisms of defense, such as projection, introjection, identification, and splitting, and their application to even the youngest (that is, pre-Oedipal) children, in whom the anxiety against which these mechanisms defend is not so much sexual as aggressive in origin. If Freud saw the child in the adult, then Klein—the first to practice genuine psychoanalysis with children—saw the infant in the child.

Karl Abraham

Along with Freud, Karl Abraham was a major influence on Klein (in 1924 Klein began a fourteen-month analysis with Abraham, which came to an end when he died; earlier she had been analyzed by Ferenczi, whom she felt did not properly analyze her "negative transference").[18] Abraham's major contribution, as Segal points out, was in the study of the pregenital phases of development.[19] Abraham also introduced the term "part object," in order to suggest that the infant first relates not to mother and father as whole individuals but only to parts of their bodies, such as breast or penis.

Freud too wrote of part-object relationships, but he did so primarily in terms of regression, as in the case of a man regressing from the desire for a woman to a desire for the breast. Freud did not, however, attach great importance to pregenital fixations, as Segal points out.[20] Abraham, on the other hand, studied these pregenital part-object relationships in great detail and was also the first to describe the loss of an internal object. Of special theoretical importance is the way in which Abraham related particular part-object relationships to particular mental disorders, such as manic depression. Today Klein's work is still called "object relations theory," although this term is frequently used to designate the work of her successors, such as W. R. D. Fairbairn and Donald Winnicott, who place more emphasis on external objects than she did. In fact, the term "object relations theory" indexes many of the issues first raised by Abraham: namely, that in the beginning the child relates to parts of his parents' bodies, rather than the whole person, and that the most severe mental illnesses, the psychoses, have their locus in these pregenital part-object relations. From this perspective, it seems quite appropriate to call Klein an object relations theorist. Klein's study of these early relationships is examined below.

The Paranoid-Schizoid Position

Klein characterizes the earliest organization of the defenses as the "paranoid-schizoid position" in order to stress both the way in which the young child's fears take the form of phantasies of persecution and the way in which he defends against persecution by splitting, a schizoid phenomenon. Through splitting, the child attempts to defend against the dangers of bad objects (that is, phantasies) by keeping these images separate and isolated from the self and the good objects. The paranoid-schizoid position begins almost at birth. It is a normally occurring psychotic state, a characterization for which Klein was often criticized.[21]

Splitting is a crucial but puzzling concept, not merely in Klein's work but throughout psychoanalysis. The puzzle begins with Freud's less than clear distinction between repression and splitting. Repression, in classical analysis, refers to the ego's removal from consciousness of an unwanted impulse and any derivatives thereof, such as memories. Ego and id are thus opposed; this is what repression means. Freud never developed a correspondingly sophisticated concept of splitting. However, in "Splitting of the Ego in the Process of Defense" (1940) Freud wrote about how the ego itself could hold two conscious, contradictory beliefs at the same time: for example, that women have a penis, and women do not have a penis. This is not repression but a division of the ego, so that the parts holding the conflicting beliefs never touch. In 1941 Fairbairn had used the term "schizoid position" to describe the way in which the infant's ego splits almost at birth into loving (idealizing) and hating (persecutory) aspects.[22] Earlier Klein herself had written of the way in which aggression is split off from love and experienced as paranoia. In 1942 she linked Fairbairn's phrase with her own, calling the earliest developmental stage the paranoid-schizoid position in order to stress the coexistence of splitting and persecutory anxiety, an anxiety that stems from the operation of the death instinct. Freud had argued that while the infant may experience anxiety, he does not, and cannot, fear death because he does not yet have an ego. Klein, on the other hand, argued that there is enough ego present at birth for the child to fear death, which it experiences as a fear of disintegration in the face of its own hatred: "The terror of disintegration and total annihilation is the deepest fear stirred by the operation of the death instinct within."[23]

Against this anxiety the infant projects the death instinct outward. However, since even the youngest infant is capable of primitive phantasies involving various part-object relationships, this projection creates a hostile externalized object—the bad breast, which seeks to destroy the infant. Much of Klein's work with adults sought to reactivate, and subsequently to integrate, incredibly primitive images, such as the phantasies of "Mr. B," in whose phantasies the bad breast bites, penetrates, and soils—a projection of Mr. B's own sadism.[24] What Mr. B had in fact done was to project not merely his anxieties and impulses but also aggressive parts of his own body into the bad object, which then came back to haunt him. Here is the foundation of talion morality, based not merely on fear of retribution, but retribution via a process that Klein termed "projective identification." Reasoning in the paranoid-schizoid position is characterized by more than thoughts of "if I am mean to you, you will be mean to me." Rather, the object is wounded by aggressively thrusting into the bad object a part of the self that was in pain and contained vicious and destructive elements (projective identification). It is this part of the self that comes back to attack the self in the paranoid-schizoid position. While talion morality always seems to involve projective identification, projective identification is not always an expression of talion morality. It may be benign.

In the past thirty years, more energy has been devoted by Kleinians to explaining and developing the concept of projective identification than to any other concept. Yet, it remains puzzling. A *Dictionary of Kleinian Thought* defines the term this way: "Projective identification was defined by Klein in 1946 [in "Notes on Some Schizoid Mechanisms"] as the prototype of the aggressive object-relationship, representing an anal attack on an object by means of forcing *parts of the* ego into it in order to take over its contents or to control it and occurring in the paranoid-schizoid position from birth."[25] The key point seems to be that it is both a part of the self and an internal object (I define this term more fully later) twinned with it that are projected into another, who is then felt to contain both. Yet, in the end it is probably not worthwhile trying to make the term projective identification more precise than it really is. As Elizabeth Spillius puts it, "I do not think it useful to distinguish projection from projective identification. What Klein did, in my view, was to add depth and meaning to Freud's concept of projection by emphasizing that one cannot project impulses without projecting part of the ego, which involves splitting, and, further, that impulses do not just vanish when projected; they go into an object, and they distort the perception of the object."[26]

While the term projective identification has been used by a number of non-Kleinians in recent years, this does not seem like a good idea. Inexact as it is, the concept loses all precision when it is removed from the theoretical context in which it was developed—the paranoid-schizoid position. Finally, it should be noted that projective identification is not necessarily a sign of emotional illness. It may, for example, represent an attempt to communicate with another by almost literally sharing one's emotions. The degree to which projective identification is associated with phantasies of omnipotent control over the object, not the frequency with which it is employed, is the key issue in determining the degree of pathology involved.

The infant projects outward not only his own aggression but also his primitive love, which through interaction with unconscious phantasy creates a good object—what Klein calls the good breast. Here we see the source of what is at once very valuable, and very problematic, in Klein. The real parents, and their reactions to the infant, whether loving or frustrating, have relatively little to do with this process. The bad breast and good breast, rather than being primarily responses to parental frustration and love, are generated internally. The aim of the infantile ego at this stage is to introject and identify with its ideal object, while keeping the bad objects away via a continuous process of projection and externalization. Segal notes that while the good object is usually perceived to be whole and intact, the bad object is fragmented into a series of persecutors. In part this is because the bad object represents externalized parts of the ego fragmented under the pressure of the death instinct, and in part because the oral sadism directed against the bad object leads to the bad object being seen as bitten into tiny pieces.[27]

The infant's foremost anxiety at this stage is that his persecutors will destroy him and his good object. The primary defense is not so much projection (already employed to create good and bad objects and externalize them) but splitting and idealization, in which the infant holds the good and bad objects rigidly apart, as though they exist in separate, watertight psychic worlds that never touch. Idealization reinforces this splitting process—in which the good breast is seen to be all good, and sometimes all powerful—so that he can provide secure protection against the persecutors (in the form of a manic, omnipotent defense). Though fixation at the paranoid-schizoid stage is characteristic of schizophrenia and other severe emotional disorders, it should be seen primarily not as pathological, but as a crucial step in emotional development, by which the infant learns to overcome his fear of disintegration by introjecting and identifying with the good breast. Splitting, in this sense, is an absolutely essential step in learning to differentiate good from bad. It is in this respect that Donald Meltzer's study of Klein's *Narrative of a Child Analysis*, her record of treating a ten-year-old boy named Richard, is extremely interesting. For Meltzer shows that Richard's core problem was inadequate splitting-and-idealization, in which he "could not keep the destructive and Hitleresque part of himself from crowding in on and taking over the good part."[28] Furthermore, because of this inadequate splitting-and-idealization (Meltzer runs the words together with hyphens as though they were a single process), Richard tended to confuse good and bad, leading to greatly heightened paranoia (for example, was the helpful maid a good object or a bad one?), hypocrisy, and confusion. In my study of groups we shall see that splitting-and-idealization also serves a useful and necessary defensive function. However, they do so at an enormous cost: they stand as a barrier to the development of reparative morality. Splitting-and-idealization is the language of *lex talionis*.

Primal splitting-and-idealization involves a delicate balancing act. In the case of too little, the child, unable to protect himself from his own aggression, lives in constant anxiety that his bad objects will overcome his good ones—and himself. Too much separation, on the other hand, will prevent the good and bad objects from ever being seen as one, an insight—the result of normal development—that is the foundation of the depressive position. Before discussing the depressive position, however, let us discuss the term "position" itself. While Klein, in her attempt to maintain continuity with Freud and Abraham, sometimes used the term position as though it were equivalent to a developmental stage, this is actually quite misleading. Position is not a chronological or developmental concept but Klein's key structural concept. As Segal points out, the term refers to a state of organization of the ego, its internal object relationships, its characteristic anxieties and defenses.[29]

Although the paranoid-schizoid position precedes the depressive position, these positions actually coexist, or rather alternate throughout life. Even quite normal individuals may manifest an ego organization characteristic of the paranoid-schizoid position when confronted with stress and loss, a manifestation that is not comparable with regression to a previous developmental stage. Thus one is not necessarily diagnosing a severe emotional disorder by saying that an individual, or group, is operating at a level of ego organization comparable to the paranoid-schizoid position, even though the emergence of a full-blown paranoid-schizoid position in an adult would be quite psychotic. In fact, Klein seems to have changed her view on positions during the course of her work, as Meltzer points out. Earlier she wrote of overcoming the depressive position. Her later works, however, stress the goal of attaining or preserving it.[30] This seems to more accurately capture the depressive position: it is a developmental achievement that must be constantly defended and regained throughout life in that stress, as well as depression itself, reinforces defenses associated with the paranoid-schizoid position.

The Depressive Position

As early as three months of age, the child begins to recognize that the bad mother who frustrates him, and whom he has destroyed in phantasy a thousand times, is also the good mother who tenderly meets his needs. It is this recognition that good and bad object are really one that is the foundation of what Klein calls the "depressive position." By helping to mitigate the intensity of paranoid anxiety, decent, loving parents may help this integrative process along. Nevertheless, Klein seems to understand the internal integration of the good and bad parent as a normal developmental sequence, driven more by the increasing sophistication of the child's cognitive apparatus (making it more difficult—but not impossible under the stress of severe anxiety—to deny that good parent and bad parent are one)

than by the responsiveness of his environment. The depressive position involves fear and concern regarding the fate of those whom the
child has destroyed in phantasy. The child attempts to resolve his
depressive anxiety through reparation: the mother and others are
repaired through restorative phantasies and actions that symbolize
love and reparation. It is the depressive position that is the foundation of morality. Klein calls it the depressive position because attempts to restore the destroyed object to wholeness are coupled with
depression and despair, since the young child doubts that he is powerful enough to make whole all that he has destroyed. If depressive
anxiety is strong enough it may lead the child to employ defenses
more characteristic of the paranoid-schizoid position, such as splitting the mother once again into good and bad. By making mother
bad, the child need not confront his own guilt and depressive anxiety (that is, that he has destroyed what he loves and depends on).
Paranoid-schizoid defenses may thus defend against depressive as
well as paranoid-schizoid anxiety, a point that is especially important to the Kleinian study of groups.

The task of the child in the depressive position is to establish a
solid relationship with its good internal objects. It is these objects
that are the grain of sand around which the pearl that is the ego is
formed. If the child fails to do this, he will be permanently vulnerable to depressive illness. New, more sophisticated defenses emerge
with the depressive position. In the paranoid-schizoid stage, the
primary defenses against persecutors are the splitting of good and
bad objects, idealization, and violent expulsion, associated with
projective identification. The depressive position involves the emergence of manic defenses, particularly in its earliest stages. As Segal
points out, dependence on the object and ambivalence are denied;
the object is controlled omnipotently in phantasy and treated with
either triumph or contempt, so that its loss is not so painful or
frightening.[31] Sometimes Klein refers to this as manic or mock reparation (a virtual synonym for manic denial), although it should be
noted that the distinction between mock and real reparation is not
equivalent to that between phantasied and real reparation. It rather
has to do with the nature of the phantasies involved, particularly
whether they serve merely to defend the child against paranoid-
schizoid and depressive anxiety or whether they also express a
genuine concern for the object qua object.[32] Ideally, manic defenses

diminish over time as the child gains confidence in his reparative powers, in part because he develops new means of expressing them—for example, hugs and kisses.

Whereas paranoid anxiety involves fear of destruction by external forces (paranoid projection), depressive anxiety concerns fears regarding the fate of others, both real and imagined, in the face of the child's own hatred and aggression. As a result of his rage and hatred, the child fears that he has damaged and destroyed all that is good in the world, as well as within himself. "He is the sole survivor and an empty shell," as Greenberg and Mitchell put it.[33] The child attempts to lessen his anxiety and guilt through phantasies and actions, directed primarily toward mother, that are restorative in nature. That is, the child attempts to recreate the other it has destroyed, first by phantasies of omnipotent reparation, later by affectionate and healing gestures toward real others. Putting it this way suggests an important point. At the early stages of the depressive position, the love and concern for others seems primarily motivated from anxiety and guilt, as in "I have destroyed those who care for me and love me; how will I survive?" However, Klein is insistent that this concern for the fate of the object soon comes to reflect a genuine concern for the object qua object, which Klein sees as stemming from the child's gratitude for the goodness it has received from the mother.[34]

Though Klein's emphasis on interpreting aggression is generally stressed (she has been called an id psychologist), the central role of love and reparation in her thinking should not be overlooked. In fact, Joan Riviere, one of Klein's earliest and most well-known associates, argues that her studies on reparation are "perhaps the most essential aspect of Melanie Klein's work."[35] Just as much as aggression, care, and concern for others are inherent features of the child's earliest relationships. "Feelings of love and gratitude arise directly and spontaneously in the baby in response to the love and care of his mother," says Klein. [36] In a word, love is neither an aim-inhibited expression of libido nor merely an attempt to identify with a powerful other. Rather, it expresses concern—*caritas*—regarding the welfare of the other qua other. Furthermore, caring is not simply a reflection of the child's great dependence on others; the child does not care for others solely to have his desires better satisfied. Care and concern express "a profound urge to make sacrifices," to make others happy out of genuine sympathy for them.[37] It is from this perspective that Klein criticizes Freud's interpretation of the Oedipus complex, arguing that he has "not given enough weight to the central role of these feelings of love, both in the development of the Oedipus conflict and in its passing . . . the Oedipus situation loses in power not only because the boy is afraid . . . but also because he is driven by feelings of love and guilt to preserve his father."[38]

Among the situations that can reactivate early depressive anxieties in later life is the loss of a loved one (two biographers have observed that the sudden death of Klein's eldest son, Hans, in 1933 probably contributed to her interest in mourning and depression).[39] Freud argues that the work of mourning consists of reality testing, in which the mourner must discover over and over again that the loved person no longer exists in the external world but that life is nonetheless worthwhile. Klein adds an additional dimension. The loss of a loved external object reactivates early depressive anxieties, in which the mourner fears he will lose his good internal objects as well. The mourner thus finds himself confronted with a catastrophic double loss, in which the threatened loss of his good internal objects leaves him once again exposed to his primitive paranoid fears of persecution. The reality testing to which Freud refers must be extended to include explorations into one's inner world in order to determine if one's internal objects are secure, whole, and undamaged, even if the external object has been lost. If the mourner has worked through his original depressive position sufficiently well to do this, the experience of mourning may be psychologically rewarding. As Klein puts it, in normal mourning

> the individual is reinstating his actually lost loved object; but he is also at the same time re-establishing inside himself his first loved objects—ultimately the "good" parents—whom, when the actual loss occurred, he felt in danger of losing as well. It is by reinstating inside himself the "good" parents as well as the recently lost person, and by rebuilding his inner world, which was disintegrated and in danger, that he overcomes his grief, regains security, and achieves true harmony and peace.[40]

As Klein elaborated the depressive position, it came to include more and more aspects of psychic life traditionally viewed from a Freudian perspective, such as the Oedipus complex. Whereas Klein had earlier suggested that greedy hatred at the mother's self-contained goodness motivates the pregenital Oedipal conflict, she came to see the conflict as part of the depressive position, in which jealousy toward the father endangers the child's relationship to the good breast, leading to heightened feelings of anxiety and loss.[41] Whatever one may think of Klein's argument, it is clear that nothing is gained by continuing to call this phenomenon the Oedipal conflict. Klein is writing about a different psychic world, whose relationship to Freud's is virtually incommensurable, at least as far as the Oedipal conflict is concerned. Klein's analysis is much more powerful when—rather than redefining Freudian categories such as Oedipal jealousy—she is developing new ones.

Envy

If the anxiety associated with the paranoid-schizoid position is not too great, one will naturally enter the depressive position. However, it is not merely anxiety but also envy that stands as a barrier to the integrative process associated with the depressive position. Indeed, Klein is the first psychoanalytic theorist to make envy—such an important experience in everyday life—a key psychoanalytic concept. For Klein, envy is an oral- and anal-sadistic expression of the destructive impulses. As such, it has a constitutional basis.[42] Klein carefully distinguishes among envy, jealousy, and greed. Jealousy seeks to exclude another from the source of the good. Its psychoanalytic paradigm is the Oedipus conflict. Envy is far more primitive and infinitely more destructive, for it seeks to destroy the good itself. Envy is also differentiated from greed, which aims at the possession of all the goodness of the object. The damage done to the object, or even to a third party, is incidental. Envy, on the other hand, actively seeks to spoil the good itself. Frequently it does so out of sheer spite: if the envious person cannot have all the good himself, if he cannot be the good itself, then no one else shall have it either. In this regard envy serves a defensive function. If the good is destroyed, then there is no reason to feel the discomfort of envy.

Envy is extremely damaging primarily because it empties the world of goodness. Excessive envy also interferes with the primal split between the good and bad breast. The building up of a good object becomes virtually impossible, in that even the good is

spoiled, devalued.[43] The individual is left alone in a world of persecutors with no good objects on which to fall back and around which
to consolidate the ego. Greenberg and Mitchell put it simply: "Envy
destroys the possibility for hope."[44] For this reason Klein states that

> there are very pertinent psychological reasons why envy
> ranks among the seven "deadly sins." I would even suggest
> that it is unconsciously felt to be the greatest sin of all, be-
> cause it spoils and harms the good object which is the source
> of life. This view is consistent with the view described by
> Chaucer in *The Parsons Tale:* "It is certain that envy is the
> worst sin that is; for all other sins are sins only against one
> virtue, whereas envy is against all virtue and against all
> goodness."[45]

As important, envy interferes with reparation, the process associated with the depressive position. Because envy hates goodness, the
envious person does not feel guilt at aggressive impulses directed
toward the good object. Envy is incompatible with the goal of restor-
ing the object to a state of wholeness, since doing so would only
enhance envy by reinforcing the recognition that the good lies outside oneself. As a result of envy the child destroys his good objects,
confuses good and bad, and in so doing heightens persecutory anxiety. For all these reasons envy stands as a barrier to the working
through of the depressive position—and thus to the consolidation
and integration of the ego. Indeed, excessive envy produces a vicious circle: the more the good internal object is spoiled, the more
impoverished the ego feels, which in turn increases envy still further.[46] Perhaps the most ironic expression of envy occurs in what is
called negative therapeutic reaction. Sometimes, says Klein, patients are unable to accept the analyst's help precisely *because* they
see the analyst as having something useful and good to offer. It is as
though the patient must remain ill in order to deny the worth of the
analyst and his technique.[47]

Kleinian Morality

Klein's psychoanalytic studies reveal a potential for morality that
flies higher than Freud's. For Klein, morality may be based on love
rather than on aggression turned back against the self (that is,

Oedipal morality) or on mere identification with others (narcissistic love). Though Klein recognizes that morality originates in aggression (the paranoid-schizoid position reflects—or rather is—a primitive talion morality, in which every phantasied act of aggression against the mother is returned in kind), this is only its starting point, not its mature basis. Klein also recognizes that love and concern for

Figure 1. Klein's System as a Moral Theory: Positions[1] and Passions

Paranoid-Schizoid Position[2]	
In p-s love, we love what makes us feel good. There is no care for the loved object; it is a greedy love that would take all, leaving nothing for the object. Such love may lead to fear of having destroyed the needed object, but this is not true guilt.	In p-s hate, we hate what pains and frustrates us. We split off the part of the self linked with the hated object and project it out. This hate returns as persecutors.
talion	morality
Love[3]	**Hate[3]**
depressive	morality (reparative)
Depressive love is *caritas*, accompanied by anxiety that we are not strong enough to protect and repair those we love. Love and guilt are linked, but *caritas* stems primarily from gratitude.	In depressive hate, we ideally hate what is truly worthy of hate. We also hate the hating self. But this is basically an undeveloped category.
Depressive Position[4]	

[1] Positions take place of developmental stages; unlike stages, positions coexist throughout life.

[2] The paranoid-schizoid position emerges at birth; aggression and hate are split off and projected out to protect self and good object from the disintegrative effects of rage.

[3] Love and hate are the primary emotions—passions. In effect they take the place of drives and psychic structure. They can perform a structural function because passions are inherently object-related.

[4] The depressive position begins as early as the third month; it stems from the insight that good and bad objects are really one.

others may be fundamentally selfish ("I love you because you make me feel so good"). Yet, this is not the foundation of Kleinian morality either but only its source. Klein reveals the potential of individuals to love and care for others out of a genuine, unselfish concern for the other's welfare. She does suggest that this concern stems from the individual's ability to identify himself with the sufferings of others. We are not dealing here with disinterested altruism or a categorical imperative. But neither are we dealing with an emotional transaction modeled on hydraulics or economics.

While Klein reveals the potential of men and women to experience *caritas*, she is quite aware that much that travels under the name of love is only a cheap imitation. This awareness did not come easily to her. For example, early in her *Narrative of a Child Analysis*, Klein seems quite impressed with ten-year-old Richard's capacity for love, including his love for his mother and his wish to protect her from the tramp, as well as his love for natural beauty. Only later, as Meltzer points out, did Klein recognize that this love was intended primarily to insure his own comfort and very much bound to his desire to possess and control the object of his love.[48] It is tempting, in light of considerations such as these, to distinguish between paranoid-schizoid love, based upon anxiety and greed, and depressive love, based upon genuine concern for the object per se. Yet, this is probably a little too neat, in part because depressive love may also be fundamentally selfish, as Klein recognizes with the category of mock reparation, discussed above. Conversely, it was Richard's capacity for increased splitting-and-idealization (an achievement of the paranoid-schizoid position) that led to his ability to express genuine love, *caritas*, for his mother and Mrs. Klein. Yet, while love comes in many guises, most of them false, Klein also found evidence of the real thing, albeit frequently mixed with its counterfeit. As Meltzer puts it, "It is precisely because he [Freud] is bound to this energetics theory that it is not possible for him to construct within its framework a conception of love that goes beyond enlightened self-interest. It remains really for Mrs. Klein's formulation of the depressive position to carry psycho-analysis over that hump."[49]

Meltzer calls Klein's a "theological model of the mind."[50] By this he means that a person's internal objects are his gods, giving meaning and purpose to his life. We might, however, extend this observation to include the recognition that Klein's basic categories are fundamentally ethical or moral in character. As Michael Rustin observes, "Kleinian theory is impregnated with moral categories, and its developmental concepts . . . incorporate moral capabilities (notably concern for the well-being of other persons) into their theoretical definition."[51] It could be argued that such a claim commits the naturalistic fallacy. This, however, would not be correct. For Klein, human nature has more to do with hypothetical features of universal relationships than it does with biology (a point noted previously in the discussion of Klein's difference with Freud regarding the status of the *Todestrieb*). Rather than deriving morality from human nature, she discovers morality in the earliest human relationships. To be sure, whether this is the right morality cannot be answered by Kleinian analysis alone.

Juergen Habermas has stated that in his last philosophical conversation with Herbert Marcuse, shortly before Marcuse's death, Marcuse said, "I know wherein our most basic value judgements are rooted, in compassion, in our sense for the suffering of others."[52] It is precisely this sense of morality whose roots Klein uncovers. It is a morality based not merely upon the desire to make sacrifices, in order to make reparation for phantasied acts of aggression; it is also based upon an ability to deeply identify with others, to feel connected with their fates. Their pain becomes our pain. In fact, such a morality may even have revolutionary implications, as Horkheimer suggests in "Materialism and Morality." Sympathy (*Mitleid*) is a potentially revolutionary force, he suggests, because it points beyond self-preservation—the highest standard of bourgeois society—to the ideal of solidarity with a happy humanity.[53] Though such an ideal is utopian, it may nevertheless, by its very existence as an ideal, help expose the contradictions inherent in bourgeois society.

Marcuse's observation that morality stems from compassion is an insight also expressed by Jean-Jacques Rousseau when he posits pity (*pitié*) as the prerational basis of morality: "Thus is born pity, the first relative sentiment which touches the human heart according to the order of nature. To become sensitive and pitying, the child must know that there are beings like him who suffer what he has suffered, who feel the pains he has felt, and that there are others whom he ought to conceive of as able to feel them too."[54] This is the morality of the depressive position—reparative morality it might be called. It depends, it is apparent, on the interaction of pity and identification.

Reparative morality is not, however, the only Kleinian morality. There is also a morality associated with the paranoid-schizoid position. This is talion morality, the morality of revenge rather than of reparation, based upon the most primitive aspects of the superego.

Like Freud in *Civilization and Its Discontents*, Klein bases morality on guilt.[55] Unlike Freud, she systematically distinguishes between two kinds of guilt. The guilt associated with the paranoid-schizoid position is experienced in terms of the talion principle, "an eye for an eye." It is not a pretty picture: "The child lives in dread of his objects' destroying, burning, mutilating, and poisoning him, because these activities dominate his own phantasies toward them. . . . Thus, in the child's psychic economy, as on the Lord High Executioner's list, the punishment always fits the crime."[56] I would add one further observation to this account: whereas these unconscious phantasies are mitigated by the reparations of the depressive position, they never disappear. They are not merely the child's unconscious fears but also those of adults when they are operating in the paranoid-schizoid position.

Analysis can serve to reduce paranoid-schizoid anxiety by showing its origins in unconscious and unrealistic fears of persecution. Analysis cannot, however, do much to reduce depressive guilt, because the analysand really did want to ravage and destroy those he loves. From this perspective one *should* feel guilty for one's phantasies, whether one has acted on them or not. Or rather, one will feel guilty about them no matter how many times the therapist says one need not. Depressive guilt can be denied, but not eliminated, because it is a product of the unconscious, in which there is no distinction between phantasy and reality. It is more productive, therefore, for the analyst to focus instead on reducing paranoid-schizoid anxiety, which may be mitigated by insight, so that the analysand's natural reparative impulses can be liberated. The real goal of analysis is not the reduction of depressive guilt but the mobilization of compensatory reparative activities.[57] In this respect, Freud's classic characterization of emotional maturity as the ability to do creative work and to love takes on new meaning. Creative work and love are signposts of maturity because they are the primary ways in which adults may make reparation, symbolic and real, in our culture.

Implications for a Theory of Groups

Melanie Klein has no social theory as such. To be sure, in "Love, Guilt and Reparation" she makes a few remarks on how bad social conditions, including unemployment, can intensify persecutory anxiety by eliciting the earliest emotional deprivations. Indeed, the harshness of circumstances in general, says Klein, has something in common with the relentlessness of dreaded parents, in which all children—under the stress of paranoid anxiety—believe. Conversely, being out of work (or, one might add, being engaged in meaningless, alienated work) also deprives the individual of an opportunity to give expression to his constructive tendencies, an especially important way of dealing with unconscious fears and guilt by means of making reparation.[58] Yet, Klein never develops these suggestions further, here or elsewhere.

Klein's comments, brief as they are, are nonetheless theoretically important. They suggest that it would be misleading to compare Klein's model of the mind with Freud's metaphor of the archaeological dig. In Klein's model, the processes associated with the paranoid-schizoid and depressive positions remain active throughout a lifetime. Indeed, this is the point of calling them positions rather than stages of development. One sees an expression of this view in Klein's interpretation of transference phenomena, which rather than being seen as living memories are interpreted as externalizations of the immediately present internal situation. Freud said that neurotics suffer from reminiscences. He assumed that giving the analysand an opportunity to reconvert repressed material into memory would give the analysand another chance to successfully work through the emotions associated with this material. Though Klein too emphasizes working through, she stresses the way in which the transference represents the activation of the analysand's *current* psychic state, his projection of current unconscious phantasies onto the analyst. Klein sees the positions of the past as alive in the present, even in normal individuals. The paranoid-schizoid and depressive positions represent not merely our archaic heritage, or developmental stages, but also ways of relating to others, and ourselves, every day of our lives.

The problem with groups, to put it as simply as possible, is that they discourage those emotional developments that lead to the ability to experience depressive, reparative guilt. By giving paranoid-schizoid anxiety an objective focus (for example, Communists or Big Business), groups legitimate and reinforce paranoid-schizoid defenses, such as splitting and idealization. The individuals in the group are made to feel less anxious, but at the cost of emotional development. It is as if the analyst said to the paranoid-schizoid patient, "You really are being persecuted. Let me help you by naming your persecutors and telling you who your true friends are, friends who are also being attacked by these persecutors. Together you and your true friends can fight the persecutors, and praise each other's righteousness, which will help you realize that the source of aggression and evil is out there, in the real world. And you thought it was all in your head!" Such a strategy, were it possible, would likely reduce the patient's anxiety, at least for a while, possibly for life. Such a defensive strategy, however, comes with a cost. The analysand will never securely enter the depressive position. The analyst has reduced the patient's anxiety by reinforcing his splitting and idealization rather than by enhancing his ability to integrate love and hate, and thus freeing his reparative powers. This is precisely what groups do.

A Reinterpretation of Klein: Passions Are Primary

Unconscious phantasy is so important to Kleinians that even the word has a special spelling (always with a *ph*) to differentiate it from other psychoanalytic views of phantasy, as well as from everyday conceptions, such as daydreaming. While the Kleinian view of phantasy is unique, there are nevertheless continuities with the Freudian account. Like Freud, Klein views phantasy as the mental expression of instincts. Freud's concept of hallucinatory wish fulfillment characteristic of the earliest stages of mental development is frequently compared with Kleinian phantasy.[59] Yet, while both Freud and Klein view phantasy as the link between instinct and mental mechanisms, the Kleinian view is more complex. The Kleinian approach to phantasy, particularly as laid out in Susan Isaacs' classic "The Nature and Function of Phantasy," is bound to the view that the infant possesses sufficient ego at birth to establish primitive object relationships and to employ primitive versions of such defense mechanisms as projection, introjection, and splitting. Unconscious phantasy, for Isaacs and Klein, is thus not merely an expression of an id impulse but a more complex combination of impulses, defenses against them, and object relationships.[60] Freud believed that symptoms and dreams represented a compromise between an impulse and the defenses against it. Klein's view of phantasy comes closer to this view, but it is not identical—and not only for the reason that Kleinian phantasy includes object relations as well. Rather than see unconscious phantasy as a compromise between impulse and defense, Kleinians believe that unconscious phantasy is itself the defense. As Meltzer observes, "Mrs. Klein's work from the very beginning was bound to unconscious phantasy and its content. Therefore in her work the unconscious phantasy *is* the defence against anxiety."[61]

Isaacs quotes the following from Freud's "Interpretation of Dreams": "Everything conscious has a preliminary unconscious stage."[62] For Kleinians this unconscious stage is phantasy. Indeed, it is through his attempt to find symbolic expressions in the external world for his unconscious phantasy that the child learns about reality. Segal emphasizes the way in which this process is similar to what Freud means by reality testing. Thinking, she says, evolves from unconscious phantasy via reality testing. While this is correct, it would be misleading to suggest that the Kleinian view of unconscious phantasy is compatible with that of classical psychoanalysis. Once again the link is more political than conceptual. In the classical view there is either reality or phantasy. Klein's view, on the other hand, stresses the constant conjunction, and constant interaction, of the two. There is never a moment in which we are not unconsciously phantasizing, never a moment in which this phantasizing is not influencing our perception of reality. In fact, Edward Glover argued not only that extending the concept of unconscious phantasy beyond regressive and hallucinatory satisfactions was tantamount to asserting that the adult is permanently fixated at the earliest pre-Oedipal stages of development; he argued further that such a view of unconscious phantasy is incompatible with key Freudian assumptions, such as the primacy of the Oedipus complex.[63] Glover is probably correct. This does not show Klein to be wrong, of course. But it

does show that the political strategy of accommodation with Freud
was becoming incoherent.

Meltzer compares unconscious phantasy to a theater in which
meaning and significance are first generated and only then projected
onto the external world. Obviously some phantasies just won't play,
as the external world cannot be given just any meaning at all and
still support human life. For example, the external world cannot
successfully—that is, in the interests of human survival—be interpreted as an ever-giving mother whose fruits require no labor or
effort. Nevertheless, Meltzer seems quite correct in stressing that
from the Kleinian point of view the world is basically empty and
formless, a screen for the projection of unconscious phantasies. One
sees an instance of this in Klein's relative neglect of actual parents.
The child's psychic world seems to live a life of its own, almost
untouched by actual variations in parental response. Indeed, the
very concept of truth in the Kleinian tradition refers almost exclusively to intrapsychic reality. Meltzer argues that because Freud's
concept of an inner world was limited to "imagoes," rather than
including an idea of a space in the mind occupied by figures with a
continuous, meaningful existence (that is, continuous unconscious
phantasy), Freud's "concept of truth could not become one of the
knowledge of psychic reality."[64] Kleinian thought is also limited,
however, in so far as "knowledge of psychic reality" is often treated—in practice if not in theory—as the only meaningful reality.

A "Platonic View"?

Meltzer calls Klein's view of the mind "Platonic," referring to the
way in which meaning is generated from within and projected onto
a formless world.[65] However, to put it this way seems to stand Plato
on his head. For Plato, only the forms (*Eidos*, or Ideas) are real, and
the forms exist quite independently of our knowledge of them. Presumably Meltzer is not invoking the doctrine of anamnesis (recollection), in which our souls may know the truth because they have
consorted with the forms (or absolutely Beauty) in another life
(*Phaedrus*, 250a–e). Rather than being Platonic, the Kleinian view,
as interpreted by Meltzer, is actually sophistic. Our mind is a cave,
and our continuous unconscious phantasies are a parade of shadows
across the back wall of that cave, which we then impose on the

external world. While the world may prove incompatible with some phantasies, such as its idealization as an ever-giving mother, all we may know for sure is the content of our own phantasies. Such a view raises a number of difficult epistemological issues, several of which will be considered in chapter 5 in the section on reparative reason. Here I want to raise only the obvious objection that the so-called Platonic character of Kleinian thought leads to an exaggerated emphasis on internal phantasy at the expense of external reality. Any social theory based on Kleinian principles will have to come to terms with this problem.

One sees an interesting consequence of this problem in Meltzer's quotation, with his own interpolation in brackets, of Klein's account of her success with ten-year-old Richard, in *Narrative of a Child Analysis:* "In the present stage of analysis, Richard's capacity to integrate the ego and to synthesize the contrasting aspects of his objects had clearly increased and he had become more able, in phantasy [not in psychic reality] to improve the bad objects and to revive and recreate the dead ones. . . . In the dream, Richard could also bring the two parents together in a harmonious way."[66] Such a perspective only confirms one's worst fears about psychoanalysis in general, and about Kleinian analysis in particular—that phantasies of reparation, dreams of harmony, and symbolic representations of reconciliation might substitute for the real thing. The way in which such a perspective leads to insensitivity regarding the claims of real people is suggested in Klein's discussion of how colonizers, having ruthlessly exterminated native populations, might make reparation: by "repopulating the country with people of their own nationality."[67] Klein's comments were made in 1936, and one could argue that they reflect no more than the spirit of the times. Yet, this would let her off the hook too easily. From a Kleinian perspective the psychological effect of an act of reparation is considerably more important than its external consequences. It is this way of thinking that leads to a certain thoughtlessness regarding real objects—that is, people.

In her later work, real people and real relationships are more important. In "Envy and Gratitude" (1957), Klein makes it quite clear that real relationships, not merely imaginary ones, are destroyed by excessive envy and greed. Yet, the issue is really more complex than this. The problem is not only the intensity of her focus on internal object relationships but also the manner of her focus.

Often she writes as though the self, the ego, is merely the stage on which internal objects destroy each other, repair each other, and generally play out their internal roles. That is, Klein sometimes writes as if internal objects lived a life of their own, impelling the individual in certain directions. "But what are our selves?" asks Klein. "Everything, good or bad, that we have gone through from our earliest days onwards. . . . "[68] The self, it seems, is little more than the container of its objects. Meltzer alludes to this aspect of Klein's thought in his comment (immediately following his discussion of Klein's characterization of Richard's improvement quoted above) that "all this sounds like an active process by the ego and not something that happens to it through the mysterious agency of the 'core of goodness' " (that is, through the influence of the good internal object).[69]

One source of these problems is Klein's neglect of psychic structure. Love, hate, and internal objects work their influence on a mind, a self, with no real attributes of its own other than being the container of these images and forces. In fact, this is probably the most fundamental theoretical gap in Klein's account. Greenberg and Mitchell comment that

> there is in her work considerable fuzziness concerning the relationship between phantasy and the establishment of character or psychic structure. . . . Klein leaves an unfilled gap between her vivid and fluid account of the phenomenology of experience and the organization of personality and behavior. Segal suggests that the most enduring features of the internal object world are the ones that have been phantasied with the greatest frequency. The simple accretion of phantasy seems, at best, an incomplete explanation for the development of character.[70]

In Klein's account, internal objects and their relationships are remarkably concrete, often almost reified. She writes as if the good and bad breast actually exist as internal objects, not just as phantasies. It is the ego, the self, and its relationships to real others in the external world that tend to be vague and abstract in Klein's account.[71]

Meltzer suggests that we must change our way of thinking in

order to come to terms with this orientation. We must come to recognize that psychic reality is the paramount reality, the locus of truth and meaning.

> Thinking about splitting processes in this very concrete way is extremely difficult if one is still hedging about psychic reality in its absolutely concrete sense. It requires an immense shift in one's view of the world to think that the outside world is *essentially* meaningless and unknowable, that one perceives the forms but must attribute the meaning. Philosophically, this is the great problem in coming to grips with the Kleinian thought and its implications. . . . Do people *really* suffer because they have *really* damaged their internal objects?[72]

In the following chapters I assume that people do indeed "*really* suffer because they have *really* damaged their internal objects." This does not mean, however, that psychic reality is paramount, only that it is real and important. Meltzer, and to a lesser extent Klein, err by ignoring society and culture, writing as if each individual endowed a meaningless world with his own private meaning.

In fact, the world is meaningless, in the sense that most (but hardly all) modern men hold that its meaning is not given by God or the movement of the absolute spirit but by the collective actions of humans in society over time. Nevertheless, most men and women experience the world as replete with meaning, filled to overflowing with it. Rather than being born into an empty cave, as Meltzer implies, we are born into a cave in which every shadow has a thousand meanings attached to it, the work of millennia of cultural history. Some of these meanings (religion, for example) may help us to be moral; others (such as nationalism) may keep us from it. What is necessary is the development of cultural values (meanings) that encourage the transformation of reparative impulses into constructive reparative activities. What is needed is a group culture that supports the acting out of reparative phantasies and channels this acting out toward those genuinely in need of reparation.

Klein tells us that humans have the capacity and need to make reparation and that doing so will make them happier and more fulfilled. One might call this a eudaemonian ethic. She also tells us that people will make reparation in a wide variety of ways—from phantasizing about it, to painting a picture, to helping their children, to feeding the poor. What's more, there is nothing in her account to suggest that one way is any more developmentally favored than another. Emotionally mature individuals do not necessarily prefer real reparation over its symbolic counterpart. They do not necessarily prefer to make reparation to exploited native populations rather than to the more privileged among their own kind. Klein's account says only—and this is nonetheless a lot!—that mature humans have an innate drive to make reparation. What is necessary is decent cultural values to channel this drive in morally praiseworthy directions. In this respect her account, interpreted as an explanation of the origins of morality, cannot stand alone. In another—and quite troubling—respect, her account can. For it may be used to empirically explain why large groups so rarely develop a reparative culture.

Three key problems in Klein's account have been identified in the preceding discussion:

1. There is a tendency to pay insufficient attention to the interchange between internal and external worlds. The problem has not merely theoretical but also ethical implications, as Klein's comments on how one might make reparation to native populations suggest.

2. Internal objects sometimes seem to live a life of their own in Klein's system. The mind—indeed the individual—sometimes (but not always) seems to be little more than a container for its autonomous objects.

3. The result is that internal objects become reified—more real and concrete than the phantasies of which they are the subject, sometimes even more real than the phantasizing individual himself. That objects are fundamentally ideas, not things, is forgotten.

These three problems, which are of course related, have a single source: Klein's lack of clarity regarding the relationship among passions, the phantasies that they generate, and the objects of these phantasies. In *The Thread of Life*, Richard Wollheim defends Klein against the charge of "misplaced internality"—that is, of attributing internality to what phantasies are *of* rather than to the phantasies themselves. According to this charge it is "rather as though she had made the opposite mistake of that of which Moore accused the Idealists when he charged them with attributing to consciousness what really applies to that which consciousness is of, with thinking, say of the consciousness of blue as itself blue."[73] In fact, says Wollheim, this criticism fails to understand Klein's purpose. Her focus on internal objects is a way of distinguishing between types of phantasies. Rather than confusing phantasies with their objects, she is categorizing phantasies in terms of their relationships to objects.[74] She is seeking to categorically distinguish between phantasies about external objects and those about internal objects, which become internal by a process of incorporation (introjection), a process that transforms the external object in accord with the needs of love, hate, and the defenses.

Were it the case that Klein employed the concept of an internal object merely in order to clarify types of phantasies, then Wollheim's defense would save the day. In fact, the problem is not so much that Klein confuses the status of phantasy and object as it is that she often—but by no means always—writes as if objects lived a life of their own, generating, rather than being the subject of, phantasies.[75] In this regard it is worth stating the obvious. Internal objects are the content of phantasies; they are what some phantasies are about. Internal objects are, in spite of Meltzer's attempt to distinguish objects from imagoes, ultimately ideas, images. What distinguishes Klein from Freud on this point is not so much the difference between an object and an imago as it is Klein's view of the object as part of a world of continuous, unconscious phantasy, a little twenty-four-hour theater in the mind. It is the dynamic character of this unconscious phantasy world—its continuous impress on psychic life, rather than its being filled with objects instead of imagoes—that sets Klein's account apart.

A strict Kleinian would not accept this view of internal objects. Strict Kleinians hold that objects originate in the young child's belief in actual physical objects located in his body, a belief that persists in unconscious phantasy. While the young child, particularly in his conscious mind, soon comes to see these objects as representations, and later as symbols, the literalness of objects seems to persist in the unconscious mind, even into adulthood. Some evidence for this position was developed by the Internal Objects Group, an association of Kleinians who met in the 1930s and 1940s to try to clarify what R. D. Hinshelwood rightly calls "this mysterious concept."[76] Very young children and schizophrenics do seem to think about objects in this way, a way that may well persist unconsciously in normal adults. Many common expressions, such as "I felt a lump in my throat," are cited by Kleinians as evidence of this unconscious persistence.

The question, of course, is whether and to what degree the origins of the internal object should determine its use as a psychoanalytic concept. We do not treat the idea of an "influencing machine" as real, because it is a common delusion. Does it make any more sense to treat internal objects as real? Edward Glover, in another context, refers to what he called Klein's "addiction . . . to a sort of psychic anthropomorphism . . . namely of confusing concepts of the psychic apparatus with psychic mechanisms."[77] And, one might add, with psychic objects. Of course, Kleinian analysts do not actually believe that physical internal objects exist. A *Dictionary of Kleinian Thought* defines an internal object as "an unconscious experience or phantasy of a concrete object physically located internal to the ego (body) which has its own motives and intentions toward the ego and to other objects."[78] Nevertheless, there is a tendency among Kleinians to treat internal objects as remarkably concrete and reified. They speak of these objects as if they actually exist, even if they know otherwise. This probably has as much to do with their theoretical commitment to the absolute reality of the internal world as with anything else. The advantage of their perspective is that it stays close to experience. The disadvantage (which I believe is much greater) is not so much that it reifies a concept as that it reifies emotional experience, depriving it of its dynamic, global character, making it something that happens to us, the result of objects living a life of their own. I see no advantage to viewing objects in this way, particularly in an approach that seeks to apply Kleinian thought in nonclinical contexts.

If objects are not primary, neither are the phantasies that are about them. The passions are primary. It is love and hate, and all their combinations and permutations, that generate and motivate unconscious phantasy (of course, phantasy may feed back to intensify, or quell, passion). Love and hate stem, at least in the young child, from experiences of pleasure and pain. As the child grows older and comes to see that the good and bad object is one, these emotions create intense ambivalence: we hate those we love. Our phantasies are attempts to resolve this ambivalence and the anxiety and pain that go with it. Phantasies of part objects, destroying objects, being persecuted by objects, or lovingly repairing objects are ways of defending against, and sometimes coming to terms with, the intense conflicts generated by our passions. Seen from this perspective, Klein and Segal are not mistaken to see unconscious phantasy as itself the psychological defense. Not unlike the dream for Freud, the unconscious phantasy is a compromise between impulse and defense. Except that in Klein's case the phantasy is ultimately a compromise between love and hate.

Putting the passions first clarifies several important points, including the relationship of objects to psychic structure. We saw that while the object-related passions take the place of psychological structure in Klein's account, internal objects themselves seem to float around quite a bit. Bringing the objects under the passions binds them to psychic structure or, rather, to its functional equivalent. Furthermore, it does so in a way that emphasizes the intercourse between internal objects and their external counterparts. In this context Wollheim makes an interesting remark, arguing that even unconscious phantasy is ruled by a logic not entirely different from that which governs ordinary life. It is not its logic that makes unconscious phantasy so different, so mysterious, but rather that it stands so much closer to our needs and fears. The unmediated pressure of these needs and fears, rather than the operation of entirely different rules of thought, accounts for the distortions of reality characteristic of our phantasies.[79]

Wollheim exaggerates, as is evident when one reflects upon Freud's characterization of the unconscious in terms of its own laws, which, for example, recognize no distinction between a wish and its fulfillment. Nevertheless, Wollheim's point is important. Unconscious phantasy is not an utterly different and mysterious world. Rather, it is a reflection of our experiences of external objects, as mediated by conflicts of ambivalence on the one hand and psychological defenses against these conflicts on the other. Such a perspective restores the connection between the internal world and external reality without rendering the former the mirror image of the latter.

Clarifying internal problems and inconsistencies in Klein's account, although important, is not the primary reason to put the passions first. The primary reason is to show more clearly the way in which love and hate make a world. One way is obvious: through self-fulfilling expectation. When we treat others with hate, they are more likely to respond to us in kind. Treating others with love may have similar self-fulfilling effects. This, though, is not the only way that love and hate make a world. Not only do these passions produce either objectively hostile or loving reactions, but they also make the world in which this objectivity is constituted. Love and hate do so via the projection of unconscious phantasy into the world followed by subsequent reintrojection, the process that Meltzer refers to as Platonic. Precisely how "Platonic" this process truly is— which means, in effect, how thoroughly our phantasies are transformed by the external world prior to their reintrojection—is not a question that can be addressed "in principle." The answer depends upon circumstances, particularly the intensity of the anxiety against which phantasy defends. What can be addressed here is the general character of these unconscious phantasies, and hence of the worlds they help to create.

While the substantive content of unconscious phantasy is evidently infinitely variable, its core structure will fall into one of two patterns. Either the phantasy will be about the splitting of objects, so that love and hate may be held separate, and the anxiety and pain of ambivalence thus denied; or the phantasy will concern the repair and restoration of objects, so that what our hate would tear asunder is restored to wholeness. Otherwise expressed, there are paranoid-schizoid phantasies and depressive phantasies, as well as various subcategories and combinations of the two—such as idealizing phantasies (which provide another way of holding love and hate apart) and mock reparative phantasies (which in their omnipotent restoration of the object evince a lack of confidence in one's real reparative powers). To say, therefore, that love and hate make a world is to say that the way in which we resolve the conflict between them, as well as the pain and anxiety that this conflict evokes, determines what sort of world we live in, via the two-fold world-making process discussed above (that is, self-fulfilling expectation and Platonic world making). All this is true only to the degree—of course—that we control the world through our own beliefs and actions, which we never do completely.

The greatest advantage of my interpretation of Klein is that it links Klein's account to artistic, literary, and commonsense insights into human subjectivity. In all three areas the passions are central. What are the great tragedies but accounts of the way in which the conflict of love and hate make a world—and destroy it? What is surprising is not that Klein's account can be interpreted so as to address this core insight of Western art and literature but that much psychoanalytic theory seems removed from this insight, as though disputes over mental structure, the status of the drives, and the intricacies of the internal object world were not mere details compared to this fundamental reality, this fundamental insight. It is the great virtue of Klein's system that with relatively little reinterpretation— and no violence to her intent—it can be made to address this fundamental reality. Only Freud, with his focus on the drives (which I have suggested are biologically based versions of the passions) comes as close as Klein to making psychoanalysis a dynamic account of human motivation rather than a classification of the mind or a theory of social integration.

Most of these proposed revisions in Klein's account (though generally only of emphasis) seek to bring her categories and focus more in touch with external reality. It might be asked, therefore, why did I not turn to some other object relations theorist who pays more attention to external reality to begin with—perhaps W. R. D. Fairbairn, Harry Guntrip, or D. W. Winnicott? (In fact, these are the analysts to whom most psychoanalytic social theorists have turned recently.) My book can fully answer this question only when taken as a whole; for it is really a question about whether the consistently inner-directed character of Klein's thought makes her work a fruitful foundation for social theory. However, several points may be noted here.

First, while it is important to appreciate the fact that passions connect us to others, it is even more important to grasp the role they play in the psychic life of the individual: that is, the way in which their intensity and ambivalence threaten to tear us apart. In this respect the passions are like the drives, a point that a Kleinian account appreciates far better than any other. The social-theoretical implication of Klein's thought is not a socially constituted self, but a self understood as the locus of the passions of love and hate, immediately experienced by the self and mediately related to others; this implication is somewhat different from that of other object relations theorists, who stress passions less and connectedness more. Second, while I have emphasized how passion generates unconscious phantasy and shown that internal objects are ultimately the subject of unconscious phantasy, these revisions are intended to provide a dynamic structure to the internal world, linking phantasy and internal objects to the self that experiences them. The importance of internal object relationships in sickness and in health, and particularly the importance of continuous unconscious phantasy, are in no way diminished. The next chapter reveals how important these two concepts are to group psychology, concepts that play a less significant role in the work of the other object relations theorists than in Klein's. Finally, there is a nascent group-psychological tradition growing out of the work of Melanie Klein that has no counterpart in the work of the other object relations theorists. I have found this tradition fruitful as well as a useful check on my own derivations of group-psychological principles from Klein's individual psychology.

CHAPTER THREE

A Psychoanalytic Theory of the Large Group

The single factor most responsible for the moderation of the child's paranoid-schizoid fears is the reality of decent, caring, loving parents. Though paranoid-schizoid fears of persecution stem from within (they are Platonic, as Meltzer misleadingly puts it), they are—unless abnormally intense—subject to correction, particularly as the child grows older and develops the cognitive capability of integrating his or her good and bad objects. The recognition that the bad parent who frustrates him is also the good parent who tenderly meets his needs helps bring the child's disjoint ideas of parents into closer accord with reality. Groups also deal with ideas of people: the idea of the good group member or citizen, the bad Communist, the trade unionist, or the capitalist exploiter, to name just a few. The difficulty is that these ideas are not as readily checked by reality. While the group member in his private life can check his idea of his neighbor with the reality of his neighbor, how is the group member to check his group's idea of Soviet leaders with their reality?[1] The way in which this leads the group to exaggerate the goodness and badness of the abstractions with which it deals is considered below.

The following question is background to most of the issues raised in this chapter. If we adhere to the postulate of methodological individualism (that is, that the behavior of groups should be explained by reference to the behavior of the individuals within them, plus any composition laws referring to the impact of the group membership on individual psychology),[2] how is one to explain the fact that while many individuals practice reparative morality, most groups do not? In this chapter, I shall pursue this question by addressing the relationship between individual anxiety and group defense. I shall also consider a case study of the "Glacier Metal Company," which demonstrates how fundamental defenses against paranoid-schizoid anxiety are to the life of the group. It also demonstrates that a focus on the reality-constitutive character of phantasy is not incompatible with a view that takes seriously the objectivity of the external world. Following this I examine the reasons why the group tends to remain stuck in the paranoid-schizoid position. Finally, I apply these considerations to explain the appeal of Ronald Reagan. Reagan is not an especially paranoid leader, as these things go. Can the principles developed in this chapter be applied to such an apparently unpromising case?

Individual Anxiety and Group Holding

For Freud, the relationship of the group to the leader is like the dependent love of the child for his parents. Similarly, the relationship of group members to each other is like the jealous rivalry of siblings. The Kleinian view of the group, while not denying this parallel, sees these Oedipal dynamics as resting upon more primitive defenses, just as it does with the individual. The group, particularly as analyzed by Wilfred Bion, devotes much of its time and energy to defending against paranoid-schizoid anxiety. To write in this way is, or course, to risk conceptual confusion. What precisely does it mean to say that the group defends against paranoid-schizoid anxiety? Bion has a long discussion of this point, in which he argues that the apparent differences between individual and group psychology are not an emergent phenomena but simply reflect the fact that the "group provides an intelligible field of study for certain aspects of individual psychology, and in so doing brings into prominence phenomena that appear alien to an observer unaccustomed to . . . the group."[3] In a word, in the group one sees aspects of individual behavior that one does not see otherwise, since these aspects are first activated in the group.

This viewpoint, while demonstrating that the study of the group can adhere to the principle of methodological individualism, does not, however, fully address the question raised above. For to say that the group defends against anxiety of a paranoid-schizoid character could mean at least two different things: (1) the group helps the individual defend against his own paranoid-schizoid fears, much as the mother helps the child defend against its paranoid-schizoid fears through her love and concern; and (2) there are anxieties of a para-noid-schizoid nature that the individual has only as a member of a group, such as persecutory anxieties about the welfare of his group vis-à-vis other groups. It is against these anxieties that the group defends. In fact, the group helps the individual defend against both kinds of anxiety. By transforming private anxieties into shared ones, the group helps the individual project his anxiety outward, where it may be confronted as an objective threat to the goodness of the group. In other words, the group reinforces the defenses of splitting and idealization. A third kind of anxiety against which the group helps the individual defend will also be discussed: depressive anxi-ety, in which the individual doubts that the group to which he be-longs is able to foster and protect the values that he and the group cherish.

An Ethnic Unconscious?

This line of argument, while conceptually unobjectionable, at least in so far as it does not postulate a "group mind" or other emergent phenomena, is nevertheless incomplete. What precisely is the rela-tionship between individual and group psychology? In order to an-swer this question, we shall first consider George Devereux's answer to another. Devereux asks how one can determine if someone from an entirely different culture is emotionally ill. If a white, middle-class American male believes that he is possessed by witches and demons, then we would probably call him mentally ill. But if a member of a so-called primitive tribe in Africa holds such a belief, would we say the same thing, particularly if the tribe as a whole believes in possession by witches and demons? Presumably not. But does this mean that no member of this tribe may become mentally ill or is mentally ill only if he believes he is possessed by radar and microwaves (that is, forces that have no place in his culture)? The relationship between this question about the cultural relativity of mental illness and the question about the relationship between indi-vidual and group psychology is apparent. Both questions concern the way in which the individual internalizes the values and beliefs of the group, using them to build his own psychological defenses.

Devereux argues that the unconscious is composed of two ele-ments: material that was never conscious, the psychic equivalent of

what Freud called the id; and material that was once conscious but
was subsequently repressed. He then goes on to subdivide the once
conscious part of the unconscious into two further categories, the
ethnic unconscious and the idiosyncratic unconscious. The individual may be said to share his ethnic unconscious with other members
of his group in so far as it is composed of material that each generation teaches the next to repress. "Each culture permits certain impulses, fantasies, and the like to become and to remain conscious,
while requiring others to be repressed. Hence, all members of a giv-
en culture will have certain unconscious conflicts in common."[4]

The idiosyncratic unconscious is different. It contains those conflicts not as readily defended against by culturally sanctioned defenses, primarily because these conflicts are those that occur very
early in life, before the child has become acculturated. In practice,
this means that the idiosyncratic unconscious is the repository of
the most primitive conflicts, those occurring during the oral stage of
development, prior to the emergence of language. In practice, however, it may be difficult to distinguish between conflicts and illnesses on this basis, for conflicts located in the idiosyncratic unconscious will often also use cultural material. For example, the content
of a delusional system will generally correspond to material available in the culture, even if the delusion is an expression of conflicts
located in the idiosyncratic unconscious. Nevertheless, says Devereux, there is a sharp, if not always easily detectable, difference:
idiosyncratic disorders just use cultural material in an improvisa-
tional fashion. This material, rather than reinforcing defenses, simply gives content to what is basically a private phantasy or
delusion.[5]

How these distinctions help Devereux to distinguish a healthy
member of the Bonga Bonga (Devereux's generic term for so-called
primitive peoples) from one who is mentally ill, even though both
believe in possession by demons, is apparent. While the healthy
member may believe that he is possessed, not only will his beliefs
correspond rather precisely to the beliefs of his group regarding possession (he will have a recognizable syndrome), but he will also be
able to utilize the defenses of his group in combating his illness,
such as the rituals of the shaman. The ill member, on the other hand,
will use cultural material in a much less patterned way. Similarly, he
will be unable to utilize the culturally sanctioned defenses. For the

ill member, culture is not a resource full of meaning and significance
but a grab bag from which to find content for his private phantasies
or delusions.

Devereux's argument seems so reasonable that one might easily
overlook the fact that from a Kleinian perspective it is quite mistak-
en, in part because it misrepresents the relationship between psyche
and culture. From a Kleinian perspective, the distinction between
idiosyncratic and ethnic unconscious is untenable. Devereux employs this distinction as a virtual synonym for, as well as an explanation of, the distinction between neurosis and psychosis, a distinction that from a Kleinian perspective has primarily diagnostic,
rather than metapsychological, significance. It is Klein's thesis that
the defenses associated with the paranoid-schizoid and depressive
positions (both of which are well elaborated by the end of the second year) penetrate even mature psychic life. Not only is the "ethnic
unconscious" (if one wants to retain this somewhat misleading
term) in constant interaction with the idiosyncratic unconscious,
but it is far more an elaboration of the idiosyncratic unconscious
than Devereux suggests. Furthermore, from a Kleinian perspective
the idiosyncratic unconscious is not so idiosyncratic after all. She
characterizes the conflicts of what Devereux would call the idiosyncratic unconscious (that is, those conflicts associated with the earliest oral stages of development) in terms of a few universal patterns,
such as splitting and idealization, and ideas, such as the good and
bad breast. It is not the content of the idiosyncratic unconscious but
the degree of conflict and integration that varies in Klein's account.
Furthermore, she assumes (surely one of her more problematic, and
certainly widely criticized hypotheses) that certain ideas, such as
the good and bad breast, are innate, requiring no environmental
stimulus or confirmation. Indeed, it is perhaps her assumption of
innate ideas, more than anything else, that justifies the characterization of her work as Platonic (Meno, 81b–86c). From a Kleinian perspective the ethnic and idiosyncratic aspects of the unconscious are
misleading characterizations of mind, generating a false dichotomy
between early and later stages of development, even though a Kleinian might find Devereux's categories a useful diagnostic tool.

An implication is that Devereux overemphasizes the distinction
between belief and delusion, a distinction that for Devereux roughly
corresponds to the distinction between the ethnic and idiosyncratic

unconscious. From a Kleinian perspective, particularly if one takes the concept of innate ideas seriously, the distinction between belief and delusion blurs. However culturally elaborated, an individual's basic beliefs—his worldview—will be structured by primitive paranoid-schizoid and depressive phantasies, phantasies that retain a delusional element in so far as their origin is primitive, private, prelinguistic, all those attributes that Devereux associates with delusion. In other words, the blurring of the distinction between idiosyncratic and ethnic unconscious implies the blurring of the distinction between delusion and belief.

This does not mean that our beliefs about the world are delusions, on a par with psychotic phantasies. Nor does it require that we question the reality of the external world. It means that we should question any sharp distinction between internally generated phantasies and collective beliefs learned during processes often called socialization or acculturation, abstract terms that could be misleading were they taken to suggest that cultural beliefs are inscribed on a psychic tabula rasa. D. W. Winnicott, an analyst strongly influenced by Klein (he was an analysand of Joan Riviere, one of Klein's closest collaborators, and was himself supervised by Klein for three years), tells of a psychoanalyst who offered her patient an apple at just the right moment in an analysis, so that the apple was filled with symbolic value: "The important thing was that the patient was able to create an object, and [the analyst] did no more than enable the object to take apple-shape, so that the girl had created a part of the actual world, an apple."[6] Here is how belief, including collective belief, is created. Collective belief is like the apple. It gives shared content, and cultural form, to the phantasies of the individual members. The culture organizes this meaning, but it does not create it. The apple holds the phantasy, shapes it, limits it, but it is not the phantasy itself. The phantasy comes from within. It is this insight that explains how love and hate, working through phantasy, make a world.

"Holding and Interpretation"

If this is so, two related questions become important. First, what gives the beliefs of groups order and coherence, such that they are truly group beliefs and not just a collection of individual phantasies? Second, what is the function of these group beliefs for the individual psyche? Winnicott has developed the concept of "holding," or what I will sometimes call containment, especially when referring to the group. Originally the term referred to the first stage of the infant's development, in which the infant and mother are symbiotic. At this stage, as Klein points out, the infant's deepest fear is of disintegration, the fragmentation of his poorly integrated ego. Holding contains this potential for fragmentation, not merely by providing security (the paradigm of holding is, or course, the physical act of cradling) but also by providing a medium through which the infant can express his needs and receive a satisfying, calming response. In the absence of proper holding, the infant will seek to "hold itself," withdrawing from any stimuli that might overwhelm his nascent ego. Here is the breeding ground of severe emotional disorder. Conversely, Winnicott suggests that proper holding is essential if the infant is to enter the depressive position, because it is the mother's holding that "enables the infant's co-existing love and hate to become sorted out and interrelated and gradually brought under control from within."[7]

At first the medium of holding is physical interaction: cuddling, nursing, rocking, and so forth. It is Winnicott's insight that far more mature, symbolically mediated interactions also constitute a form of holding. For example, an insightful, well-timed analytic interpretation is a form of holding, for it recognizes the analysand's deepest anxieties and responds to them. Conversely, when the analyst's attention lapses, Winnicott says that "the mind has dropped the patient."[8] In a similar fashion, Winnicott regards the analytic session itself as a holding medium, in which primitive anxieties are given linguistic form (though not exclusively linguistic; the body also remains important even in analysis). The potential for disintegration produced by these anxieties is contained by the analyst's responsiveness to the patient, a responsiveness that includes understanding—that is, analytic insight—as well as love.

Group culture is a form of holding, of containment, in Winnicott's sense. This is not merely an analogy. If an analytic session can be a form of holding, so too can a group experience, such as the president's State of the Union Address. If an analyst's interpretation is a form of holding, so too is a culture's explanation of, for example, the meaning of death and disease. Like the analyst's interpretation, cultural explanations (for example, "The plague was sent by the gods to punish man's hubris") give anxiety a name, a locus, and a meaning, all of which help distinguish anxiety from the self experiencing the anxiety. This mitigates the anxiety, rendering it less overwhelming, less prone to disintegrate the self, and hence more manageable. In this sense, group holding functions like Devereux's ethnic unconscious, with the difference that the group holds its members' most primitive and private phantasies, not merely their socially sanctioned beliefs. Or rather, the Kleinian perspective sees no fundamental difference between these categories. It is this view of the group as holding and interpreting its members' anxieties that connects individual and group psychology.

The Group as Screen and Process

In the United States today, group therapy is generally conducted in groups of four to twelve members. While this is the norm in England as well, group therapy with very large groups—from forty to 120 members—is more common there. These large groups are often, but by no means always, composed of in-patients and staff in hospital psychiatric wards. While a therapeutic ethos underlies such groups, an experimental ethos is even stronger, though often tacit. What happens when one places between forty and 120 persons in a group with virtually no direction other than that of several "facilitators," who are present primarily to protect vulnerable individuals from the group? Much of this section is drawn from analyses of these groups. While the possibility of genuine therapy in such large groups appears doubtful, this is not a drawback for our purposes.

One could argue that because much of this data comes from psychiatric patients, it is tainted. While this is possible, it should not be overlooked that Freud gathered his data from neurotics and then generalized to humanity at large. He generalized on the basis of his assumption that neurotics differed only in degree from ordinary people. We all face the same psychic conflict; neurotics are just less effective in dealing with them than others. The Kleinian perspective extends this insight to even the most severe emotional disturbances. Psychotic phantasies, the paranoid-schizoid position, are a part of

normal mental life as well. Though there is certainly a sharp difference between psychotic and normal, it too is a difference of degree,
not kind. Referring to projective identification, Bion characterizes
the continuity between normal, neurotic, and psychotic in terms of
"the degree of fragmentation and the distance to which the fragments
were projected as a determining factor in the degree of mental dis-
turbance the patient displayed in his contact with reality."[9] Though
he does not clarify the term "distance" (perhaps he means that the
normally high degree of projective identification associated with
intimate relations would be pathological were it to characterize
more distant, casual relations), the basic idea is clear. Projective
identification is itself neither sick nor healthy. Sick or healthy refers
to the degree to which this defense fragments and impoverishes the
ego, and this is a quantitative, rather than qualitative, distinction. As
discussed in the previous chapter, sick or healthy also refers to the
extent to which projective identification is associated with phantasies of omnipotent control over the object. But this too is a question
of degree.

There is another advantage to focusing on the large group. Most
psychological studies of group processes have been based upon experiences with small therapy groups. Among the most well known
of these, at least from a Kleinian perspective, is Bion's *Experiences
in Groups*. Such small groups are generally, though not always, composed of individuals who are not especially disturbed. If the theorists of the large group are correct, however, this is not a key issue.
Rather, the key issue is size. At some point the group becomes so
large that face-to-face interaction with each member is impossible. It
is at this point that group dynamics changes decisively. The small
group really stands closer to individual psychology (or at least to
individual psychoanalysis) than it does to large-group psychology,
for the small group recapitulates family dynamics. In the large group
this too changes.

The large group actually more closely resembles the Kleinian
view of how the infant perceives his parents: not as persons, not
even as part-objects, but as blank screens on which he projects his
love and hate. It seems possible that for this reason Klein's is actually a more satisfactory account of large-group than of individual psychology. Bion's contributions will not be ignored. His view of the
group as defending against what are basically psychotic anxieties is

a cornerstone of my account. Nevertheless, it is not Bion, but several theorists of the large group, who are central to my account. Most of the groups that are socially and politically significant are large. Once the limits of the small group are exceeded (that is, once one exceeds the number of individuals who can know each other personally), it may be that all group dynamics are essentially the same.

Pierre Turquet argues that the individual in the large group never seems to establish his boundary "at the skin of his neighbor." Either the individual draws into alienated isolation or is submerged into the group. There are several reasons. One is that the categories that the large group employs to characterize its members (whom it does not know as individuals), such as career woman or sailing enthusiast, are too vague and general. Like the object of projective identification, the group member is forced into categories that fail to recognize his individuality.[10] Another reason is that the large group, as Freud also points out, has no sense of the past.[11] Consequently, it responds to its members as though they had no history, as though they were only group members, with no identity prior to, or outside of, the group.[12]

However, the primary reason that the large group is so incompatible with the identity of its members, and hence so threatening to them, is what Turquet calls "response bombardment." Too many different individuals offering too many different responses that are of low quality (for example, responses that show no appreciation of individual uniqueness, are not based upon having listened to the individual, or are disjointed) lead the individual to withdraw from the group, even as he may use the group as a container to hold some of his unwanted aggression via projection.[13] Even this last strategy, however, which must always deplete the ego to some degree, is more problematic in the large group than in the small. One reason individuals employ projective identification is to stabilize the other, to make the other like the self, literally a holder of parts of the self, so as to know what to expect, by virtue of being able to identify more fully with the other. In the small group these "caretakers of aspects of the self" are identifiable others, with whom one has a relationship. In the large group these caretakers are generally anonymous, many, and frequently quite unpredictable, in large measure because this "mutual endowment" (as this process is called in the language of group psychology) is not really mutual but merely parallel—that is, everyone is projecting, but no one is receiving because of response bombardment. This may lead to a vicious circle in which more and more aspects of the self are projected onto anonymous others in the vain hope of controlling them, leading to an increasing fragmentation of the self, with the resulting perception of a further loss of control, leading to even more projective identification, and so forth.

The result is the depletion of the ego of the group member, as more and more of the self is given up to others in projective identification. Reality testing is impaired, since the agent of reality testing—the ego—is weakened, fragmented, and dispersed. Depersonalization occurs, in which the damaged powers of thought and identity lead to a perception of the world as somehow more real and alive than the individual himself. In attributing his powers to the group or leader, the individual renders the group aggressive, powerful, and capable, himself weak, vulnerable, and in danger from the group. The group becomes more magically alive than any of its members. "In such nightmarish situations appeasement, flight, warding off the magic by desperate counter-magic, the seeking of allies, or a leader, and so forth, may take place. This is the world of psychosis and of extreme industrial and civil strife."[14]

Apparently inspired by Turquet's analysis, Otto Kernberg has elaborated upon this process, further clarifying the way in which the group threatens individual identity.[15] In matters that affect the group, says Kernberg, the group seeks to substitute itself for the member's ego and superego, much as Freud described in *Group Psychology and the Analysis of the Ego*. Against the psychic imperialism of the group, the individual responds with aggression, a response that threatens both individual and group. It is to defend against his own aggression that the individual binds himself ever more closely to the group. This is, or course, ironic, as it is the group that threatens the individual in the first place. As Kernberg puts it, to follow the idealized leader "permits protection from intragroup aggression by this common identity and the shared projection of aggression onto external enemies, and gratifies dependency needs by submission to the leader."[16] Aggression against one's own group—on which the adult often depends almost as much as the infant does on his mother; in a complex society most require the constant cooperation of others—is split off as aggression against other groups in order to allow a more secure, dependent attachment to one's own group.

This is, of course, the same defensive process analyzed by Klein, that of splitting and idealization. What Kernberg adds is a further appreciation, entirely consonant with the principles of methodological individualism, of why the individual in the group behaves so differently from the individual at home: in order to protect himself from the aggression that he feels against the group, the individual identifies with the group, purposefully (if not consciously) using the group's defenses against other groups as his own, in order both to belong to the group and to defend himself against it. Group psychology is, one might say, a compromise formation, a compromise solution, not entirely unlike the process that Anna Freud called identification with the aggressor.

Whereas Turquet emphasizes individual withdrawal as the key defense against the group (that is, establishing one's boundaries deeply inside oneself), Kernberg emphasizes immersion in the group to accomplish the same purpose (establishing one's boundaries deeply inside the "skin of his neighbor"). Here is the "dialectic" of large group life. Large groups are so threatening to the individual that they generate a series of extreme choices, with alienation at one extreme, deindividuation at the other. Graham Little, in his recent *Political Ensembles: A Psychosocial Approach to Politics and Leadership*, concurs. Social life, he says, "is the outcome of the interplay between fear of isolation and fear of losing individuality."[17] It is this dilemma, the seeming impossibility of finding a reliable midpoint, that "underlies political and social life."[18] It is Bion, however, who puts it best, suggesting that while man is indeed a group animal, it is the nature of this animal to be torn by conflict in the face of the demands placed on it by the group. "The individual is a group animal at war, not simply with the group, *but with himself for being a group individual* and with those aspects of his personality that constitute his groupishness."[19]

Against this harsh assessment it might be argued that when one actually looks at large groups one only infrequently sees such extreme conflicts and choices. Such an observation is correct, because most large groups are not loosely organized therapy groups but highly organized bureaucracies. Bureaucracy and organization mediate between the individual and the group, mitigating response bombardment and projective identification. In other words, bureaucracy and organization serve a defensive psychological function (which does not, of course, deny that they also serve the objective function of coordinating the actions of large numbers of people; the psychological function works through the institutional function) by standing between the individual and the group. For example, by controlling the direction and flow of communication, bureaucracy and organization prevent response bombardment within the group from overwhelming the selves of the members.

In individuals, the excessive use of psychological defenses may inhibit emotional growth and learning. The same thing may occur in bureaucracies. The ideal of the therapy group, large and small, is that free and unstructured communication, while perhaps at first heightening emotional conflict, will eventually lead to the release of repressed emotions (for example, envy at a successful group member). Made public, these emotions may then be integrated by the members in a way that repressed and split-off emotions never can be. This is how emotional learning takes place. Occurring rarely enough in the therapy group, it occurs hardly at all in bureaucracies. Or rather, if it occurs in bureaucracies, it occurs only in spite of their organizational structure. Bureaucratic restrictions on the direction of communication (information up, policy down), the fragmentation of communication in the name of specialization and division of labor, as well as norms that encourage the repression of emotion in the name of professionalism and efficiency all assure that communication will not lead to emotional learning. The defensive functions of bureaucracy overwhelm any contribution it might make to group learning—by facilitating the flow of information, for example. The outcome is not a pretty picture.

> Intelligence succumbs to coercion; hierarchical pyramids, far from being flattened, grow even higher; affiliative communication gives way to hierarchical blocking, leadership of ideas and trends gives way to the pressure of personalities in authority and "leaders," obfuscation rules the day and the large group, rather like a large vulnerable animal, is subjected to all sorts of violations, when it is in fact a most highly sensitive instrument whose enormous potentials we can at present only very dimly envisage.[20]

Later in this chapter I will argue that this inhibition of learning also affects the emotional learning that leads from paranoid-schizoid to depressive morality.

Bion

From the screen perspective, the group is essentially empty, a container (primarily in the sense of a dustbin) for unwanted parts of the self. Indeed, it is the emptiness of the group, its utter unresponsiveness to the individual qua individual, that makes it so threatening. The process perspective is different. It views the group as an entity in its own right. Perhaps the best way to grasp the process perspective is to imagine that all the conversation in a group came from a single individual, as though he were talking to himself, trying to make up his mind about something, for example. How would one characterize this monologue? Many observers of group processes argue that this "group monologue" is fundamentally schizophrenic, at least at first. It is characterized by fragmentation, disjointedness, one assertion (one speaker) not responding to another, topics rapidly changing with only the loosest association between them, obviously false assertions going unchecked, and so forth. For example, one of the most frequently heard comments in the large group, particularly in the beginning, is "I want to go back to my previous point," because the intervening points were unresponsive, following another train of association.

Bion exemplifies the process perspective, in which group processes take on a life of their own, a life that Bion regards as latently psychotic. What happens, asks Bion, in the small therapy group when the analyst does not intervene? Are there patterns to the way in which the group organizes itself? He answers that the group tends to organize itself in one of three ways, which he calls basic assumptions. These assumptions concern the aims of the group. They stand in no hierarchical or temporal relationship; the group may change its basic assumption almost minute by minute. The first basic assumption is that the group comes together to fight against, or flee from, external enemies. This is the *fight-or-flight* group. The second basic assumption is that the group comes together to obtain security from one individual upon whom the entire group can depend. This is the *dependent* group. The third basic assumption is that the group comes together to witness the romantic relationship of a pair. The group's relationship to this pair is intensely ambivalent, involving both the unconscious hope that the pair will produce a child who will save them (a Messiah) and great hostility at the way the pair (or imagined pair) hold themselves separate from the group. This is the *pairing group.*

Each of these assumptions reflects primitive, pre-Oedipal fears that may be characterized in roughly Kleinian terms. The fight-or-flight group is a response to anxieties of a paranoid-schizoid character, in which primitive aggression is projected outwards, where it may be fought or fled from. The dependent group is the counterpart of this first group, in which aggression and hatred split off and attributed to others allow a secure attachment to an idealized leader. While the pairing group seems to more closely resemble Oedipal dynamics, the process it represents is a good deal more primitive, involving phantasies of a little child as savior of the group. In addition, the group seems unconsciously to view the paired couple as though they were one, virtually fused—a phenomenon similar to what Klein called the combined parent figure. Here the emotional dynamic seems to come closer to that of vicarious participation in a powerful and indivisible alliance, the parents as united and invincible protectors.[21] Indeed, from this perspective all three groups involve dynamics familiar from Freud's description of the Oedipus complex (aggression, fear, dependence, and jealousy), but pushed back, as they are in Klein's account, to the earliest, pregenital stages.

Most groups that we are familiar with in daily life do not, of course, resemble the basic assumption group. Most are what Bion calls work groups, oriented toward a particular task. It is this task orientation, and not just bureaucracy and organization, that prevents regression to the basic assumption group. This avoidance of regression in objective activity is not, however, automatic. It requires repression, work, which generally expresses itself as the sheer denial of the reality of emotional life in groups. That such repression might inhibit emotional learning in groups is apparent, to say the least. Nevertheless, there is really no choice in the real world of groups. In this regard Bion's argument is similar to Freud's in *Civilization and Its Discontents.* Repression may be psychologically costly, but there is no alternative. The attempt to translate basic assumptions into action may well threaten the physical survival of the group. Basic assumptions reflect the principles of unconscious (that is, primary process) thinking, in which there is no time, no delay, and no reality check. In particular, the basic assumption group cannot wait; consequently, it can never learn from experience.[22]

Though Bion uses the term basic assumption, it could be misleading were it taken to suggest that these assumptions reflect the most fundamental psychological processes. Basic assumptions are themselves defenses against more fundamental anxieties of a basically psychotic character. As Bion puts it,

> Approached from the angle of sophisticated work-group activity, the basic assumptions appear to be the source of emotional drives to aims far different either from the overt task of the group or even from the tasks that would appear to be appropriate to Freud's view of the group as based on the family group. But approached from the angle of psychotic anxiety associated with phantasies of primitive part-object relationships, described by Melanie Klein and her co-workers, the basic-assumption phenomena appear far more to have the characteristics of defensive reactions to psychotic anxiety. . . .
> I consider the latter [perspective] to contain the ultimate sources of all group behavior.[23]

From this viewpoint, the organization of groups, as well as the tasks that they perform, serves two functions. Organization and tasks help master a recalcitrant world, without which there would be no survival. Organization and tasks also may be seen as second-order defenses against psychotic anxiety, preventing the employment of even more primitive defenses (that is, the basic assumptions), defenses far less adaptive for individual or group. To say that the organization and activity of the group serve to defend against psychotic anxiety is not, therefore, to diminish the real-world achievements of groups but only to note that these achievements are directed against inner nature as well as against its external counterpart. It is this general perspective of Bion that I draw upon in the sections that follow, rather than upon his specific hypotheses regarding the content of group aims, hypotheses that may be more appropriate to the small group than to the large one.

Bion does, however, make two substantive points about leadership that will be useful in the Reagan case study. First, he notes that the group often seems to choose its sickest, most paranoid-schizoid member as leader. Bion speculates that this is because the group recognizes how dependent it is on the leader. In picking its sickest member as leader, it is picking a leader who will be equally dependent on the group.[24] However, there exists a less subtle explanation for the group's attraction to paranoid leaders. Such leaders are best able to give internal anxieties a compelling external location and focus because they have had more practice at this way of thinking than most. In other words, the paranoid leader may be simply more imaginative at generalizing his own paranoid-schizoid defenses to the objective problems faced by the group and at selling this interpretation to others. In doing so, the paranoid leader best "holds" the group, objectifying members' paranoid-schizoid anxieties in a more convincing fashion than others. If this is so, then the key variable is not intensity of his paranoid anxiety but imagination: the ability to interpret his anxiety via the symbols of the culture.

Second, Bion argues that the leader of the group is often not that distinct, sharply etched figure he is frequently taken to be. Rather, the leader is often an empty vessel, a compliant personality upon whom the group can project its own needs.[25] Freud argued that the group member identifies with his leader in his ego ideal and superego. The leader represents what the member would most like to be, as well as what he should be. Such an account, says Bion, stems from a view of identification as a process of introjection by the ego, a mature—that is, neurotic—defense. However, if one sees the process of identification with the leader as more akin to projective identification, then it is not the strength of the leader or his ideas that are decisive but his character as a "blank screen" upon which members may project parts of themselves—in this case, their own ideals and illusions.

In arguing that screen and process views are "complementary," I use this term in its everyday sense to suggest that they enrich each other. Not all psychoanalysts use the term in this sense. Heinz Kohut, for example, uses it to refer to the necessity of employing two mutually incompatible assumptions (Freudian drive theory and his own self-psychology) in order to fully explain psychic phenomenon.[26] From the screen perspective, the group is a container for unwanted parts of the self. Aside from this, it has almost no life of its own. In this respect it is a fiction. The group contains (in the sense of a dustbin) the primitive paranoid-schizoid and early depressive anxieties of its members, as well as some of their primitive idealizations. The process view begins where the screen view leaves off. The process perspective asks what happens to the split-off anxieties and idealizations projected onto the group. They do not just die but rather go on to live a life of their own, a life that feeds back to influence the members.

A simple example will clarify this point. When individuals project their paranoid anxieties onto the group, the group becomes an arena in which it is considered appropriate to express anxieties of this nature, provided they are translated into the language of the group culture (Winnicott's "holding and interpretation"), such as business versus labor, the free world versus communism, God versus Satan, and so forth. Not only can such a group culture act to reinforce the anxieties it is supposed to contain (as members learn from each other only variations on the theme of how dangerous the outside world truly is), but the group may act so as to bring about what it most fears. The arms race is exemplary. From this perspective it would be absurd to see the group as a fiction. Quite the contrary. The group creates (even if it is not the ultimate origin of) the world in which its members live.

Group Theory as Role Theory

Before considering an extended example of how the group reinforces both paranoid-schizoid anxiety and its defenses, an important issue remains to be resolved, an issue with which this chapter began. The principle of methodological individualism asserts that the behavior of the group must be explicable in terms of the interaction of its members. Does this mean that when a group acts in a paranoid-schizoid fashion, its individual members (or a majority of them, or the most important members, or whatever) must be operating from the paranoid-schizoid position? Money-Kyrle, in "Psycho-Analysis and Ethics," in effect answers yes. The reason that Britain did not respond to Hitler until it was almost too late, he implies, is that most Britons had never securely entered the depressive position. Thus, they employed defenses characterized by idealization and manic denial, defenses associated with the paranoid-schizoid position.[27]

Surely this is sometimes the case. Some cultures seem to encourage their members to remain in the paranoid-schizoid position in almost every aspect of their lives. Yet, this does not seem an adequate explanation. There is nothing in Klein's writings to suggest that she believes that most individuals have failed to enter the depressive position. A somewhat more sophisticated version of Money-Kyrle's argument might be that it is only under the stress of difficult international circumstances that most Britons reverted to paranoid-schizoid defenses. But, did they do so in their private lives as well? Did most husbands and wives, friends and family, begin to relate to each other along fundamentally paranoid-schizoid lines at the time Hitler took Czechoslovakia? Presumably not. Although Klein notes that many of her patients were made more anxious by international events (and Klein's biographer notes that Klein herself was quite fearful of a German invasion),[28] she nowhere suggests that this anxiety was sufficient to produce a qualitative psychological change. A more plausible explanation must, it seems, invoke a version of role theory. It is only in their roles as group members (citizens) dealing with another group that the majority of Britons employed paranoid-schizoid thinking (if, that is, Money-Kyrle is correct in the first place).

Yet, while this comes closer to the mark, it can hardly be a complete explanation, for much of the preceding analysis has focused on how the group becomes a container for individual anxieties. If we are to employ some version of role theory (as I believe we must), then it must take into account that much of the paranoid-schizoid anxiety that the group confronts stems from the individual anxieties of its members. That is, it must take into account that the boundary between private and public is remarkably fluid. The concept of group holding and interpretation implies that the group provides psychic services to its members, objectifying their anxieties, and so reinforcing defenses based upon splitting and idealization. From the holding and interpretation perspective, it appears that public life serves what is an essentially private psychological function. If this is so, what must be explained is what holds the roles of public and private citizen apart in the first place.

One of the most important forces holding the roles of individual and group member apart is the way in which group holding and interpretation perform their psychological functions. In effect the group says to its members, "You may defend yourself from your internal persecutors by giving them the name our culture has chosen, which is currently 'Nazis.' In fearing and fighting Nazis, you will be able to preserve a large section of your private life from constant invasion of your own persecutors." Keeping the roles of group member and individual citizen separate, then, is part of the group-sanctioned defense in the first place. It is what makes the defense work. Otherwise expressed, it is the role theory that we employ to explain how paranoid-schizoid anxieties can be confined to group life without spilling over into private life *that is itself the defense against this spillover.* Group members hold their private and public lives separate—that is, they enact role theory—because it is only by doing so that they can take advantage of the defenses the group offers. Role theory is not so much why group "holding" works as how it works. In a word, role differentiation reinforces splitting. Obviously, none of this denies that the differentiation of roles may have other, more objective functions in a complex society. Here is another example of how a psychological function (defense) works through an institutional, bureaucratic function—in this case, the division of labor.

There is a final irony to this account. Both Turquet and Kernberg stress that it is the group itself that often constitutes the greatest threat to its members because of response bombardment, ignorance of individual uniqueness, and the like. Individuals thus take advantage of the defense offered by the group (group holding) to defend against individual anxiety, an individual anxiety that is heightened by the group itself. The group, at least, pays its debts. And the cost, once again, is the emotional growth of the group members in their roles as group members.

Ten-year-old Richard's analysis (*Narrative of a Child Analysis*) took place during the German bombing of England. This was reflected in Richard's play and drawings, which featured a great many wartime themes, in which Germans were invariably the persecutors. Richard's fundamental problem, we recall, was inadequate splitting-and-idealization. He "could not keep the destructive and Hitleresque part of himself from crowding in on and taking over the good part," as Meltzer puts it.[29] Had Richard been older, and perhaps a little less anxious, he might have had an easier time of it. As an adult citizen or soldier he might have made better use of all the cultural defenses available, defenses that help keep Hitler walled up—or rather, projected outwards, which amounts to the same thing—where he belongs.

My argument could be criticized as being out of touch with reality and, as such, filled with unintended irony. Hitler was, after all, a real persecutor. Even paranoids have real enemies, and Hitler was it. But this is precisely the point. Though I have emphasized the creation of enemies who are not real, Money-Kyrle's example concerns the denial of enemies who are. It is paranoid-schizoid anxiety that, if Money-Kyrle is correct, led Britons to deny a real threat in order not to have to confront what was even more threatening: this real threat (terrible as it was) intensified by primitive persecutory fears. Although Money-Kyrle does not specify the exact process involved, presumably he is referring to what Klein calls manic defense, associated with the early depressive position, which may be employed to deny anxiety, particularly anxiety in which realistic and paranoid-schizoid elements are mixed, reinforcing each other. For example, Klein uses this defense to explain the "apparent lack of fear" of some Britons toward the German bombing. "Analysis revealed that the objective danger-situation had revived . . . early phantastic anxieties to such an extent that the objective danger-situation had to be denied."[30]

Before proceeding, a possible objection must be addressed. From the structuralist perspective in sociology, roles are the rules of behavior that individuals are expected to follow when performing certain socially recognized activities. Understood thus, roles do not reach very deeply into the psyche of the individual. Individuals do not so much become the roles they play as accommodate themselves to them.[31] Such a view of roles could not, of course, support my argument. There is, however, another way to look at roles that, influenced by the school of symbolic interactionism, focuses upon how individuals make roles—transforming, creating, and enacting them so as to serve their own needs, albeit within the constraints set by the array of roles recognized by the culture. The problem with some versions of this approach, however, is that it makes roles run deep into the psyche only by making the psyche shallow. Erving Goffman's perspective, in which the individual is his role, with virtually nothing left over, is exemplary.[32] However, other role theorists influenced by symbolic interactionism, such as Turner and Zurcher,

take the relationship between role and identity much more seriously, recognizing that while identity is not defined by its roles, roles
nonetheless serve an important function in helping to secure individual identity.[33] This is not my perspective either, since it fails to
appreciate fully the ways in which roles serve emotional needs, as
Bernard Meltzer and John Petras suggest.[34] Nevertheless, it comes
closer by recognizing that roles are created by individuals to serve
psychological needs.

Role theorists generally believe that individuals organize their
roles into a hierarchy, some roles being much more important than
others. Seen from this perspective, one would not expect the role of
citizen to be dominant in our culture (even though it might have
been in fifth-century Athens). Yet, the order of a hierarchy is not
given; it depends on one's perspective. And from the perspective of
psychological function, it may well be that the role of citizen is quite
important, as it contains and walls off the aggression and anxiety
that threatens to disintegrate the self and contaminate other roles.
Seen from the top down (that is, from the perspective of social structure), occupational and family roles are dominant. Seen from the
bottom up (from the perspective of psychological need and defense),
other roles may be equally important. These remarks do not, of
course, exhaust all the issues raised when one considers the relationship between depth psychology and role theory. My argument is
only that there are theoretical grounds to believe that some roles
reach deeply into the psyche and as such may interact with the
phenomena with which psychoanalysis is concerned. As usual,
Freud figured this out first. His answer to how the little boy quells
his castration anxiety—by identifying not merely with his father but
also with his own future social role (as a man who will have authority, a wife, and give her babies)—fully appreciates the way in which
roles may reinforce a psychological defense, as well as how deeply
these roles must penetrate the psyche in order to do so.[35]

Yet, I am aware that my argument raises as many questions as it
answers. For example, do those individuals with greater paranoid-
schizoid anxiety, who presumably invest the role of citizen with
more aggression and fear than others, experience greater role conflict (which occurs when the demands of two or more roles conflict;
the working mother, for example, may be torn between the demands
of family and profession) between the roles of citizen and loving
family member? Perhaps not. It may be that splitting and projection

are quite functional here in holding these roles rigidly apart, and thus in reducing conflict, albeit at a cost. One would also like to know more about the psychological mechanisms involved in role "investment." Presumably projective identification plays a major role. But why is it that roles often enrich rather than deplete us? Probably because we reintroject that part of ourselves projectively identified with the role, enriched by various cultural meanings associated with the role. And do those with the greatest paranoid-schizoid anxiety, who use the role of citizen, for example, to contain this anxiety, reintroject less (in order to keep this anxiety outside) and hence live out more impoverished roles? Perhaps, but these must remain questions for further study. They seem particularly fruitful questions, however, in that they lend themselves to empirical, not just theoretical, research. This research could contribute much to group psychology, as long as it avoids defining the individual as tantamount to his roles and so producing a comprehensive theory only by flattening the subject.

Internal Threats, External Threats

Nothing in my analysis denies the existence of real threats, real enemies, or real persecutors. Though the screen perspective focuses on how we create these threats, some enemies are born, not made. The real point is that paranoid-schizoid thinking, reinforced by the group as a defense against the individual anxieties of its members, leads the group to misperceive its environment. From a Kleinian perspective, psychological factors constitute a world, a world built out of our phantasies (screen perspective). However, this world does not exist in a vacuum. It interacts with a real one, the world as it really is, a world that is at least in part constituted by the effects of our phantasies (process perspective). From this viewpoint, some psychological worlds are more functional than others, because they correspond more accurately with the objective world. Perhaps this sounds too pat, but consider the alternatives: that we may apprehend the world in a direct, unmediated fashion (logical positivism); or that the world of our phantasies is the only world (absolute idealism). The following case study, as well as the study that concludes this chapter, should further clarify the relationship between internal and external worlds.

The Glacier Metal Company: A Case Study of Paranoid-Schizoid Defenses

Elliott Jaques examined a relatively peaceful labor-management dispute from a Kleinian perspective. One of his conclusions was that individuals in both labor and management had come to use the organization of the company as a psychological defense. They took "those impulses and internal objects that would otherwise give rise to psychotic anxiety, and pool[ed] them in the life of the . . . [company]."[36] This did not lead Jaques to conclude that the Glacier Metal had become psychotic, whatever that would mean exactly. However, Jaques did find in the relations of the group manifestations of unreality, splitting, and paranoia, behavior that he regards as the social counterpart of—although not identical to—what would appear as psychotic symptoms in individuals "who have not developed the ability to use the mechanism of association in social groups to avoid psychotic anxiety."[37] One reason the reorganization of the company was so threatening, therefore, is that it required individuals in both labor and management to reorganize their own defenses against psychotic anxiety as well.

Labor dealt with this threat by dividing management into various constellations along the lines of good and bad. Often these constellations were quite complex, but the basic pattern was straightforward: good management meant those managers who dealt with labor on a daily basis; bad management involved those managers removed from the shop floor and negotiating table. This allowed labor to negotiate with management in a peaceful and fruitful manner, by locating the source of threat elsewhere, in split-off and emotionally distant "bad management." Splitting and idealization-devaluation allowed labor to negotiate with an entity it deeply feared. As important, splitting protected day-to-day relationships between management and labor on the shop floor from the threat posed by management-sponsored reorganization.[38]

Management's concerns were different. Management was less fearful of labor, more concerned about whether the workers could be relied upon to do their jobs properly. Management dealt with this essentially depressive anxiety (about the goodness of the object) by means of manic denial. Labor was idealized. This, though, did little to improve relations between them: "The more the workers' representatives attacked the managers, the more the managers idealized them. . . . The greater the concessions given by management to the workers, the greater was the guilt and fear of depressive anxiety in the workers, and hence the greater the retreat to paranoid attitudes as a means of avoiding depressive anxiety."[39] Management's idealization of the workers promoted depressive anxiety among the workers, in part because they felt guilty at not living up to management's ideals. More important, management's idealization of the workers showed management to be a fundamentally humane and responsive entity. This made it more difficult for labor to split management into good and bad. It also generated depressive guilt— namely, that labor had attacked an essentially good object with the unconscious hope of destroying it. Indeed, perhaps labor's recalcitrance regarding reorganization would end up destroying management, and with it labor itself. The company on which all depended would go under, and with it the source of goodness and security in the world. In order to defend itself against such depressive anxiety, labor resorted to paranoid-schizoid defenses. This illustrates an important point. Paranoid-schizoid defenses may be employed to defend against depressive as well as paranoid anxiety.

A key Kleinian assumption is that mental life is characterized by a continuous stream of unconscious phantasy. Jaques argues that group life is influenced by such phantasy, particularly as group members may come to share certain phantasies about the organization. What Jaques calls the "phantasy social form and content of an institution" is a virtual parallel organization, which may either reinforce or contradict the aims of the actual organization. Bion's basic assumption groups are exemplary, although Jaques states that he does not find Bion very useful in this regard, as the relationship of basic assumption groups to the paranoid-schizoid and depressive positions remains unclear.[40] In the case of Glacier Metal, the content of the group phantasies closely paralleled the paranoid-schizoid and depressive defenses outlined above (recall that for Klein the phantasy *is* the defense) and were focused on a committee of representatives from management and labor. The semisecret nature of this committee may have made phantasizing about it easier, and Jaques believes that its members were unconsciously quite aware that they were the objects of a great deal of phantasizing. When the committee had little of importance to do, this arrangement was actually quite

functional. The management-labor committee could become the repository of all the fears and hopes of management and labor, allowing their day-to-day relations to be conducted on a more realistic
basis. After the reorganization, however, the management-labor
committee was given some difficult and important tasks and proved
utterly incapable of accomplishing them. The reason, concludes
Jaques, is that the committee members were so busy acting out the
unconscious phantasies of the group (Jaques explains this process in
terms of projective identification) that they could not free themselves to perform real work.

While Jaques raises a number of issues that are helpful in understanding group life, five are central. First, paranoid-schizoid defenses—splitting and idealization-devaluation—can be quite functional for group life. Indeed, this is a key reason it is very difficult to
move beyond this stage. These defenses work, allowing group members to interact with something deeply feared, albeit at the cost of
emotional growth: entry into the depressive position. It also appears
that the unconscious phantasies projected into leadership may severely constrain it, preventing it from successfully undertaking
complex challenges. Second, paranoid-schizoid defenses are doubly
favored. They are evoked not only by (possibly) objectively threatening events, such as the reorganization itself, but also by friendly
gestures by management, albeit for different reasons: fear in the first
case, guilt in the second. What Freud remarked about neurotic
symptoms applies to paranoid-schizoid defenses as well: they are
overdetermined, evoked by quite different stimuli.

Third, were an observer to attempt to predict the psychological
response of either management or labor by assuming that groups
respond as they are treated (relational symmetry), he would be mistaken. Group psychology is not a mirror model. Fourth, even if
Bion's basic assumptions are rarely seen in the groups we run across
in everyday life, his hypothesis, shared by Jaques, that groups help
the individual defend against his most primitive and profound anxieties—what Jaques calls psychotic anxiety—is important. From a
Kleinian perspective, the paranoid-schizoid position (whose full-
blown emergence in the adult would indeed be psychotic) never
disappears and is never fully repressed. It always hovers in the
background, even in the normal adult. Indeed, this is why groups
are so psychologically important, as Jaques suggests. They reinforce

individuals' defenses against paranoid-schizoid anxiety: splitting and idealization.

The fifth point concerns a possible counterargument. It might be argued that labor *should* distrust management. Even when management is forthcoming and friendly, its motive is only to further its long-term interests, interests objectively hostile to those of labor. Yet, even if one holds this position, this case study should be cause for concern. Jaques's key point is not so much that labor was able to cooperate with management only via splitting and idealization-devaluation but that the anxieties of its members prevented labor from accurately assessing the intentions of management. This failure in reality testing must be deleterious to labor's interest, no matter how one defines these interests.

The Trouble with Groups

If it is no reification to speak of group psychology, then it is not misleading to speak of group morality. Group morality is the conduct of individuals—in their roles as group members (for example, union leader, union member, soldier, bank president, member of an ethnic group)—toward other groups and individuals, in so far as this conduct may be said to be right or wrong. From a Kleinian perspective, the key problem with the morality of groups is that it tends to remain fixated at the paranoid-schizoid position, in part because paranoid-schizoid defenses against anxiety are particularly efficient—but therefore no less morally problematic—when reinforced by others, as in the group. The very effectiveness of paranoid-schizoid defenses, characterized by splitting and projection, discourages the integration of good and bad necessary for the development of reparative psychology and morality. By reparative morality I mean a morality based upon *caritas*, a love and concern for the object for its own sake. The outlines of such a morality, as well as its psychological basis, were laid out previously. One way in which paranoid anxiety may inhibit reparative morality is suggested in Robert Coles' study of wealthy children, *Privileged Ones*. Coles notes with surprise the large number of children of the wealthy who fear that all will be taken from them by the poor. Drawings and discussions revealed that many of these children, none of whom were clinically disturbed, saw their houses as fortresses, besieged by the greedy, criminal masses. Coles speculates that it is guilt, generated by the children's recognition that their advantages are shared by so few, that produces such paranoia.[41] Klein tells us that paranoia, by splitting the good and bad, stands as a barrier to reparative impulses. She goes on to suggest that this paranoia will be greatest among the downtrodden, whose harsh circumstances reinforce primitive anxieties.[42] Coles, who found far less paranoia among underprivileged children, suggests the opposite conclusion: it is paranoid fears among the elite that social theorists interested in greater fairness must address. This Klein-cum-Coles perspective might more fully explain (I assume that issues such as this are always overdetermined) why social change in the direction of greater equality is so difficult: greed and the pleasures of privilege are reinforced by paranoid anxiety. A Kleinian perspective also reveals why greater equality is so important: not only is it desirable in itself, but it may also act to reduce paranoid guilt, thus possibly paving the way for the emergence of a reparative morality among elite groups.

Three Barriers to Reparative Morality

If one takes Klein seriously, one will not, however, be terribly optimistic about the emergence of a reparative morality among elite—or any other—groups. Groups tend to remain stuck at the paranoid-schizoid stage. In the child, the development of reparative morality depends upon the child's ambivalent love for his mother (or primary caretaker), a love coupled with hate that leads to guilt and remorse over the harm that he has done to her in phantasy. This is the beginning of the depressive position, as well as of the morality of reparation. Its development depends upon three things: first, love for a concrete other; second, a decrease in splitting; third, that depressive anxiety itself not be too severe. In each of these areas the group is deficient.

Regarding the first point, Meltzer makes an interesting remark, arguing that only in intimate relationships, in which our passions are fully and concretely engaged, "can we experience the conflicts of emotional meaning which contribute to the growth of the mind." Primary among these conflicts, as we have seen, is that we love and hate the same person, an ambivalence that ideally leads to the integration of these powerful emotions in the depressive position. Our other relations, Meltzer continues, "are really relationships that contribute nothing to our growth and development."[43] In fact, Meltzer exaggerates. Through identification and the transference, individuals are able to use imaginary relationships with others (whom, perhaps, they have never even met) to generate the conflicts, especially ambivalence, that foster emotional growth. Think, for example, of how we may use a teacher, whom we may not know very well, as an emotional stand-in for a parent. Klein suggests that such relations may, in fact, be especially conducive to emotional growth. Because our feelings toward the stand-in will likely be less intense, the chances of integrating the emotions evoked by the stand-in are greater. "Just because his feelings towards these new people are less intense, his drive to make reparation, which may be impeded if the feelings of guilt are over-strong, can now come more fully into play."[44]

Yet, if Meltzer does not quite capture the dynamics of emotional learning, his comments nonetheless fit the large group exceptionally well. Response bombardment (too many stimuli of too low quality), the threat posed by the group to the self, the difficulty of establishing one's boundaries at the "skin of his neighbor," the tendency of projective identification to distribute parts of the self too widely in the large group—all this and more diffuses emotion so widely in the large group that no particular relationship, real or imaginary, develops the intensity necessary for emotional learning. To be sure, organization and bureaucracy generally control this diffusion. However, the cost is identical. Bureaucracy and organization, as we have seen, restrict communication and interaction so severely that emotional learning never begins. If the unorganized large group diffuses the emotional intensity necessary for learning, bureaucracy represses it. The outcome is the same in either case. The group member, qua group member, tends to remain fixated at the paranoid-schizoid level.

This does not mean, however, that group emotions are therefore pale and vapid. To the contrary, it means that emotions associated with the activities of the group tend to remain at a primitive—that is, paranoid-schizoid—level, even if these emotions are not always consciously experienced and expressed. In the group, emotional learning is thwarted because its primary condition is not present: love for a concrete other. Freud wrote of how it is psychologically

almost impossible to "love they neighbor as thyself." Love of abstract others, he went on to say, must be a feeble love indeed.[45] We
see now more fully the consequences. Our relationships to abstract
others become not less intense but simply more primitive, governed
by principles more closely associated with talion morality than with
the morality of reparation.

Splitting and idealization-devaluation, the second barriers to
reparative morality, are the dominant defensive strategies of most
groups. They are such pervasive defenses in part because they often
lack an obvious reality check. Once a certain level of cognitive maturity is reached, it becomes more and more difficult (but not impossible under the pressure of severe anxiety) to deny that good mother
and bad mother are one. But, how is the average individual to evalu-
ate the group-sanctioned distinction between "aggressive Soviet
leaders" and "peace-loving Soviet people"? Furthermore, groups are
abstract, divisible entities to begin with. As such, they lend themselves to splitting—Soviet leaders and the Soviet people really *are*
different things—in a way that individuals do not. The other reason
this defense is so pervasive is because it works. It really does reduce
anxiety. Indeed, splitting is often quite functional, enabling us to
peacefully interact with something deeply feared, as Jaques's study
reveals.

Klein recognized that splitting in the very young child serves a
useful purpose, analogous to the function of splitting in the group.
Splitting protects a portion of the very young child's ego from his
own fears, enabling the child to develop a relationship to the good
object. In the group, splitting protects the members of the group
from their own aggression, often enhancing group solidarity. However, Klein also recognized that the benefits of splitting were limited.
Carried on too long, it can seriously weaken the ego, preventing its
eventual integration during the depressive position. Fortunately,
love and cognitive maturity generally curtail splitting. This is not
the case in the group. What can sometimes be an effective strategy
for managing anxiety and aggression generally becomes, in the
group, a socially sanctioned worldview that prevents the development of reparative morality.

The third barrier to the development of reparative morality is the
intensity of depressive anxiety itself. Depressive anxiety emerges
when the child realizes that good mother and bad mother are one.

The child fears that he will never be able to restore her to wholeness, to repair the damage he has done to her in phantasy. If this anxiety is too intense, the child will once again resort to defenses associated with the paranoid-schizoid position, such as splitting. Generally, however, the mother's continued love, coupled with the child's developing ability to show love and concern in new, realistic ways (for example, words, hugs) prevents this regression. Once again, however, these barriers to regression are less powerful in the group. Unlike mothers and fathers, other groups rarely return love for hate. Furthermore, even when other groups do, this may paradoxically serve to heighten paranoid-schizoid defenses against depressive anxiety, as the Glacier Metal Company's idealization of its workers suggests. Paranoid-schizoid morality (that is, *lex talionis*) is thus doubly favored: it may be employed to defend against paranoid-schizoid fears, and it may be reverted to in order to defend against depressive anxiety.

Caveats and Qualifications

There are many different types of groups. It must, therefore, be somewhat misleading to treat them all in terms of Kleinian principles. Yet, while this is surely this case, it is not quite clear what types of groups a Kleinian account is best suited to explain, with one exception. It seems that a Kleinian account is better able to explain the behavior of large groups (in which every member no longer interacts with every other member) than of small ones, because the large group more closely resembles the Kleinian parent: a screen. Bion's account of the small group might seem to be an exception to this generalization. Certainly he sees himself as using Kleinian principles. Yet, as Jaques points out, Bion is never able to integrate his basic assumption groups with Klein's fundamental categories, the paranoid-schizoid and depressive positions.[46]

One might argue that the degree of formal, bureaucratic organization is the key variable, much as Freud does in Group Psychology and the Analysis of the Ego. Yet if my thesis is correct, the key difference is that highly organized groups are simply more efficient than less organized ones at defending against paranoid-schizoid anxiety by means of splitting and projection (for example, "Our problem exists in a complex world that is to be mastered by our

techniques; it does not lie within ourselves") and denial (bureaucratic busyness with tasks and routine as an escape from the internal
world of the psyche). That is, the key difference between a less and a
more organized group is that the latter helps its members contain
their anxiety better than the former; thus, we see less anxiety in
organized groups to begin with. Highly organized groups have transformed those cultural meanings that usually "hold" paranoid-schizoid anxiety into procedures and rituals of an especially orderly and
methodical character. Bureaucracy and organization are the rationalization of the cultural containment of anxiety. Needless to say, this is
not the sole, or even primary, function of bureaucracy and organization. It is, however, an important function that is generally given
insufficient attention.

Certainly some groups are reparative. The American Friends Service Committee (the social action arm of the Quakers) comes readily
to mind. In addition, in most towns and cities there are organizations, frequently voluntary, whose goals include feeding and hous-
ing the poor, fighting fires, and saving lives—all reparative activities. Yet, it would be easy to overestimate the number of reparative
groups. A paranoid-schizoid orientation toward the world is not
incompatible with genuine love and concern for aspects of it. Indeed, this is precisely what splitting and projection allow: namely,
that some groups may be treated well by exaggerating their differences from other groups, which become (via paranoid projection)
the source of all evil. Probably the best indicator of a group's paranoid-schizoid character is not its hatred and aggression (which are
often suppressed) but the degree of idealization it practices. Excessive idealization—of one's own group, values, or favorite person (for
example, God)—is almost always a sign that intense persecutory
fears are bubbling under the surface. Idealization, as Klein points
out, is a corollary of persecutory anxiety, an attempt to protect the
good object from aggression by isolating it.[47]

Idealization, and the intense love and commitment that it often
inspires, is often quite attractive. In this respect paranoid-schizoid
morality should not be underrated. It is not merely about hatred and
fear. Nevertheless, one should not overlook the costs of such a morality, in which moral goodness stems not so much from a desire to
make reparation but from the displacement of aggression onto others. In the paranoid-schizoid position, every act of care and concern

is purchased by an act (or phantasy, which redounds as fear of persecution: talion morality) of aggression and hatred against others. Here, at least, the economic model holds: the more we love some, the more we must hate others, in order to protect the loved ones from our own aggression. Furthermore, even the love and care associated with the paranoid-schizoid position is problematic, in that it tends to be rigid and one-dimensional, concerned more with the idea of the good person or group than with the reality. The individual in this position loves not a complete other but only his or its idealized good aspects. The complexity of the other is not respected; shades of grey disappear as the all-good aspects of the other are idealized and its all-bad aspects are split off and parceled out. Here is the true ground of the rigid authoritarianism that Money-Kyrle associates with the paranoid-schizoid position.[48] This perspective on idealization may also help to explain the factionalism and charges of deviation that seem to characterize so many ideological groups, in which conformity or schism become the only options. The idealization of the beliefs on which the group is based becomes so extreme that reinterpretation and revision are tantamount to consorting with the devil.

Reparative Leadership, Reparative Groups?

At the conclusion of *Civilization and Its Discontents*, Freud speculates about the possibility that cultural development might lead men and women to master their aggression.[49] Even such a tempered expression of optimism is surprising, given the melancholy tone of the book, and one is reminded once again that Freud was a man of the Enlightenment. Can one find comparable grounds for tempered optimism in the Kleinian account of groups? One must look very hard, for the Kleinian account suggests that the issue is not cultural development per se but the very structure of groups, especially the way in which this structure reinforces the most primitive defenses. Perhaps it would be more fruitful to turn our attention briefly to the question of leadership.

Herbert Marcuse has suggested that responsible political leadership today consists largely in resisting the aggressive urges of the population.[50] The Kleinian study of groups adds a corollary to this

statement. Responsible political leaders will recognize that the public is scared to death: of its own aggressive urges, as well as of the
enemy. Responsible leaders will therefore not exaggerate the goodness of their own group and the badness of the other. Talk of the
opposition as an "evil empire" only encourages splitting and projection. In fact, Ronald Reagan's designation of the Soviet Union as the
focus of evil in the world exemplifies both phenomena especially
well. Conversely, a political leader who recognizes that "the only
thing we have to fear is fear itself" expresses deep insight into the
political psychology of the group. By calling the enemy by its right
name—not only some evil group, but also our own anxiety—such a
leader may help the group minimize its use of paranoid-schizoid
defenses. In so doing, he or she might turn the group's attention
toward the restoration and protection of its own goodness—that is,
the restoration of threatened group values. Could such a leader encourage the development of a reparative morality within the group?
It seems as though he or she might.

Who is a reparative leader? One for whom the opposition, no
matter how intensely fought, remains part of a moral or ethical
whole to which all people belong. As part of this whole, the opposition partakes of the good; it is not simply the evil other. Such a
leader also recognizes that his own group's claim to goodness is
incomplete. The reparative leader does not protect either his leadership or the unity of his group by demonizing others. Rather, his
leadership is based upon his ability to interpret the group's moral
tradition in such a way that it includes the opponent, without utterly remaking the opponent and denying his otherness. The last clause
is important; otherwise the leaders of the Crusades could be called
reparative. Gandhi and Martin Luther King come readily to mind as
genuine reparative leaders.

In the United States today, one hears grave doubts about the nation's ability to protect and live up to its ideals. In fact, it is depressive anxiety regarding the nation's ability to protect its good objects
(values), rather than a paranoid fear of external persecutors, that
most influences contemporary public life (this assertion is supported in the next section). A truly reparative leader might be able to
interpret our anxieties with sympathetic accuracy sufficient to less-
en them. He might be also able to interpret our political tradition in

such a way as to make past reparative achievements, such as the Civil Rights Legislation of the mid-1960s, an inspiration for national policy. This outcome is unlikely, however, not merely because reparative leaders are rare (although they are) but also because the group is so susceptible to appeals aimed at mobilizing its paranoid-schizoid defenses. It is also susceptible to the mock reparative leader, who reinforces phantasies of denial. In an environment in which leaders compete by heightening anxieties on the one hand, and by denying real dangers on the other, there is little ground for optimism—not because these leaders are bad (they are just as scared as the rest) but because the group is so vulnerable to appeals to its paranoid-schizoid defenses, for all the reasons mentioned.

Ronald Reagan and the Politics of Mock Reparation

With all the emphasis on paranoia, persecutors, and so forth, one might think that the Kleinian explanation of the group applies only to hostile and aggressive groups led by truly paranoid leaders (recall Bion's claim that the group usually picks its sickest member as leader). In fact, the implications of a Kleinian analysis are more subtle, a point revealed in the following case study of the appeal of Ronald Reagan. This case study is also intended to give substance to a number of otherwise rather abstract claims about groups. In spite of his talk about an "evil empire," Reagan appears not to be especially paranoid, and the American electorate, while apparently quite scared, is not terribly aggressive, at least in historical perspective vis-à-vis other powerful nations. These points too are addressed by my Kleinian group theory.

In a fascinating psychoanalytic study of political leadership, Vamik Volkan interprets Atatürk, the father of modern Turkey, as a reparative narcissistic leader (a category that differs from what I call a reparative leader). By this term Volkan means a leader who enhances the integration of his grandiose self by idealizing a group of others whom he then includes as an idealized extension of himself.[51] I shall argue that Ronald Reagan is a mock reparative leader. Mock reparation, it will be recalled, is a defense against early depressive anxiety. One fears that the good object upon which one depends has been destroyed by one's own greed, selfishness, and aggression and that one is not strong enough, good enough, or self-possessed enough to put the good object back together. Mock reparation denies dependence on the good object. Accordingly it is closely associated with manic denial. Mock reparation is also often coupled with phantasies of being able to repair the damaged object magically. Because mock reparation involves phantasies of total independence and autonomy, often coupled with phantasies of omnipotence, it may be seen as having a strong narcissistic element. While phantasies of narcissistic perfection (for example, "I am so perfect that I need no one") and omnipotence are not themselves equivalent to mock reparation, these narcissistic phantasies are a psychological reservoir readily drawn upon in times of depressive anxiety to provide content to mock reparative defenses.

With the term *group (die Masse)*, Freud referred to any assembly of individuals more organized than the crowd but less organized than the army or Catholic church. Because the crowd lacks direction and leadership, it is not a true group. On the other hand, if a group is more organized than the army or church (Freud is primarily concerned with the relationship between leaders and followers in these organizations, not the internal structure of the high command), then it functions, according to Freud, more like an individual, at least in so far as bureaucracy and organization provide a measure of central direction and control.[52] The American electorate, especially in the era of mass media, seems to readily qualify as a large group in Freud's sense. The electorate responds to leaders but like the enlisted man or laity is not in a continuous bureaucratic relationship with the high command.

In *The American Voter*, Campbell et al. concluded that opinions about specific policies play a modest role in voters' choices of a presidential candidate. Other studies seem to support this view, suggesting that the candidate's personality, particularly whether he is perceived as a capable leader, is the single most important factor.[53] Today, however, it is widely held that positive judgments about Reagan's policies contributed significantly to his victory, both in 1980 and 1984. Yet, closer examination reveals how truly difficult it is to separate judgments about policy from those about personality and affect. In one of the most sophisticated studies of the 1980 presidential election, Miller and Shanks attempt to distinguish the relative effect of general feelings about the candidates ("net affect") from the effect of candidates' policies.[54] They find policies more important, but not greatly so. For example, net affect has a more significant impact than the candidates' views on taxes or employment.

However, Miller and Shanks have no way of distinguishing the symbolic appeal of a policy (for example, "A low tax rate makes me proud to be an American, for a low tax rate respects individual initiative") from its material appeal ("A low tax rate will make me rich"). Since studies have shown that most voters do not vote their pocketbooks in any straightforward sense (for example, those in deteriorating economic circumstances are generally only slightly more critical of the president than those doing well),[55] it does not seem farfetched to conclude that the symbolic appeal of Reagan's policies is a significant factor. These policies appeal to traditional American values and thus make voters feel good, regardless of the actual material affect of these policies. If this is so, then voters' judgments about a particular policy and their feelings about the president who promotes them (net affect) are not two separate things but aspects of the same appeal. Policy creates affect, and approval of policy is an expression of affect. This view is supported by studies of the importance of "policy projection," in which voters attribute desirable policies to candidates with high net affect, regardless of whether the candidate actually holds these policies.[56]

The point of these considerations is not to promote a sort of political-psychological scepticism—that is, we don't know why people find one candidate more appealing than another, they just do. It is rather to suggest that it is not misleading to view the appeal of Reagan's policies in symbolic terms, as an attempt to assuage voters' depressive anxieties and, in this sense, as intimately bound up to how voters feel about the president: his personality and affect. This view does not, of course, imply that voters' material judgments about policies are unimportant. It does, however, imply not only that it is enormously difficult to separate the material from the symbolic but that in most studies the result of this difficulty has been to underestimate the symbolic for all the reasons mentioned. Psychological and material explanations need not conflict with each other. As discussed previously, the psychological effect works through the material effect.

Anxiety, Illusion, and the American Dream

In his autobiography, Where's the Rest of Me? Reagan tells the story
of one of his first jobs, that of "re-creating" baseball games. He was
not present at the game but received brief coded messages by telegraph of each play. Reagan's job was to give life to the game, to
describe it as though he were actually there. Yet, no one was fooled;
indeed, occasionally the public was invited into the studio to watch
him "visualize" the game. One day the telegraph went dead in the
middle of the game, and Reagan was forced to improvise plays. He
tells us that it was terribly important that the audience not know
that the line went dead.[57] Why, since the audience was aware that
Reagan was not out at the ballpark? Garry Wills suggests the answer
in Reagan's America. Even though all knew that Reagan's presence
at the game was an illusion, there was "complicity in make-believe."
All—broadcaster and audience—knew it was vital that the illusion
be maintained, that neither remind the other that it was all pretend,
lest the pleasure in the performance be shattered. For many claimed
that Reagan's re-creations were better, more dramatic, than the actual game.[58]

Freud claims that illusions are wish-fulfillment phantasies. As
such, they stem from our anxieties: with our wishes and illusions
we seek to alleviate an anxiety.[59] Klein makes the same point about
unconscious phantasy. The anxiety that Reagan addresses is a feeling of helplessness: that America's economy and society is out of
control. More precisely, the anxiety is that Americans have lost control over their collective lives. Consider the following signs of national decline (whether these signal an actual loss of mastery or are
only widely perceived as such is not important here), as reported by
a series of surveys in Public Opinion regarding the concerns of
Americans: cities have become ungovernable; the service economy
no longer provides good quality services; the national economy
seems perpetually vulnerable; student achievement scores are lower; the quality of American-made products often seems lower than
that of the foreign competition; businessmen and Wall Street find it
difficult to think beyond the next quarter; the American worker is
complacent and ill prepared compared to his foreign counterpart;
drugs and crime have invaded the schools, professional sports, and
executive suite.[60] Troublesome enough in themselves, these signs
share an even more alarming quality. None is simply the result of

outside forces beyond America's control. Rather, they are the result of Americans' own greed, selfishness, and aggression.

To frame the issue in the language of Kleinian psychoanalysis, many Americans fear that they have destroyed the good object on which we all depend for our prosperity, even our lives: America. Many Americans also fear that we continue to be so greedy and selfish that we cannot work together to repair America. In response to this depressive anxiety, many Americans have turned away from public life to their own private affairs. It is my thesis that this withdrawal (which may be individually quite rational) is quite often accompanied by an unconscious phantasy, similar to what Jaques calls the "phantasy social form and content of an institution." The phantasy is one of utter autonomy: that individual Americans need no one, no group, not even their own country. It is in this psychological context that Reagan is so appealing, for he labels narcissistic retreat into phantasies of omnipotence a return to the traditional verities. He calls our retreat from repairing America a return to traditional values. In so doing, Reagan translates manic denial into the language of the American dream.[61]

Since Garry Wills has so clearly shown how the myths of American history that Reagan evokes (they are myths not because they are false but because they equate a partial truth with the whole) serve to deny Americans' dependence on any one or any thing, I will not repeat this effort here. The key point is that many of our national myths focus solely upon individual initiative and thus deny the contribution of group effort to national achievement. For example, the American frontier was settled not only by lone cowboys and pioneer families but also by federal troops, civic organizations, community posses, and railroad combines. "The West was not settled by the gun but by gun-control laws," says Wills.[62] That is, the West was settled by cooperative, not merely individual, effort. Today, says Wills, we want to retain what we never had, a mythical frontier life, an America in which merit and hard work were the only paths to success, and in which the government did not interfere with the workings of the market's invisible hand. One sees Reagan's appeal to this myth nowhere more clearly than in his State of the Union speeches. These speeches have instituted a virtual cult of the hero, singling out individuals whose bravery reveals by contrast the torpid, stifling character of government action.[63]

Reagan's appeal to this myth is also seen in what has come to be known as The Speech, versions of which he has been giving for over twenty-five years.[64] In the version printed as an appendix to his autobiography, Reagan refers to specific government programs twenty-one times. These include farm programs, TVA, welfare programs, and social security. Every reference is critical, and every criticism is the same: collective government activity is inefficient, is beyond rational control, stifles individual initiative, and renders its intended beneficiaries passive, helpless, and dependent. Surely this is often the case or at least often a significant part of the story. That is, The Speech contains a plausible assessment of America's difficulties, and there is no reason to think that voters who found Reagan capable on the basis of this assessment were judging irrationally. Yet, The Speech is so one-sided in its attack on government (though Reagan obviously approves of some government activity, it finds no mention here; the Defense Department is mentioned only in so far as it runs 269 supermarkets that are said to lose $150 million annually) that it does not seem inappropriate to read it also as a way of addressing Americans' concerns regarding the decline of national mastery by denying the value of government activity in general.

The way in which the myth of American individualism serves an ideological function is familiar. It puts the onus for economic failure on the individual, not the economic system. In so doing it denies that the middle class and wealthy frequently depend upon government programs as much as the poor. What may not be so familiar is how the myth of American individualism is related to the issues we have been considering. Those who suffer depressive anxiety often find it especially difficult to acknowledge their dependence on another, lest they be forced to confront their deepest fear: that in their greed they have damaged beyond repair the other upon whom they depend. Even mature, realistic dependence on others, which in the social realm generally takes the form of collective activity (since we recognize that as a member of a group we can do much that we cannot do alone), is threatening. Reagan appeals to an electorate suffering from depressive anxiety. He addresses it by promoting a compensatory phantasy, a phantasy of manic denial: the illusion of total autonomy.

One sees an instance of this illusion in a surprising place—in Reagan's comparison of government to a needy baby: "Government is like a baby, an alimentary canal with an appetite at one end and no sense of responsibility at the other. If you keep feeding it, we will be up to our neck in something. . . . Debt."[65] With this comparison Reagan is suggesting that the need, the greed—and above all the helpless irresponsibility—are not ours but government's. This is the defensive reasoning of a small child, that of pure manic denial: "It is not I who am dependent on Mother; it is she who is dependent on me." Not merely communism but also the American government itself becomes an object on which to project our anxieties. Unlike communism, however, the American government must first be made an alien entity, totally unlike ourselves, the Other. This is the purpose of The Speech.

It is always difficult to link particular presidential policies with general attitudes held by the president, as responsible psychobiographical studies continually emphasize.[66] There are so many intervening factors (economic, political, social, as well as psychological) that any policy appears vastly overdetermined in retrospect. Nevertheless, several examples suggest themselves. Reagan's failure (though it is not his alone) to deal with the deficit may itself be a form of denial. It is as though Reagan has given Americans permission to refuse to pay for all they really want from government in order that they may deny their own need and greed. Translated into the language of unconscious phantasy, Americans' anxieties about the deficit might be couched in the following terms: "In our need and greed we have sucked the object on which we depend dry, taken more than it had to give, taken more than we were ever willing to put back. Now the good object is terribly weakened, and we shall all suffer terribly for it." How could Americans defend themselves against such depressive anxiety? One way is to render government incompetent by refusing it funds sufficient to support itself. In so doing we make our dependence on government less apparent—that is, we deny it utterly—as if to say, "How could I really need and depend upon something as incompetent, as unable to control itself, as all that?"

A second example is Reagan's Strategic Defense Initiative (SDI), which promises total autonomy, total independence. We need not depend upon the goodwill of the Soviets, their rational self-interest, or even their sanity. We need not depend upon the Soviets at all. We can guarantee ourselves total security without the cooperation of anyone else. We shall need no one. Indeed, we do not even need to rely on our *own* self-restraint, our ability to control our anxiety and aggression. Our cleverness will overcome our inability to trust others, as well as our lack of confidence in our ability to control ourselves. How such a phantasy serves as a manic defense against depressive anxiety, in which we doubt our ability to protect those whom we love from utter destruction at the hands of our own anxiety and aggression (thermonuclear war triggered by an American first strike, perhaps in response to a false alarm about a Soviet attack), is apparent.

At issue here is not the technical feasibility of SDI. In his March 1983 speech, Reagan presented SDI as a technology that would free us from dependence upon Soviet will. In his radio address of March 12, 1988, he reiterated this point, emphasizing the way in which SDI would protect us all from the scourge of nuclear war. That SDI might have a realistic, but far more limited, role to play in strategic defense is not at issue here. At issue is the way in which scientific and technological progress supports manic denial. The psychoanalyst Janine Chasseguet-Smirgel believes that it is "legitimate to take into account the external activating factors (which nonetheless have their roots in the individual psyche of every human being) of this ancient wish for reunification of ego and ideal, by the shortest possible route, namely Illusion. The development of the pathology I have attempted to outline is to be set to the account of those factors which take progress made by science as confirmation of the possibility of an immediate reunification of ego and ideal."[67]

Following Freud, Chasseguet-Smirgel treats the ego ideal as the avatar of primary narcissism: a standard of perfection, wholeness, and autonomy. While the ego ideal represents a standard inspired by primary narcissism, in health it is modulated by experience and reality and integrated with the superego. In depressive anxiety, on the other hand, narcissistic illusions of omnipotence (especially as they idealize an autonomy so perfect that the cooperation of others is redundant) are not well integrated. Rather than serve the ego as a source of ideals and inspiration, these illusions serve to deny the reality of interdependence. They defend a threatened ego with a phantasy. Perhaps only a nation suffering from depressive anxiety would take the purveyor of such an illusion seriously. For in many respects SDI is the perfect mock reparative phantasy, combining utter freedom from dependence with transcendence of the need for self-control.

Most of my examples have concerned domestic policy, in part because Reagan's ability to project American anxieties outward, onto foreign enemies, has been more thoroughly studied. I have been more interested in the way in which Reagan employs splitting and projection domestically, projecting national anxieties onto American government, which is then split off from individual Americans. Indeed, in this respect Reagan's strategy exemplifies an important Kleinian principle. Splitting is a complex mental phenomenon. It may take place along a number of different planes, and it may be employed iteratively, as when the good breast is split into good breast and bad nipple.[68]

Although the splitting is not so involved, a word about Reagan's foreign policy may nonetheless be helpful here. While it would not be mistaken to see Reagan's foreign policy as an assertion of frustrated American grandiosity on a world stage, it is significant that in most of Reagan's assertions of American power little is actually risked. America has tested herself primarily against easy targets, such as Grenada or Libya. When the going got tough, as in Lebanon, the tough went home. The model here is the 1984 Summer Olympics in Los Angeles, where Reagan led the cheering for America victorious, overlooking the fact that the toughest competitors, the Soviet Union and many of its allies, had stayed home. It is as though the American people desperately need confirmation of their goodness and strength (that is, reparative powers) but are not sufficiently confident to test themselves against the strongest or best, lest they risk another humiliating defeat. With Reagan the nation found a perfect president for such times, one who would provide an illusion of goodness and strength without putting too much at risk.

While my conclusions are hardly cause for optimism, it should not be overlooked that there seems to be a rational and healthy core in the attitude of Reagan and many Americans, suggesting that neither has fundamentally lost touch with reality. Consider the consequences were the nation to become convinced, as other nations have been, that it could overcome its fears of national weakness only by systematically conquering other lands! Sometimes illusion protects the ego, serving, rather than defeating, its reality-testing function. Indeed, there is cause for hope in the fact that so many Americans value a mock reparative leader. It suggests that many Americans are struggling with depressive anxiety. They have not regressed to the

stage of employing strictly paranoid-schizoid defenses against depressive anxiety. Demonizing other countries, or scapegoating domestic minorities for America's ills, would be examples of such
paranoid-schizoid defenses, defenses that Reagan, in spite of his talk
about an "evil empire," has not systematically evoked. In seeing
the enemy as "big government," Reagan at least retains some connection between us and the sources of our anxieties. It is only a partial
split.

Leadership and Complicity

Bion's characterization of the leader as often the sickest, most paranoid member of the group does not fit Reagan well. To be sure,
Reagan is quite skilled at using American myths to reinforce the
basically paranoid-schizoid strategy of splitting off a part of ourselves, labeling it bad and other (government), and making it the
repository of our anxieties. However, the way in which it is employed by Reagan seems not terribly sick as these things go. Another
of Bion's remarks about leaders may be closer to the mark. Bion
argues, as we have seen, that the leader is often not that unique,
hypnotic figure he is frequently made out to be. Rather, the leader is
more akin to an empty vessel, which the group members can fill up
with projected versions of their own needs. This leadership function
is best fulfilled by a compliant personality. If this applies to Reagan,
however, it does so only with major qualifications.

Reagan is a master at using American myths to reinforce group
defenses. This is an active, creative process, not the project of a
compliant personality. Reagan also seems to stand for something, to
be stubborn in his commitment to his basic values, even when doing
so is politically inexpedient. Yet, this sharply etched aspect of Reagan's character is mostly confined to the realm of symbols and values. There is widespread agreement, even among his supporters,
that Reagan is strikingly casual, even passive and withdrawn, in
attending to the details of how these symbols and values might be
realized in practice.[69] Perhaps this is because Reagan—and the remarkably tolerant voters—unconsciously realize that it is really the
symbolism that counts. It is the symbolism that reinforces psychological defenses, not reality (at least in the short run). In this sense
there may be an element of complicity between Reagan and many

voters—they both know it's really a game. In eagerly fostering and participating in this complicity (as Reagan did "re-creating" baseball games), while not mastering the details of what it would take to implement his policies, Reagan may be seen as a partially empty vessel. He is filled with symbolism that he articulates and uses far better than the average citizen. However, he seems to lack the consistent application of attention necessary to transform ideas into reality, perhaps because deep inside he shares with many voters the recognition (actually, the illusion; even symbolic politics has real consequences) that it is really all pretend. "Facts are stupid things," said Reagan (in a wonderful Freudian slip) in his valedictory address to the 1988 Republican National Convention.

Is there any theoretical (that is, psychoanalytical) basis to support the suspicion that Reagan and many voters are conspirators in a game of make-believe? Perhaps there is. Meltzer calls attention to a brief passage in Klein's *Narrative of a Child Analysis*, in which Klein tries to reassure Richard, who distrusts her because she is foreign. The question Klein asks is why should her reassurance decrease Richard's anxiety, as it did, since Klein knows (from subsequent events) that Richard is not really reassured in the least. Indeed, he is made even more suspicious by her reassurance, along the lines of "If she were really honest, she would not have to say how honest she is." Klein answers that while her reassurance did not convince Richard one whit, it reinforced his splitting and idealization by giving his need to idealize something to work with, even if it was only an unbelievable (to Richard) reassurance. Richard's anxiety was reduced by Klein's unwitting reinforcement of his paranoid-schizoid defenses.[70] Even falsehoods known to be such may reduce anxiety by supporting splitting and idealization, in which the known lie is itself split into conscious "truth" and unconscious lie. Here is the source of the perennial appeal of politicians and their promises. They make us feel better, even when we don't believe them, by giving our idealizing phantasies something to work with. This would explain too why the public always seems to come back for more.

Throughout this chapter the problem of group psychology has been posed in terms of the group's fixation at the paranoid-schizoid position and of the great difficulty it faces in entering the depressive position. This is because my primary concern is group morality, which has a fundamentally different character in each of these positions. Yet, from the perspective of the pure problem-solving efficiency of groups—how well they cope with internal and external demands—this may not be the key issue. Rather, the key issue is whether what Jaques calls the "phantasy social form and content of an institution" is in accord with its objective mission. Within limits, a paranoid-schizoid orientation toward the world may be quite functional for most groups, which really do live in a hostile environment. Nations, for example, really do have enemies; sometimes they even have persecutors. Of course, these limits may readily be exceeded, leading to misperceptions of reality sufficient to destroy the group. What counts is whether the group phantasy is roughly in accord with the objective demands placed on the group, its task in the world. A strictly reparative "phantasy social form and content of an institution," were the institution the American labor movement in the 1930s, might well have led to its destruction.

Seen from this perspective, the social phantasy that Reagan promotes—that America and Americans need no one—is self-defeating because it is out of touch with reality. We really do depend on each other, a lot. When collective activity and mutual interdependence are denied and downgraded, and strictly individual solutions emphasized, we become less adept at collective activity. This is true whether we actually withdraw from collective activity, or whether—as is usually the case—we continue in this activity but deny the interdependence involved. As we know, much "individual" economic activity takes the form of lobbying Congress and other government institutions to pass laws and regulations benefiting one group against another. In either case, we fail to self-consciously practice mature interdependence.

The result is a public world even less manageable, less subject to human mastery and control. It is this perception, in turn, that exacerbates individual withdrawal from the public world into the private. When the public world is perceived as beyond repair, most individuals do not abandon their attempts to make reparation and restore goodness—that is, they do not regress to the paranoid-schizoid position in every aspect of their lives. Rather, they simply shrink the realm to which reparative morality applies, generally to family and a few friends. This is, of course, the same dynamic by which groups become morally impoverished. While Reagan's appeal to the myths of rugged individualism may have a temporary (and perhaps temporarily necessary) soothing effect, in the long run this appeal is quite dangerous. For it encourages solutions—an actual or imagined withdrawal from public life—that can only make public life even less manageable, an outcome that can only encourage further withdrawal. In turn, such withdrawal eliminates any chance that public life might be inspired by reparative morality.

CHAPTER FOUR

Art and Reparation: Or, Poetry after Auschwitz?

Aesthetic formation proceeds under the law of the Beautiful, and the dialectic of . . . consolation and sorrow is the dialectic of the Beautiful.
—Herbert Marcuse, *The Aesthetic Dimension*

In an older and more ambitious philosophical tradition, art is not merely the topic of a special branch of philosophy called aesthetics. Art is instead the key to grasping the basic structure of the world. We come closest to apprehending the order and harmony of the world when we experience it through art. In the Neoplatonic tradition, "man's sense of his place in the universe is due to his judgment about the beautiful."[1] To be sure, some moderns have left aesthetics at the center of philosophy. Generally they have done so, however, by subjectivizing philosophy itself, reducing it to a matter of taste. For Nietzsche, art represents the primordial subjective experience of the world, an experience that accepts the mystery of being, rather than seeking comfort in the illusion ("aesthetic Socratism," he calls it)[2] of reason.

There are exceptions to this generalization. Heidegger, for example, seems to give aesthetics the objective function of creating a space within which Being might appear. Yet, while art is important to Heidegger, it is certainly no longer at the center of philosophy in his account. It is Croce's view of aesthetics as a branch of general linguistics concerned with the expression of human feeling that best captures the modern view. Or, as Susanne Langer puts it, art is a symbol of feeling.[3] Below I consider aspects of the aesthetic theory of the Frankfurt School, which stands in an interesting relationship to this larger tradition. On the one hand, the school, and especially Marcuse, grants art—which Marcuse calls the aesthetic sensibility—a role it has rarely played in the modern world: it becomes the medium by which a new order of reality is apprehended. On the other hand, both Marcuse and Adorno are concerned that art is too indiscriminate: that it will find beauty and pleasure where it should really find—if it is to be true to reality—ugliness and suffering. That is, they are concerned that art will be too transcendent, too eager to reveal a higher order, paying insufficient attention to this one. Marcuse and Adorno are also (but not merely) materialists.

It is in Adorno's famous comment about the barbarism of writing poetry after Auschwitz that the Frankfurt School's concerns about art are most dramatically expressed.[4] To be sure, Adorno came to argue that literature must resist the cynicism that his own comments about Auschwitz and lyric poetry express.[5] Nevertheless, this concern about art—that its beauty will cause us to forget the horror and the suffering—runs like a thread throughout his works. The aesthetic principle of stylization, he says, "make[s] an unthinkable fate appear to have had some meaning; it is transfigured, something of its horror is removed."[6] In the end this concern about art inhibits both their aesthetics.

My goal is to defend the truth-telling function of art, while recognizing that the subjective experience contained in art is valid in itself, not to be measured strictly in terms of how close it takes us to Plato's Ideas. Relevant questions include whether these two functions are in conflict. If not, what must the world be like, and what must we be like, so that the subjective function serves—or at least does not contradict—the truth-telling function? It may seem that in expressing it this way the terms of the debate have been subtly changed by quietly introducing a third term, for the subjective experience evoked by art is not the same thing as transcendence. While this is surely the case, they are nonetheless related. For the Frankfurt School, it is the subjective experience of eros, of which art is an almost pure—albeit highly sublimated—expression, that is the source of transcendence. It is the desire for pleasure that leads us to other, more beautiful worlds. This is, of course, not merely the position of the Frankfurt School. Plato too saw eros—the desire for beautiful bodies that leads us to the desire for Beauty per se—as the ground of transcendence (*Symposium*, 210e–212b; *Phaedrus*, 249d–252b). These are the considerations that lie behind my decision to treat the subjective, experiential aspect of art as closely related to, albeit not identical with, the quest for transcendence. A consequence is, of course, that the less this subjective experience is centered on eros, the looser this relationship to transcendence becomes. In arguing that art should be seen less as an expression of eros, more

as an expression of the desire to restore a shattered whole, I in effect
weaken (but do not obliterate) the link to transcendence, while
strengthening the truth-telling aspect of art.

The problem of art and suffering is actually part of a larger problem confronted by the aesthetic theory of the Frankfurt School: the
proper relationship between immanence and transcendence; Hegel
and Kant; negation and affirmation; critique and utopia. Immanence
risks not being able to see beyond the suffering, disorder, and chaos
of this world. It risks reifying this world, providing no vision of an
alternative. Under these circumstances, art becomes a fetish, an
echo of a disintegrating society, as Adorno believed surrealism to be,
and as some critics believe Adorno's aesthetics to be.[7] Transcendence, on the other hand, risks forgetting the pain and opportunities
of this world. It risks implicitly countenancing injustice in the name
of an ideal other in which all contradictions are resolved. Transcendent art may perpetuate the lie, the illusion, that a society worthy of
humanity actually exists. Both Adorno and Marcuse insist that art,
and cultural criticism generally, must remain between these poles,
emphasizing one, then the other. As Adorno observes, "To insist on
the choice between immanence and transcendence is to revert to the
traditional logic criticized in Hegel's polemic against Kant."[8] Furthermore, a work of art may at one time strike the right balance, at
another it may not. For example, Adorno believed that Schoenberg's
twelve-tone row challenged the feigned naturalness of bourgeois society. Yet, Adorno seems to have come to feel that at the hands of
Schoenberg's students the twelve-tone row mirrored the instrumental rationality of society so closely that it lost its critical edge.[9]

The relevance of these abstract considerations to the problem of
art and suffering is apparent. The strictly immanent representation
of suffering may fail to escape the desperate cynicism expressed in
Adorno's statement about poetry and Auschwitz. The strictly transcendent representation of suffering may render it merely beautiful.
In his own work neither Adorno nor Marcuse loses the appropriate
balance, though in general Adorno surely risks the errors of immanence, Marcuse of transcendence. Yet, it is hard to avoid the impression that neither is very surefooted in striking the balance, in part
because both Marcuse and Adorno see art as sublimated eros. Although Adorno criticizes the psychoanalytic interpretation of art, he
too locates its origins in desire.[10] As an expression of eros, art would
avoid suffering if it could.

Several followers of Melanie Klein have developed an aesthetic theory based on her work. This theory sees art as an expression not merely of eros but of *caritas*, which leads to a need to make reparation. How such a view of art might overcome the theoretical problem addressed above, in which art either avoids suffering or risks beautifying it, is apparent. In fact, a key reason that Marcuse and Adorno must be so dialectically nimble is that they lack what Klein provides: an account of art that has a place for love, not just desire. For what else is the wish to speak for those who suffer silently but love? Guilt, perhaps, but Klein reveals how mature expressions of guilt are themselves an instance of love. Unlike Marcuse, for whom "history is guilt but not redemption," Klein finds a place for redemption, not just transcendence or infinite regret.[11]

Yet, the Kleinian account is not without problems of its own. The love and reparation that it expresses remain abstract, a projection of unconscious needs unattached to the real world. Reconciliation with one's internal objects in phantasy sometimes seems more important than—or rather, seems interchangeable with—reconciliation with external objects: people. In the language of the present discussion, Klein's account risks the errors of transcendence. Yet, in another respect she also risks the errors of immanence. While a focus on suffering avoids false positivism, a false optimism, and thus generates a certain resistance to the world, this need not lead to criticism, as Adorno points out.[12] These two risks are, in fact, related. The achievement of transcendence in phantasy, in which one restores one's internal objects to perfect wholeness, may lead to a lack of concern with repairing real relationships, real people—that is, the errors of immanence.

In response to this problem I develop an alternative aesthetic theory that, while still concerned with reparation, addresses how men and women may come to be at home in the world as well as with their passions, both of which sometimes seem so alien. In this account, art helps us become reconciled with both our external and internal worlds. The basis of this reinterpretation—as well as what makes it still Kleinian—is my revision of Klein so as to make the passions central. It is the passion of art, so often concerned with love and hate, that links it to the external world in a way that the aesthetic theory inspired by Klein does not always appreciate. The result is an aesthetic theory somewhat closer to Adorno's than Marcuse's in so far as it confronts, rather than transcends, the sheer ugliness of so much in the world. In the discussion that follows, however, more attention is paid to Marcuse than to Adorno, primarily because Marcuse's view is less dialectically subtle and hence more clearly an example of the limits of an aesthetic theory that fails to distinguish eros from love. My goal is not to make aesthetic theory more practical or more relevant to the real world. On this point Marcuse and Adorno seem correct: especially in the modern world, in which the social state seems capable of integrating everything, it is the autonomy of art, its sheer impracticality, that makes it critical. Rather than make aesthetic theory practical, I seek to show how it reveals the power of the unconscious needs and defenses that Klein uncovers, a power that may change the world but that also requires—if we are to integrate ourselves—that we come to terms with the world as it truly is.

Marcuse's Aesthetics

Like Adorno, Marcuse sees aesthetic form as the key to the emancipatory power of art.[13] By form Marcuse means those stylistic qualities, such as harmony, rhythm, and contrast, that make a work a self-contained whole with a structure and order of its own. It is by subjecting the particular events with which it deals to the requirements of form that art renders these events universal. The task of form, then, is to transform the particular into the universal and so to create a separate reality, in some ways more real than everyday reality, precisely because its principles are universal. As Marcuse notes, "The illusion is in the reality itself—not in the work of art."[14] Form transforms reality by interpreting particular events in terms of what Marcuse calls universal Ideas, the most important of which are Eros and Thanatos. Through artistic form, the power of Eros and Thanatos to constitute reality is heightened (or rather, made more apparent) by stripping away all those mundane events that distract us from this power.

It seems fair to call this a Platonic-cum-Freudian view, in which aesthetic form expresses universal Ideas, ideas that constitute a world and in turn are constituted by the play of the life and death instincts. But if this is a Platonic-cum-Freudian view, it also finds a place for Aristotle. As is well known, Aristotle defines tragedy as the representation of action that, enriched by various artistic devices, uses pity and fear to bring about the katharsis of these emotions (*Poetics*, c. 6). Marcuse is, of course, writing not only about tragedy. It is therefore necessary to expand the definition somewhat, even though the Aristotelian core remains: art engages our emotions, including those of love and desire—eros—as well as pity and fear, and in so doing subjects these emotions to katharsis, bringing us closer to peace and contentment. As Marcuse observes, "This catharsis is an ontological rather than psychological event. It is grounded in the specific qualities of the form itself, its non-repressive order, its cognitive power, its image of suffering that has come to an end. But, the 'solution,' the reconciliation which the catharsis offers, also preserves the irreconcilable."[15])

Here is the source of art's power, as well as its limit. Through beauty, art has the power to create another world, a better world, and in so doing to challenge the poverty and ugliness of this one by showing this world as contingent—neither necessary nor universal. Yet, precisely because this power is obtained through catharsis, it risks premature reconciliation with, and acceptance of, pain and suffering. Adorno makes a similar point in *Aesthetic Theory*, arguing that purgation reinforces repression, allowing substitute gratification to take the place of the real thing. In this sense, says Adorno, Aristotle's view of tragedy, no less (albeit more subtly) than Plato's view of art, serves the powers that be.[16]

Marcuse recognized this problem for some time, although he was never able to solve it. As early as 1955, in *Eros and Civilization*, Marcuse states that through its commitment to the value of form, art risks adulterating its negative, critical potential. "This element of semblance (show, *Schein*) necessarily subjects the represented reality to aesthetic standards and thus deprives it of its terror."[17] To be sure, Marcuse did not always stick to this position. In *An Essay on Liberation*, a book in which Marcuse's utopian hopes seem less restrained than in any other, he suggests that the artistic representation of suffering might itself help redeem suffering by giving it meaning. Art, he says, serves "to indict that which is, and to 'cancel' the indictment in the aesthetic form, redeeming the suffering, the crime. This 'redeeming,' reconciling power seems inherent in art, by virtue of its being art, by virtue of its form-giving power."[18]

Yet, Marcuse soon came to change his mind, returning to the position taken in *Eros*, a position from which he never subsequently

wavered. To speak of art as "canceling" or "redeeming" human suffering is to risk the artistic transfiguration of suffering. In *Counterrevolution and Revolt* (1972), Marcuse argues that art must do no
more than represent suffering in the hope of memorializing it.[19] In
order to do this, art must stand back from its suffering subject. For
art to engage itself emotionally with its suffering subject, it must risk
subjecting this suffering to premature catharsis. A statement in his
last book, *The Aesthetic Dimension*, reveals Marcuse's belief that
this difficulty would not be resolved: "Art is powerless against this
reconciliation with the irreconcilable; it is inherent in the aesthetic
form itself. Under its law . . . a representation of the most extreme
suffering 'still contains the potential to wring out enjoyment.' "[20]

To be sure, Marcuse assures us that by approaching suffering at a
respectful distance, the artistic catharsis may preserve the irreconcilable; that it need not succumb to affirmation. He never tells us
why, however. Marcuse's is an assertion about the proper way to
approach suffering, an assertion steeped in the subtleties of the dialectic of negation and affirmation, as well as his own sensibility.
However, it has no grounds in his aesthetic theory (the same conclusion applies to Adorno). To the contrary, Marcuse's aesthetic theory
says that art will tend to do one of three things: (1) avoid suffering
because suffering is unpleasant, antierotic; (2) avoid suffering because in dealing with suffering art risks "subjecting it to aesthetic
form, and thereby to the mitigating catharsis, to enjoyment"; or (3)
affirm suffering as somehow noble, fine, and beautiful.[21] Each of
these tendencies is problematic, to say the least. And none really
comes close to the respectful, albeit somewhat distant, approach to
suffering that Marcuse has in mind. Avoidance is not respectful distance but merely avoidance.

Why Marcuse faces a virtual trilemma is apparent. The tendency
of art to avoid suffering, or affirm it, stems from Marcuse's view that
the transcendent power of art, its status as the carrier of universal
Ideas, depends upon the power of Eros, a power that expressed in
artistic form concerns "the ever recurring, desiring Subject." In a
word, eros—the foundation of the pleasure principle—would rather
avoid suffering altogether; if forced to confront it, however, eros will
try anything to make the suffering more beautiful. Such a view finds
little support in Freud. While Freud certainly saw art as sublimated

eros, he paid far more attention to the way in which art is an expression of the artist's attempt to overcome his internal conflicts and thus to embrace reality more fully.[22]

Kleinian Art Theory

Klein never developed an aesthetic theory. The task has been left to others, among whom Adrian Stokes is probably the most well known.[23] In fact, of all the psychoanalytically oriented aesthetic theories, the Kleinian, along with Gestalt theory, is the most developed. To be sure, Klein interpreted several works of art from a psychoanalytic perspective. A study of her interpretation of Aeschylus' *Oresteia* trilogy concludes this chapter. However, it is her associates—above all Hanna Segal in "A Psycho-Analytical Approach to Aesthetics"—who transformed Klein's insights into systematic aesthetic principles.[24]

Art, says Segal, is an expression of the depressive position. Like Marcuse, Segal sees the task of the artist as the creation of a world, arguing with Roger Fry that great art may be defined in terms of how well and how thoroughly it creates another reality. In this world the artist mourns for lost people and experiences that have given meaning to his life. Segal goes on to describe an episode in the last volume of Proust's *Remembrance of Things Past*, in which Proust explains his decision to devote the rest of his life to writing. Upon coming back to see his old friends after a long absence, Proust finds them to be mere shadows of the ones he had known—useless, silly, ill, on the threshold of death. Some had died long ago. Realizing that his former world exists no longer, Proust decides to sacrifice himself to the re-creation of the dying and the dead. It is through his art that he can give those persons and things he cares about eternal life.[25]

"What Proust describes," says Segal, "corresponds to a situation of mourning."[26] He sees that his loved ones are dead or dying. Writing a book as an act of mourning, in which these loved ones are given up as they exist in the external world and re-created in an inner world—in a work of art. All creation, says Segal, is really the re-creation of a once loved and once whole, but now ruined and lost, object, a ruined internal world. What makes this situation especially poignant, Klein reminds us, is that at an unconscious level the death and destruction of a beloved object is seen as a result of one's own hatred and aggression. Unconsciously, mourning is experienced as punishment—living in an empty world—for having destroyed what was good in it. In Freud's account, mourning is a process of reality testing, in which the mourner must discover over and over again that the loved person no longer exists in the real world.[27] Klein adds another dimension to this account, as was shown in chapter 2. The mourner is not only deprived of an external source of support and satisfaction through the loss of the object, but he also fears that he will lose his internal good objects, objects with which the loved person was identified. Mourning is thus not merely a matter of reality testing. It also involves reinstating one's internal objects, becoming once again convinced of their presence and goodness via creative phantasies.

The appeal of a work of art is that it allows the viewer to vicariously experience the artist's depression at having lost (destroyed) all that he loves, as well as the artist's joy at having re-created and restored his loved objects to an internal world. While Segal uses Dilthey's term *nach-erleben* (to reexperience) to capture this process, the connotations could be somewhat misleading if this term were taken to suggest that something like *verstehen* (imaginative understanding) is at stake. What Segal really means is that one who truly appreciates art projectively identifies with the artist's struggle, which is a more intense psychological phenomenon than *verstehen*. Art is about destruction, loss, and restoration. It is a successful act of mourning. Out of chaos and destruction, caused by his own greed and rage, the artist is able to recreate and restore a world that is whole, complete, and unified. Through an act of creation the artist asserts that his love is stronger than his hate, that his powers of care and concern are stronger than his aggression, that he can repair what he has virtually destroyed. It is this assertion that helps him—and those who can vicariously participate in his works—overcome his depressive anxiety: that because his love is not strong enough to overcome his hate, he must live in a cold and empty world, in which all his good objects are dead.

Like Marcuse, Segal focuses on literature, though she makes some attempt to integrate music into her account as well. Not unlike Marcuse, she tends to regard those works of art that do not fit into her account, such as much of modern art, as less great, less beautiful, less "aesthetic." Segal, like Marcuse, sees aesthetic theory not as an account of what separates art from other activities, but as an account of the psychological appeal of beauty, clarifying what true beauty really is. Like Klein, Segal draws many of her examples from classical tragedy, in which the wholeness and perfection of the artistic form promises the restoration of an order destroyed by the protagonists' hatred, greed, hubris, and aggression. Poetic speech, restrictions on time (for example, the requirement that events unfold within twenty-four hours) and on place, as well as many other formal requirements of plot and presentation stand in sharp contrast to the utter destruction and chaos depicted in the narration of events, suggesting to the audience that even the most intense hatred and aggression need not destroy all order. "Without this formal harmony the depression of the audience would be aroused but not resolved. There can be no aesthetic pleasure without perfect form."[28]

The analysis of reparative motifs in art cannot be undertaken in a vacuum or in isolation from conventions of style. As Ernst Gombrich points out in "Norm und Form," there is a classical solution to certain stylistic problems in painting, a solution emphasizing symmetry and harmony.[29] To interpret this classical solution as a reparative motif, without understanding how the classical solution evolved as a response to certain technical problems, not just psychological ones, would be absurd, just as it would be absurd to ignore the objective functions of bureaucracy while analyzing its subjective, psychological ones. Ignorance of stylistic conventions simply reduces aesthetics to psychology, rather than enriching the former discipline with the insights of the latter. On the other hand, the fact that symmetry and harmony are part of a classical aesthetic solution does not mean that their appeal cannot be illuminated by reference to psychological factors. That a phenomenon serves an objective aesthetic function does not render psychological explanation irrelevant. Conversely, that formal conventions of symmetry and harmony reflect psychological needs does not make these conventions mere epiphenomena of these needs. As the psychological function of bureaucracy works through its institutional function, so the psychological function of style works through its technical, aesthetic function.

Kleinian Aesthetics and the Frankfurt School

For Marcuse, form represents the subjection of the particular to the universal Ideas of Eros and Thanatos. In a similar fashion, Segal argues that the death instinct (understood as aggression, rage, and hatred) is denied less in great art than in any other human activity. "Beauty is nothing but the beginning of terror that we are still just able to bear," says Rainer Maria Rilke.[30] Such an insight, implies Segal, appreciates that behind every work of art lies the narrowest of victories over Thanatos. Though Segal, unlike Marcuse, tends to see the death instinct as operative in all those forces which oppose, or stand in contrast to, aesthetic form, rather than as operative in the form itself, both see art as the field in which eros and Thanatos play out their eternal struggle. The difference is that Segal understands eros not merely as the desire for gratification but as an expression of love, the desire to make reparation. For Marcuse, hatred and aggression are overcome by an overflow of eros into every aspect of life and art, so that peace, joy, and contentment leave no place for death. "Make love, not war," as though enough gratification for everyone would simply leave no room for aggression. An element of manic denial is present in such a viewpoint (as eros would deny suffering), as though hatred and aggression could be overcome by simply filling the world with joy and happiness. In two books and several articles, I have criticized the psychological assumptions that Marcuse must make (a version of Freudian libidinal hydraulics) to support such a view of eros, and I shall not repeat this analysis here.[31] Suffice it to say that Segal more fully appreciates the way in which hatred and aggression are forever active, forever threatening to overcome love, forever requiring that we make reparation for them—for ourselves.

Marcuse, like Adorno, and Segal (for whom Proust epitomizes the aesthetic attitude), sees art not as simple recollection but as the recollection of a lost unity and wholeness. In what does this lost wholeness consist? Here Marcuse and Adorno differ, as Martin Jay points out.[32] For Marcuse, this lost wholeness is the lost unity of subject and object, a state of primordial oneness with the world. "The utopia in great art . . . is grounded in recollection," he states.[33] Though Marcuse does note that this recollection may be of an ideal, a hope, not an actual state of affairs, the ideal or hope still concerns a unification of subject and object. For Adorno, on the other hand, the wholeness and unity to be remembered in the work of art are the wholeness, unity, and integrity of the object itself. In art, and perhaps in art alone, can this wholeness be grasped, because art is less conceptual than philosophy: art lets the object be (mimesis), it reveals the object in its totality, rather than seeking to understand and control it by forcing it into fixed categories. Art, in other words, avoids the dialectic of Enlightenment, in which virtually all thought becomes an expression of instrumental reason.

Adorno's view comes closer to Kleinian aesthetics, in which art expresses concern for the integrity of the object, an object destroyed by greed and aggression. Indeed, in Adorno's characterization of "idealism as rage" at a world too sparse to be dominated, one sees an almost Kleinian version of the *Dialectic of Enlightenment*, fully appreciative of the sources of even philosophical aggression in frustration, hubris, greed, anxiety, and desire.[34] To be sure, the wholeness that art expresses in the Kleinian view involves a reconciliation between subject and object, and in this sense a wholeness in Marcuse's sense as well. Nevertheless, in Marcuse's view there is a certain lack of concern for the integrity of the object qua object in its own right. Once again, this seems to be a consequence of Marcuse's failure to distinguish between eros and love. Eros is truly concerned not with the object in itself but with the object only as it is, or may become, a source of satisfaction to human wishes and desires. Could it be that eros, in its pursuit of pleasure, really defends against the pain of sympathy (what Germans call *Mitleid*—literally, suffering with another) by refusing to engage itself fully in the pain of others? Eros, whatever its virtues, is not unselfish.

Yet, if Marcuse's aesthetics does not strike the right balance, neither does Segal's. Though Kleinian aesthetics respects the object, it actually respects the *idea* of the object, an internalization of the object as constituent of one's psychic world. To be sure, one would not expect art to capture the thing in itself. Nevertheless, the reparation that Kleinian aesthetics seeks is ultimately an internal, symbolic act, quite removed from the repair of actual people. Kleinian aesthetics focuses on the idea of suffering, its internal representation as guilt, rather than on the suffering object. The problem is apparent: an aesthetic theory that substitutes the symbolic repair of one's internal world for the symbolic repair of real others comes too close to the selfishness of eros. Kleinian aesthetic theory exaggerates a tendency in Kleinian psychoanalysis (counterbalanced somewhat in her later works by greater attention to real relationships) to treat symbolic objects, of which internal objects are one instance, as more real than actual ones. We saw a curious example of this tendency in Klein's discussion of how one might make reparation for the extermination of native populations—by repopulating the land with one's own people.[35] For Klein it is the internal, psychological activity of reparation that matters, not its results.

To be sure, painting a picture commemorating the destruction of natives, or writing a novel about it, is not going to repair any real natives either. Nevertheless, there is a difference between these creative acts and mere phantasied reparation, a difference not fully grasped in the Kleinian account. The artistic representation acknowledges the external world, even as it goes on to create another one. In creating another world of perfect wholeness and reconciliation, art calls attention to the contrast between this perfect world and its damaged, fragmented, empirical counterpart. It is in this contrast between fantasy and reality that the emancipatory power of art resides—the image of perfect harmony indicts a miserable reality, at least for those who would look or listen. A familiar example is utopian fiction, frequently intended by its authors to criticize this world by implicitly contrasting it to an ideal one. Reparation in phantasy is different. Rather than creating another world of perfection, reparation in phantasy may substitute the repair of internal objects for external ones. Rather than heightening the tension between a perfectly restored ideal and reality, reparation in phantasy may diminish this tension by rendering reparation in phantasy tantamount to reparation in reality. Or, by treating real people as little more than symbolic stand-ins for internal objects, reparation in phantasy may imply that one act of actual reparation (for example, to white Europeans) is as good as another (to natives). Though art need not terminate in premature catharsis, reparation in phantasy likely will.

Klein's and Marcuse's aesthetics make the same mistake. (It is their similarity, even to making some of the same mistakes, that makes a Kleinian perspective on Marcuse so fruitful.) Both stress the achievement of wholeness, restoration, unity, and completeness (even if they understand these attributes somewhat differently) to such an extent that the idea of art telling us the truth about a broken, fragmented reality, except by complete contrast, tends to be lost. To be sure, the idea of a torn and fragmented reality is perhaps inconceivable without the idea of its opposite. Furthermore, Kleinian aesthetics, especially, appreciates the way in which it is human aggression that rends the unity of the object. Nevertheless, both Marcuse and Segal stress the ideal of wholeness and reconciliation—this is the meaning of aesthetic form for both—so heavily that the idea of art as messenger and truth teller about a fragmented world tends to be lost. Complete contrast, if it is too complete (that is, based on the portrayal of only perfect worlds), too untouched by reality, may turn us away from this world, in part because we can see no connection between them. This is, of course, the error of transcendence. If art is to tell the truth (albeit, not necessarily literal, empirical truth), then certainly part of the truth is that aspects of the world are so deformed and ugly that no reconciliation with them is possible or desirable, a point Adorno seems to appreciate more fully with his aesthetics of the ugly (*haesslich*).[36]

The Tasks of Art

In *Languages of Art,* Nelson Goodman argues that far from being a passive, contemplative representation of the given, art is an active, intellectually assertive attempt to know the world through emotions, not just intellect. "The aesthetic 'attitude' is restless, searching, testing—is less attitude than action: creation and recreation."[37] In the aesthetic experience emotions have a cognitive function. They help us learn more about the real attributes of the world. Emotions are a means of knowledge, and art helps mobilize these emotions in the name of knowledge. At first glance, such a view would seem to be quite the opposite of the aesthetic theories discussed so far. Goodman's view challenges any conception of art as imitation, even Adorno's, which appreciates the active, creative moment in mimesis.[38]

Yet, while Adorno certainly does not see art as mere representation or passive reception, he would probably regard Goodman's account with horror, as though art too had become but one more instrument by which to better apprehend the world. This is so even though Adorno clearly appreciates that art is itself a form of cognition and, as such, partakes of reason, albeit a noninstrumental reason that lets itself be guided (but not determined) by the object. "The continued existence of mimesis, understood as the non-conceptual affinity of a subjective creation with its objective and unposited other, defines art as a form of cognition and to that extent rational. . . . Art expands cognition into an area where it was said to be non-existent."[39]

Not only does Goodman's account of art as knowledge not fit very neatly with Adorno's account, it does not fit neatly with Klein's either. Whereas Goodman makes emotion a tool of knowledge, one could argue that Kleinian aesthetics does the opposite, viewing knowledge of the world strictly in terms of how it serves emotional reconciliation. However, aesthetic theory, even when psychoanalytically informed, is not psychoanalysis, and there is no reason not to blend these approaches eclectically if it seems helpful. The result, formulated below, is an account of art that renders it more choosy, more selective in its love, more discriminating in its objects of reconciliation and reparation. Such an account is especially suited to correcting Marcuse's aesthetics, in which the beautifying power of eros risks promiscuity, loving even the ugly and evil. By virtue of its concern with reparation, my account may help contain the intellectual aggression that Adorno might find in Goodman's version.

Unlike Klein's and Marcuse's accounts of art, mine does not suggest that art is about just one thing—such as reparation or transcendence into a realm of joy and beauty. In my view art does at least four things: it helps to make us more at home in the world; it helps us to clarify our emotions, making us more at home with ourselves (this view comes closest to art as reparation); it plays with the world and so creates a realm of personal freedom in an unfree world; and it tells us the truth about the world, even when this truth is unpleasant. These four tasks of art (and there are surely others) stand in no hierarchical or systematic relationship. A work of art may express all four tasks, just one, or any combination. Its greatness is not necessarily measured by how well it integrates these tasks; perhaps all great works of art are one-sided, or perhaps only some are. Unlike the aesthetic theories of Segal and Marcuse, my art theory does not seek to explain what makes a work of art great, or beauty a source of pleasure and value. It rather seeks to characterize art, to explore what it shares with psychoanalysis, without reducing art to psychoanalysis. From this perspective a painting of Elvis on black velvet is just as much art as Michelangelo's Moses. Bad art is still art;

it is just bad art. In this respect my account stands closest to Goodman's, who makes a similar argument.[40] At the conclusion of this section I point out how art may help make us more moral. This, though, is not one of the tasks of art, just its occasional effect.

In allowing us to use our emotions, not just our cognition, to know the world, art lets us see the world in a way more in accord with our unconscious impressions of it. In so doing, art helps us to be more at home in the world, rendering the world more deeply human, less alien. Art does so by representing the external world as an expression of our deepest needs—and fears. In psychoanalytic terms, art projects our deepest needs and fears into the world, allowing us to experience the world as imbued with these needs and fears. The psychological mechanism involved is that Kleinian favorite: projective identification. In relating to other people, as Turquet points out, we employ projective identification to stabilize them, to render them more predictable and less threatening, by making them more like ourselves. They become literally caretakers of the parts of ourselves that we attribute to them.[41] In so doing, we are at least as likely to attribute the bad parts of ourselves to others as the good parts. The psychological goal here is the creation of familiarity, not goodness. Needless to say, this is largely an unconscious process.

The result, particularly when aspects of nature are the object of the artist's projective identification, is an aesthetic experience akin to what Freud called the uncanny (*unheimlich*). The unconscious experiences a work of art as "disturbingly and unexpectedly familiar" because it recognizes a part of itself in the art.[42] The landscapes of Edvard Munch, such as *Summer Night on an Oslo Fjord,* are striking examples of the power of works of art to evoke this experience. Ironically, even the *unheimlich* can help us to be more at home in the world by rendering it less the unresponsive, capricious other and making it instead more like us, possibly even a caretaker of part of us. Such a perspective is the counterpart to Weberian rationalization and demystification, the opposite of the scientific worldview, in which all comes to be explained in terms of natural processes that know and care nothing for human needs and fears. Is this not pure anthropomorphism, it might be asked, and as such an expression of primitive denial of the otherness of the objective world, including nature? The answer would have to be yes, if there were no more to art than this. However, the clarifying, playful, and truth-telling functions of art may mitigate this tendency, even if they do not eliminate it.

Katharsis

Seen from this perspective, art may be interpreted as promoting katharsis, expressing our needs and fears and finding a place for them in the world. However, it is katharsis in quite a different sense from Marcuse's, with its connotations of emotional purging leading to peace and contentment ("its image of suffering that has come to an end," as Marcuse puts it).[43] Aristotelian katharsis, argues Martha Nussbaum, is better seen as the use of our emotions to obtain *clarification*, insight into the true nature of reality.[44] Nussbaum begins her analysis by examining the historical use of katharsis and related words (*kathairo, katharos,* and so on). In pre-Platonic texts, she notes, these words frequently refer to water that is clear and open, free of mud or weeds. Or they refer to a cleared area, to winnowed grain free of chaff, or to speech that is not marked by obscurity or ambiguity. The medical use of the term, referring to purgation, is a secondary and derivative usage. Plato, she says, preserves this pattern. The primary way in which he uses katharsis and related terms is to refer to clarity, freedom from admixture, or absence of impediment: "In the case of the soul and its cognition, the application of the word-group is mediated by the dominant metaphors of mud and clean light: the eye of the soul can be sunk in mud (*Republic,* 533d1; *Phaedrus,* 69c), or it can be seeing cleanly and clearly."[45]

By the time Aristotle wrote, says Nussbaum, katharsis was employed as an epistemological term directly, without need for metaphor. When, in his *Prior Analytics,* Aristotle writes of a need to "examine and indicate each of these things with clarity (katharos)," it is obvious that the reference has nothing to do with purification or purgation (50a40). One sees this too in his theory of rhetoric, in which the term is applied to speech that is clear and free of obscurity (*Rhetoric,* 1356b26, 141413). When Aristotle defines tragedy in terms of the concept of katharsis (*Poetics,* c. 6), he is therefore not writing about emotional purgation at all but rather about how experiencing pity and fear at an artistic performance allows us insight into the nature of these emotions. The function of tragedy is to accomplish through the experience of pity and fear a "clarification (or illumination) concerning experiences of the pitiable and fearful kind."[46] Nussbaum goes on to emphasize that katharsis does not mean intellectual clarification about these emotions. It means simply clarification—emotional experience is employed to gain emotional understanding about emotions. This, she notes, is something new in Aristotle. Plato would have seen the issue in terms of using emotions to obtain intellectual clarification, as he does in the *Symposium* (201d–12c).

Goodman's account comes closer to Plato's on this point, mine closer to Aristotle's. For while both see the emotions represented in art, as well as the viewer's emotional reaction to these emotions, as leading to genuine knowledge of reality, Goodman stresses how emotion serves intellectual and cognitive goals. My Kleinian-inspired account, on the other hand, stresses how the experience of pity and fear may lead us to better understand these emotions in ourselves. For fear is the predominant emotion of the paranoid-schizoid position, pity the dominant emotion of the depressive position. Art, at its best, allows us to work through—that is, to obtain emotional clarification about—our fear so that we can realize our potential to feel pity, the ground of reparation. This working through is, of course, quite different from mere purgation, just as Kleinian psychoanalysis is quite different from therapies aimed at promoting emotional catharsis. Working through is a combination of insight (illumination) and emotional integration of love and hate, evidently the same type of emotional experience that Aristotle had in mind in his definition of tragedy.

Much of modern art, especially painting and sculpture, seems to be nothing more than play, an expression of the desire to transform reality for its own sake, and for the sake of freedom. The sculptures of Henry Moore are exemplary, as are many of the portraits by Picasso. (If Arianna Huffington's controversial new book on Picasso is correct, this assessment may have to be revised; rather than being expressions of play and freedom, Picasso's portraits would also have to be seen as representing his perception of the world's ugliness.[47] Of course, the viewer may find play and freedom where the artist saw only ugliness, and vice versa. *Pace* Segal, the viewer's response need not mimic the artist's in order to be valid.) How does this fit into my account? Marcuse provides the answer in a 1933 article, *"Ueber die philosophischen Grundlagen des wirtschaftswissenschaftslichen Arbeitsbegriffs,"* in which he argues that labor must forever be a burden, no matter how it is socially organized, because in labor man must conform to the "law of the thing" ("*Gesetz der 'Sache'* "), the objectivity of the natural world. Play is the sole realm of freedom, because in play man can substitute his laws for those of nature (or at least he can pretend to do so; the ball will still not roll uphill unaided, and the butterfly does not rush to meet the collector's net) and thus play solely for himself as he can never labor just for himself.[48] In play, man both accepts the objectivity of the natural world (if the world were not objective, there would be no need to distinguish work and play) and rejects it for a world in which his rules, and not nature's, prevail. This too is reconciliation with an alien world, in which we accept its brute givenness and at the same time seek to create alternative worlds of utter freedom, as if to say that the world is not really as given as it appears to be. Or rather, what we experience as entirely man-made—the rules of the game— we know to depend on the givenness of nature's rules as well, and in this way nature's rules become somehow less alien, more an expression of our own, even if there is perhaps an element of wishful thinking in such a perception.

The latter way of expressing it, however, is not so much Marcuse's as my own. For Marcuse, the ultimate goal seems to be not reconciliation with the objectivity of nature but rather the triumph over it, via the unlikely combination of technology and the aesthetic sensibility. Since I have dealt with this aspect of Marcuse's program at length elsewhere, I shall not do so here. Suffice it to say that much of modern art seeks not to transcend nature but to play with it, and in so doing to create a small measure of freedom in a harshly objective world. *Capricorn,* the sculpture by Max Ernst that depicts the droll king and queen of the sea subjugating but one small animal, exemplifies this spirit of play that recognizes the limits of its own freedom. Adorno's appreciation of Johan Huizinga's suggestion in *Homo Ludens* that mythical cosmologies obtain much of their power from a "half-joking element verging on make-believe" expresses a similar insight.[49] To approach a culture's mythic (or scientific) account of worldly objectivity in a spirit of play is not so much to deny objectivity as it is to say "I must accept the world; but I will not give up my freedom to come to terms with it in my own way, for this is the dearest freedom that I possess." Adorno makes what I believe is the same point in another context, stating simply that "philosophy is the most serious of things, but then again it is not all that serious."[50]

On the other hand, not all modern art is playful. Much of it is shocking, unpleasant, ugly, and often more alien and alienating than the world itself. How could an artistic representation of giant, dead, rotting insects, for instance, express reconciliation? In so far as art teaches us about the world by calling attention to our emotional reactions to it—reactions that are often unconscious—art may be seen as telling us what we already know but have been unable or unwilling to formulate. In the case of the artistic representation of ugliness, art reconciles us to what we frequently recognize but will not admit: that the world, including sometimes even our closest relationships, is filled with hate, ugliness, despair, and emptiness. The portraits by George Grosz and Otto Dix (*Die Irrsinnige*, for example) are exemplary, as are the plays of Eugene O'Neill. So too, albeit in a more subtle fashion, is the series of paintings by Donald Sultan entitled *Black Lemons*, which transforms piquant, limpid fruit into "standardized lemons, products of the terrifying consumer society."[51] In telling us things like this, in reminding us of what we already know about our world but will not admit, art reconciles us not with this ugly world but with that part of ourselves that knows the world to be ugly but will not call it by its right name.

In so doing, art helps prevent what Adorno calls (referring to Lukács' *Wider den missverstandenen Realismus*) "extorted reconciliation" ("erpresste Versoehnung"), in which one is asked to love and come to terms with something that is not worthy of reconciliation.[52] Art, in this sense, is even more about truth than beauty. Or rather, it finds a certain beauty in the truth, even when the truth concerns the ugliness of the world. Consider, for example, Manet's *The Execution of Emperor Maximilian of Mexico*, in which the contortion of Maximilian's face lacks any semblance of beauty, and the observers behind the wall, showing neither joy nor sorrow, seem to testify to this truth.[53] If truth is beauty, and beauty truth, then the truth of ugliness is beautiful because it is the truth, because it has the courage to call a spade a spade. This is the only alternative to the conclusion that the ugly is itself beautiful, a conclusion that both Marcuse and Adorno believe art always risks. Marcuse would have art turn away from the truly ugly and horrible, lest it beautify it. My perspective avoids this, stressing the way in which even the unpleasant truth can be the subject of reconciliation. Most of the longer stories of Kafka exemplify this point, in which the world is revealed

as so flat, fragmented, and ugly that the only possible object of reconciliation remaining is the truth itself.

Art and Morality

Why bother to become reconciled with the unpleasant truth, one
might ask. One answer is that facing even unpleasant realities is the
mark of a noble character, an expression of one of the finest (if sel-
dom realized) human capabilities: the will to truth. How difficult
but important this is, even in aesthetics, is captured by Rilke in his
Letters on Cézanne: "First, artistic perception had to overcome itself
to the point of realizing that even something horrible, something
that seems no more than disgusting, *is,* and shares the truth of its
being with everything else that exists. Just as the creative artist is not
allowed to choose, neither is he permitted to turn his back on anything: a single refusal, and he is cast out of the state of grace and
becomes sinful all the way through."[54] The artist is cast out because
in denying the ugly he does not transcend reality, or even become
reconciled with it; he only escapes from it, as eros would. Furthermore, such an escape can never be truly successful, since the unconscious knows the truth anyway. Denying evil and ugliness can only
divide man against himself, thus robbing the artist of the psychological potential of his art, "the ever-returning proof to himself of his
unity and genuineness," as Rilke puts it.[55]

There is another, albeit closely related, reason to come to terms
with evil and ugliness. It may help to make us more moral. Splitting,
Klein points out, leads to decreased responsibility for our own actions, in that we deny our ugly and evil impulses and deeds rather
than seek to make amends for them.[56] Abramson makes a similar
point regarding Freud. Freud, he notes, generally rejects any connection between therapy and morality. For example, Ernest Jones
reports Freud as saying that "analysis makes for unity, but not necessarily for goodness."[57] Yet, Freud's position is actually more complex than this, for Freud also writes that "anyone who has succeeded
in educating himself to truth about himself is permanently defended
against the danger of immorality, even though his standard of morality may differ in some respect from that which is customary in society."[58] Behind Freud's assertion, as Abramson points out, is the

insight that repression isolates our desires from the possibility of rational reflection. Consequently, desires are neither integrated with the maturing self nor subject to the influence of others. Recognizing the intensity of our desires, as well as the ugliness of our greed, hatred, and envy—something art may help us do—at least establishes the possibility that they might become the subject of conscious influence and choice. Abramson quotes Paul Ricoeur: "There is . . . opened up a clearing of truthfulness, in which the lies of the ideals and idols are brought to light. . . . This truthfulness is undoubtedly not the whole of ethics but at least it is the threshold."[59]

Freud's position on how insight may defend us against immorality contains more than a hint of the Socratic "no one ever does wrong knowingly," a position that simply does not accord with most of what Freud says about the way in which the mind is divided against itself, a point Abramson appreciates. As Aristotle points out against Socrates, we may know what is right and still be unable to do it (*N. Ethics*, 1110a–11b). However, perhaps even this inability might be addressed by psychoanalysis. One reason that people do wrong is because they are fearful of disobeying others, even if this fear is unconscious. Analysis, by showing that this fear of authority is reinforced by persecutory fears of an unrealistic, phantastic character, may better enable us to resist malevolent authority, as Money-Kyrle indicates.[60]

Could art, by clarifying the intensity of our fear as well as our desire for the wholeness and integration that is denied us by our fear, lead us to this same insight? Rilke suggests that it might in the following observation: "Surely all art is the result of one's having been in danger, of having gone through an experience all the way to the end, to where no one can go any further. . . . Therein lies the enormous aid the work of art brings to the life of the one who must make it,—: that it is his epitome; the knot in the rosary at which his life recites a prayer, the ever-returning proof to himself of his unity and genuineness."[61]

From a Kleinian perspective, the danger that takes us perilously close to the edge is the danger posed by our own hatred and rage, which threatens to destroy all that is good in the world, making it a place not worth living in. In creating something beautiful, however, we make reparation for our hate, as well as adding to the goodness of the world. In this way we prove to ourselves that we have not been made permanently false (hypocritical) and fragmented (schizoid) by our own hate. Perhaps this insight is available not merely to the creative artist but also to one who appreciates art, one who can reexperience the artist's passion—or rather, what he imagines the artist's passion to be.

Too Much Eros, Too Little Love

Seen strictly in terms of the balance between immanence and transcendence, my view comes closer to Adorno's than to Marcuse's. Adorno, without rejecting the ideal of transcendence altogether ("semblance is a promise of nonsemblance"),[62] appreciates the way in which art respects the independent reality of the object, the world. He also appreciates the way in which the "de-aestheticization of art" (art that not only knows itself to be illusion but shows itself as such to all) allows it to capture the alienated, fragmented character of modern life. What is lacking in Adorno is a theoretical basis in aesthetic theory for this balance. His aesthetic theory, as several critics have pointed out, is an extension of the philosophy of negative dialectics to the world of art—with the difference that since art is noncognitive, it may occasionally represent utopia without extorting reconciliation. Art, says Adorno, "is meant to assist the nonidentical in its struggle against the repressive identification compulsion that rules the outside world."[63] Yet because Adorno sees art as the continuation of philosophy and history by other means, he in effect abandons this assistance program. Or rather, his philosophical and historical view of art is incompatible with the goal he sets for it: to assist the object in revealing itself.

Peter Uwe Hohendahl argues that "the late work of Adorno tends to identify philosophy and art."[64] Comments by Adorno in *Aesthetic Theory* (unfinished at the time of his death), such as his assertion that "aesthetic experience must pass over into philosophy or else it will not be genuine," do little to refute such criticism.[65] Russell Berman states it more stringently, arguing that Adorno's "aesthetic theory must be understood as camouflaged social theory in self-imposed exile."[66] The best evidence for this charge is Adorno's own complaint about the later works of Bartók, which do not fit the social categories that Adorno assigns to modern music: "Partial responsibility for this is borne by the naiveté of the professional musician who goes about his business without partaking in the movement of the objective spirit."[67] If works of art are "philosophical sundials of history," as Adorno calls them, then it is the artist who is to blame if he does not keep the correct time.[68]

Against Adorno's position that in order to apprehend a work of art one must see it as an instance of philosophy, Lucien Goldmann states that "the work of art is a universe of colors, sounds and words, and concrete characters. There is no death, there is only Phaedra dying."[69] It is clear why Marcuse would criticize Goldmann, since Goldmann's position downplays the transcendent dimension of art. However, Richard Wolin's suggestion that Adorno would have accepted Goldmann's critique as a compliment does not seem quite right.[70] Or rather, even if Adorno had accepted Goldmann's assertion (for it fits Adorno's concern for the object qua object), it is an assertion that accords with only one pole of Adorno's thought, a pole fundamentally inconsistent with his virtual equation of art, philosophy, and social theory. Seen from this perspective, the question is, Why would Adorno stress this equation so heavily, given his goal of assisting the object to become itself? Assisting the object seems quite incompatible with a view of art as a philosophical sundial. For how could the sundial view apprehend the object in any way except as a reflection of human cultural history?

Why would Adorno hold two apparently incompatible views of art? Perhaps because while he wants to assist the object, he fears even more the indiscriminate eros of art, an eros that seeks reconciliation with the irreconcilable, an eros that might seek to make—if just for an almost forgotten moment—even the evil and ugly beautiful. As Adorno puts it, "The moral of . . . art, not to forget for a single instant, slithers into the abyss of its opposite."[71] Transforming art into philosophy is part of Adorno's attempt to contain eros, the result of which is to sublimate the eros of art in cultural history. As an instance of cultural history, art is once again subject to rational interpretation and control. Art becomes historiography, says Adorno.[72] By transforming art into history and philosophy, we can intellectually apprehend this promiscuous tendency in art—to indiscriminately render everything beautiful—and prepare ourselves to reject it, just as Odysseus had himself tied to his ship's mast because he knew he could not otherwise resist the Sirens' call.

Adorno turns from art to philosophy because he, like Marcuse, is frightened of the irrationality of art, a consequence of its origins in the pleasure principle. Thus, Adorno would in the end harness art to philosophy (sacrificing its power to help the thing reveal itself), whereas Marcuse would have art stand back from certain realities, lest it fail to do justice to them. What makes Kleinian aesthetic theory different is its greater confidence in the morality of the nonrational. It is this insight that my adaptation of her account rests on; it is what makes my adaptation still (albeit loosely) Kleinian. While fully appreciating the primitive character of our unconscious needs and desires, Klein sees them as more sophisticated, other-directed, and other-concerned than the Frankfurt School (drawing on Freud) ever does. Consequently, our emotions and passions can be trusted—but not always, not completely, and not to the exclusion of rational reflection. Moral philosophy is still necessary, but for the purpose of guiding our desire to make reparation, not constraining it or rendering it less selfish. I will come back to this difficult topic in chapter 6.

If the passions can be trusted within the limits noted above, then the transcendent character of art may be reinterpreted. Our emotional reactions to the artistic representation of reality are not something that we have to guard against in order to prevent the distortion of reality. Rather, these reactions are the best source from which to learn the truth about reality. Here is the source of art's transcendence. Art transcends the conventional, everyday, socially accepted interpretation of reality in order to show it to us as we really know it to be in our deepest—often unconscious—hopes and fears: beautiful, ugly, evil, banal, pointless, wondrous, and so forth. What art properly transcends is thus not reality itself—art grasps reality—but the lie that this reality is fit for man or even necessary, not merely contingent. Art does this by telling us the truth about our emotional reactions to reality, which frequently reflect our unconscious awareness of society's lies, lies that we will not admit even to ourselves. Seen thus, the transcendence of art is not a threat to truth but its ground. Art transcends the truths of convention to apprehend the deeper truths that stem from our own passionate encounter with reality. It is in this sense that art promotes katharsis, clarification regarding reality.

Klein and the Tragic Worldview

Aristotle, as we have seen, defines tragedy as the artistic representation of action, which by means of pity and fear clarifies (katharsis) these emotions to us. Klein is concerned with precisely this. Pity, whose most primitive expression is depressive anxiety regarding the welfare of the good object, and fear, whose most primitive expression is persecutory anxiety, divide the world in a Manichaean fashion: good and bad. These powerful emotions also divide the self against the self. The restorative process—clarification—begins when it is recognized that the good and bad objects are one. It is this recognition that leads one to integrate aspects of the self devoted to these two emotions. Klein's account does more than explain tragedy. It is tragedy by Aristotle's definition.

Other commentators on tragedy, such as Hegel and Nietzsche, have also stressed its restorative character. For Hegel, the hamartia (a tragic flaw) that defines the tragic hero stems from his adherence to one moral claim above all others. The outcome, in which the tragic hero frequently dies, nonetheless contains "an aspect of reconciliation," in which the wholeness—the complexity—of the moral order is affirmed against one who would emphasize only one aspect.[73] For Nietzsche, Greek tragedy reconciles the Apollonian with the Dionysian, as is well known.[74] Yet, if this is so, if the balance is restored, then what makes this view tragic after all? Is it merely that the protagonist frequently suffers and dies to make this point? No, it is rather that the balance is fragile, tentative, exceedingly subject to disruption.

Richard Sewall, in *The Vision of Tragedy*, sees tragedy as rooted in humanity's terror when confronted with the meaninglessness of existence and the irrationality of the universe.[75] Art can address this terror by making the world less alien, more meaningful. Our considerations suggest, however, that this terror may have deeper roots. If the Kleinian perspective—in which all meaning stems from the projection of unconscious phantasy into the world—is correct, then the world is naturally filled with meaning. The world possesses a surfeit of meaning, the result of projective identification, in which we make the world like us in order to make a home in it. Rather than finding ourselves thrown into a world already void of meaning, we empty it ourselves via our envy, greed, and hatred, taking from the world all the goodness that might make it a decent home for humanity. Behind

the terror of meaninglessness is humanity's terror at its own irratio-
nal aggression, its penchant to destroy the good and the meaningful,
as well as the bad. Here is the real tragedy: it is we who make the
world the empty, unresponsive place it so often is.

The Oresteia Complex

The tragic character of Klein's vision is most clearly revealed in her
study of Aeschylus' *Oresteia* trilogy. This is one reason why I have
chosen to comment upon it at some length. The other is that it
illuminates Kleinian aesthetic theory especially well. Unlike Segal's
systematization of Kleinian aesthetic principles, Klein's study of the
Oresteia is an application of these principles, albeit to a work of art
that seems especially well suited to explanation in terms of these
principles. The following discussion is neither a summary of Klein's
interpretation nor an interpretation of my own, but a combination of
the two. Using notes or references in the text, I try to indicate which
contributions are distinctly Klein's. Her interpretation of the *Oresteia* is comparable to Horkheimer and Adorno's interpretation of the
Odyssey in *Dialectic of Enlightenment*. Both Klein and the Frankfurt School use classic Greek myths to illustrate their key themes:
the cunning of instrumental reason in the case of the Frankfurt
School, the way that love and hate make a world in the case of
Klein.

Aristotle (*Poetics*, c. 13) defines the tragic hero as basically noble, with a singular weakness in character (hamartia). In many Greek
tragedies, this flaw is hubris—overweening pride and arrogance.
About hubris, Klein says that it is experienced as sinful because it is
fundamentally an expression of greed: the desire to have all the
glory, honor, and approbation in the world, a desire that stems from
the infant's unlimited desire to possess all his mother's riches. The
result, says Klein, is a paranoid fear of punishment by the mother,
which if excessive can lead to even greater splitting as a defense.[76]
The outcome is a self unsure of its ability to protect those it loves
from its own aggression, and hence unable to love.

From this perspective Klein contrasts Agamemnon's lack of guilt
for the suffering that he has inflicted on Troy, as well as on his own
people (his is the only ship to return to Argos), with Orestes' guilt at
having murdered his mother to avenge his father, Agamemnon. To

be sure, Agamemnon expresses fear of the gods and a desire to avoid appearing hubristic. However, this reveals only his persecutory anxiety. Orestes' guilt, on the other hand, is evidence of a degree of emotional maturity: he can recognize that Clytemnestra, who sent Orestes away in order to take a lover and later murdered Orestes' father, was at the same time a good mother who sometimes met his needs. Thus, Orestes feels guilty, not merely persecuted (although he certainly feels this too). It is because Orestes feels guilt that Athene is able to help Orestes overcome what can only be called his psychotic break, characterized by the paranoid delusion of persecution by the Furies, who punish matricide. That no one but Orestes can see the Furies (at least in the *Libation Bearers*) seems to support the supposition that his persecution stems from internal rather than external sources.[77]

In *The Eumenides (Furies)*, the Olympian gods are frequently reminded by the Furies that the Furies stem from an even older and more primitive time. They represent "the mind of the past" (line 838). The morality of the Furies is, as it were, pre-Oedipal, concerned strictly with the relationship between mother and son—that is, blood relationships. Apollo (who ordered Orestes to avenge his father), on the other hand, represents the morality of civilization (Oedipal morality) in which a social institution (marriage) takes precedence (lines 215–30; 603–08). The primitive character of the Furies is seen in the tortures with which they threaten Orestes: decapitation, castration, the gouging-out of eyes, and the sucking of blood (lines 185–95). We are told that their breath is "as a fire flung far and wide" and that poisonous vapors emanate from their bodies. Klein relates these tortures to the primitive oral- and anal-sadistic phantasies of young children, in which biting and attacks by flatus, urine, and feces predominate. She argues that the character of Orestes' disorder reveals a mental state associated with the transition between the paranoid-schizoid and depressive position. At this cusp, guilt is experienced in an especially primitive way—as persecution. The moral principle represented by the Furies is pure *lex talionis*. Like Freud's account of the superego, the Furies represent the child's aggression turned against himself.

Yet, the "Oresteia complex" is not just another version of the Oedipus complex. In Klein's thinking, this guilt—primitive as it is—expresses an innate desire, as powerful as aggression, to make amends to the injured object, to repair it. Orestes is apparently able to mobilize these feelings because he once experienced love from his mother (or from his wet nurse, who, along with Athene herself, seems to represent the good aspects of mother) whom he has introjected as a good object. Because Clytemnestra was both good and bad, and because Orestes can see these attributes as belonging to a single person (he has entered the depressive position), he is able to identify with her suffering in a most profound way, almost as though it were his own suffering. It is this ability that is the foundation of morality. Conversely, the inability to work through the depressive position—and consequently—(like Agamemnon)—to feel only persecutory anxiety but no guilt—is the basis of a number of severe emotional disorders.

It is Athene who helps Orestes work through the depressive position. Athene helps make the Furies milder, less harshly punitive, more concerned with those aspects of justice that take circumstances into account. For the individual's own furies to become milder requires that his good objects, epitomized by the good aspects of mother, be firmly established in his unconscious. That Orestes' good internal objects are not secure is suggested by his clinging to the statue of Athene in fright (*Eumenides*, line 258). Evidently, suggests Klein, it is Athene's steadfast fairness in mediating between Orestes and the Furies that helps Orestes establish his good objects more firmly. Why good internal objects are so central in mitigating the furies of the paranoid-schizoid position is apparent. Although Klein does not express it this way, it appears that in identifying with its good objects the ego comes to care for itself as it would for its good objects. In a word, the ego too may become the object of reparation.

What is it about the Greek tragedies that is so compelling? Part of the answer, surely, is that they are so spare, so stark: they seem to capture the power of human passion with nothing left out—and nothing left over. What are these passions? Love, hate, jealousy, greed, envy, guilt, retribution, expiation, and atonement certainly head the list. These are, of course, the passions that dominate Klein's account of mental life. Some have argued that she attributes to the young child far more complex mental processes than he is capable of. Perhaps such criticism is correct, but it really does not matter here. Klein's is fundamentally an account of the internal dynamics of the passions. She identifies the essence of emotional life with this dynamic. This is why her account is so brightly illuminated by an analysis of Greek tragedy.

The process by which love and hate, and hence the different parts of the self, are integrated is not easy, even for one who has firmly established his good objects. This is represented by the trial of Orestes, in which revenge and reparation receive an equal number of votes. About this ambivalent outcome, which Athene resolves in favor of Orestes, Klein says, "I would conclude that the opposing votes show that the self is not easily united, that destructive impulses drive one way, love and the capacity for reparation and compassion in other ways."[78]

Orestes' reaction to his liberation from the Furies reveals that he has indeed integrated love and hate. Orestes resented his mother not only because she murdered his father but also because she deprived him of his patrimony: his kingdom. In reclaiming his kingdom Orestes stresses not the power and the glory that once were his father's, and are now his, but the fairness and gratitude with which he will exercise his rule. That is, Orestes does not act as if he had won an Oedipal victory over his father (his kingdom is now Orestes'), nor does he exalt over the defeat of Clytemnestra's ghost, who still seeks revenge. He instead looks toward the future and in doing so projects the reparative feelings that he is now able to feel toward his family onto a larger family, his kingdom. Orestes exits the play at this point, but the play is not yet over, as Klein points out. It ends with a celebration of the integration of the Furies into the community. That is, the play ends not with the repression of hate but with its integration with love. This is the key theme. The "mind of the past," as the Furies call themselves, will not "be driven under the ground, out cast, like dirt!" (lines 838–39, 871–72). Rather, the Furies will live on as the Eumenides, benevolent spirits of justice. The state—the ego—is capable of living with these impulses and civilizing them, even if they are never fully tamed. While they are given an honored place in the community, it remains a place "deep hidden under ground that is yours by right where you shall sit on shining chairs beside the hearth to accept devotions offered by your citizens" (lines 804–07). The Furies are not driven underground. They are not violently suppressed; their existence is noted, even respected. However, the Furies remain too primitive to be allowed to wander freely in the light of day. They are brought out from the unconscious and integrated into the community of the mind, but they remain children of the night, to be repressed once again but not denied.

Aeschylus' *Eumenides* (along with Sophocles' *Oedipus at Colonus*) involves a greater degree of cosmic reconciliation and divine participation in the katharsis than any other Greek tragedy of the middle period. Yet, even in *The Eumenides* the order restored is fragile, only temporary. The play ends not with Orestes' return to health but with a celebration of the integration of the Furies into the community, a celebration that is both intense and poignant in part because it represents a narrow victory (by only one vote), and in part because it will have to be won again and again. Next time, perhaps, there will be no capricious goddess of morality to sway the jury and the outcome in favor of love and reparation over hatred and revenge. If the essence of tragedy is the terror of being truly alone in the world, then perhaps this terror is exacerbated by internal sources: the fear that within ourselves there is insufficient love to overcome our own hatred and aggression. We are left alone with our own aggression and hatred. In the *Oresteia* it was a close call. Will we fare well in a world in which the gods no longer intervene?

Critical Social Theory and the Tragic Worldview

Klein is not the only analyst to have seen the psychoanalytic significance of the myth of Orestes. In *The Age of Desire: Reflections of a Radical Psychoanalyst*, Joel Kovel compares Orestes with Frank, the child of lower middle-class Irish and Italian immigrants to the United States. Both, he says, have overly identified with their mothers, owing in part to the absence of their fathers. This creates in both young men such confusion, anxiety, and emotional chaos that matricide seems the only way to achieve separation. Yet, the outcome for Frank, even though he only phantasizes matricide, is quite different than for Orestes. Orestes "is ultimately redeemed by Apollo in a reconstructed patriarchy for which the Mother God becomes tamed and phallic Athene. Frank, on the other hand, being a proletarian in late capitalism, can expect no such salvation. All he has at his disposal is a mental-health clinic with a good-sized waiting list and shifting, inexperienced personnel."[79] The question, or course, is whether any mortal can expect the salvation of Orestes.

To be sure, Kovel is probably correct in his assertion that Orestes' (and Frank's) particular illness would not arise in a society not characterized by patriarchal domination. But while such a society is certainly to be desired, it is unlikely to be our salvation either. The Kleinian account suggests that the problem of integrating our love and hate is so profound—and so constitutive of reality—that it will remain a severe problem in any imaginable society, even as it may take different forms. As Kovel observes in a sober moment, "Different historical epochs will select different pathologies."[80] "Different pathologies," not "no pathologies," because the source of emotional distress is ultimately neither material scarcity nor social inequality (even though both may make things worse), but the way in which our love and hate divide us against ourselves, and thus create a world in this image. One reason, therefore, that Klein's account is tragic is because there is no redemption: not for Frank, not for any of us.

Tragedy, says Aristotle, represents people as better than they are, comedy as worse (*Poetics*, c. 2). While Marcuse and Adorno surely do not have a comic vision, it is not truly tragic either, in spite of their great concern with human suffering. Focusing on eros and transcendence, Marcuse is not so concerned with real human beings as with human beings as carriers of universal Ideas. Marcuse defines aesthetic form in terms of how it universalizes individual experience. For Marcuse there is only Thanatos; there is no place for Phaedra dying. Adorno, while concerned with objects (that is, human beings) in a way that Marcuse is not, has no tragic vision either. In part this is because he transforms art—which if Goldmann is correct is properly concerned with the suffering of concrete individuals— into philosophy and history. Even when he does not take this approach, Adorno is so concerned to reveal the fractured, split, and rent character of human existence that the notion of the tragic hero rising above the sum of his parts finds almost no place in his work.

To be sure, Orestes is hardly a whole and complete figure either. But neither is he utterly at the mercy of the Furies that divide him. He is able to take advantage of the resources that his culture makes available in order to tame the Furies. Orestes is neither the mirror of a rent society nor merely the vehicle by which this society is to be transcended. He is a suffering individual with a potential for wholeness—relative, partial, and fragile as it is. Contrary to Kovel's reading of the story of Orestes, Klein's sees in Orestes an individual who can participate in his own salvation; or rather, since we no longer live in an enchanted world, an individual who can participate in the integration, incomplete as it always is, of his own furies. Marcuse's view of the individual, on the other hand, is not so much tragic as pathetic. The pathos of his project, as Wolfgang Fritz Haug points out, is that in the end it is only humanity who stands in the way of utopia; but for the way to be cleared humanity must be utterly transformed, down to its instincts.[81] A Kleinian perspective holds out little hope for such a transformation. Nevertheless, it finds in human nature as it is currently constituted cause for hope—a hope, to be sure, that remains tragically unfulfilled, especially in the large group.

CHAPTER FIVE

Reason and Reparation

Central to the program of the Frankfurt School is its critique of the dialectic of Enlightenment, sometimes called the critique of instrumental reason. In Lukács' augmentation of Marx's concept of alienation, the concept refers to man's alienation from himself as producer. People become like the things they produce; they also become like the production process itself. The Frankfurt School radicalized this critique, extending it to include not merely exchange relationships under capitalism but also the history of Western reason since (and even before) Socrates. For the critique of instrumental reason, it is not merely productive relationships under capitalism that promote reification. Reason itself becomes reified, in the sense that it comes to mimic the most rigid, aggressive, and fragmented aspects of nature itself in order to control it. This is mimesis in its least erotic, least creative aspect. The unique and the particular—in nature and in those men and women who employ instrumental reason—are broken up into uniform, meaningless parts in order to control them. The capitalistic production process, as well as the rationality that it exemplifies (instrumental reason), is but a reflection of this larger, world-historical development, the dialectic of Enlightenment. In this dialectic, the potential of reason to be more than an instrument is split off as idealism, where it remains impotently confined to higher realms.

In order for Klein to be relevant to the concerns of the Frankfurt School, it must be shown that her psychoanalytic theory can successfully address this issue. If the Kleinian account is to be an improvement on the work of the Frankfurt School, it must also suggest a solution to the dialectic of Enlightenment. For in posing the problem of instrumental reason in such radical terms, the Frankfurt School rendered its solution virtually unimaginable. I shall argue that the Kleinian categories of love, hate, and reparation can better explain the dialectic of Enlightenment. Instrumental reason can fruitfully be interpreted as an expression of paranoid-schizoid aggression and anxiety, the result of which is rigid, constrained, one-dimensional symbolization. The alternative is what I shall call reparative reason. Although reparative reason is based on love, I shall not emphasize the way in which it seeks to repair and make amends. I shall instead stress the way in which reparative reason is sensitive to the complexities and nuances of objects, rather than forcing them into rigid, prefabricated categories. It is this attribute that makes reparative reason relevant to the critique of instrumental reason.

First I review and analyze the Frankfurt School's critique of the dialectic of Enlightenment. I emphasize the way in which the school's embrace of Freud's version of the Oedipal conflict contradicts their critique of instrumental reason. In the next section I show why it is more fruitful to interpret instrumental reason as originating in paranoid-schizoid anxiety. Following this, I develop a Kleinian-inspired alternative to instrumental reason—called reparative reason—showing that it avoids certain problems the Frankfurt School could not overcome. Though reparative reason does not express a romantic view of nature, it too sees reconciliation with nature as worthwhile, as will be demonstrated. Finally, I attempt to render the idea of reparative reason more concrete, showing how it is expressed in what Carol Gilligan calls "a different voice," but not in what Juergen Habermas calls discourse.

Dialectic of Enlightenment

Science, according to the Frankfurt School, epitomizes instrumental reason, in which the laws of nature are learned only by slavishly imitating the lawfulness of nature itself. This is the real story behind Homer's *Odyssey*, according to Horkheimer and Adorno in *Dialectic of Enlightenment*.[1] Odysseus outwits nature and returns home safely. In order to do so, however, he must reject the erotic, Dionysian aspects of his own nature. For instance, he must have himself tied to his ship's mast, because he knows that he lacks the strength to resist the Sirens' call—a call that represents the desire to abandon oneself to primitive, Dionysian desires. Odysseus is rational enough to think ahead, to outwit his own nature, his own needs. But his sailors, like most men, must have their ears stopped with wax—they must never learn of their deepest needs—lest they cease their laborious rowing altogether. This episode, says David Held, "symbolizes the mode in which crews, servants and labourers produce their oppressor's life together with their own. . . . Their master neither labours nor succumbs to the temptation of immediate gratification. He indulges in the beauty of the song. But the Sirens' voices become 'mere objects of contemplation'—mere art."[2]

The *Odyssey* represents the transformation of comprehensive reason into mimesis as the price of survival. Man was once weak and ignorant, whereas nature was powerful and mysterious. Man came to master nature, but only by imitating her most rigid and routinized aspects. One sees this in experiments in science, in which the researcher subjects his every action to the stringent discipline of experimental controls. Reason comes to be defined in terms of a single task: the prediction and control of the given. In defining reason thus, man slowly learns to dominate nature, but at the price of renunciation. Man must subject himself to a terrible discipline, under which he is forced to reject those facets of human nature that are incompatible with the controls of the scientific experiment, as well as with the order and regularity imposed by the factory. For Horkheimer and Adorno, the discipline imposed by the industrial system is merely the latest stage in the scientific conquest of nature. The outcome is the diminution of the concept of reason itself. Reason, in so far as it is concerned with the potential of things to become more than they are, is split off as idealism, where it comes to represent little more than "an imaginary *temps perdu*" in the real history of mankind, as Marcuse calls it. A reason powerful enough to ensure human survival and comfort in a hostile world is purchased at the price of Reason itself. Originating in human weakness, instrumental reason overcomes nature only by renouncing the Dionysian aspects of human nature, as well as the potential of reason itself. Reason becomes powerful only by becoming an instrument.

One of the key aspects of instrumental reason, according to Horkheimer and Adorno, is the way in which it forces reality into categories, categories that define objects in terms of how they may best be manipulated or controlled. They call this type of thinking "identity thinking," the assumption that the concept is adequate to the object—that is, it tells us all there is to know about the object—if the concept allows us to predict or control its behavior.

Dialectical thought is the opposite: "The name of dialectics says no more, to begin with, than that objects do not go into their concepts without leaving a remainder, that they come to contradict the traditional norm of adequacy. . . . It indicates the untruth of identity, the fact that the concept does not exhaust the thing conceived."[3] Dialectical thought is reconciling, because it seeks to come to terms with the object, to let it be, to let it reveal itself. The cognitive utopia, says Adorno, "would be to use concepts to unseal the nonconceptual with concepts, without making it their equal."[4] Presumably reconciliation with nature would involve an understanding of nature that lets nature set the terms under which it is conceptualized. What precisely this would mean is, to be sure, unclear.

In the face of such a comprehensive indictment of reason, many have asked what the alternative might be. A return to a strictly objective concept of reason is clearly not the answer. In today's world, Horkheimer and Adorno both believe that Neoplatonism can only be ideology.[5] Neither nominalism nor essentialism is an acceptable alternative. Indeed, the division of reason into categories such as this is precisely the problem that Horkheimer and Adorno are addressing. In Habermas' view, Horkheimer and Adorno have exhausted all alternatives. Nothing cognitive remains. Their project terminates in a cul-de-sac. Adorno's alternative to instrumental reason is, says Habermas, a nonrational, imitative, highly sympathetic, snuggling (*anschmiegen*) relationship to nature. While expressing genuine human needs, such a relationship lacks intellectual content. It is the "pure opposite" (*bare Gegenteil*) of reason: pure impulse.[6] Elsewhere Habermas states that Adorno practiced "ad hoc determinant negation."[7]

Habermas exaggerates, however. Adorno explicitly rejects the imitative dedifferentiation of man and nature that Habermas sees as the noncognitive core of Adorno's program. As Adorno observed in one of his later essays, "The picture of a temporal or extratemporal original state of happy identity between subject and object is romantic, however—a wishful project at times, but today no more than a lie. The undifferentiated state before the subject's formation was the dread of the blind web of nature, of myth; it was in protest against it that the great religions had their truth content."[8] Nevertheless, Habermas is correct that Horkheimer and Adorno's alternative to instrumental reason seeks reconciliation with nature, rather than mastery over it. Precisely what reconciliation would look like remains unclear, but the hope seems to be that a less repressive organization of society would better satisfy members' erotic, Dionysian needs. In such a society, in which individuals would behave less aggressively toward each other, men and women could lead less fearful, angry lives. They would, consequently, be less aggressive toward nature, less aggressive in forcing it into categories. For aggressiveness toward nature—what Adorno calls *"verwilderte Selbstbehauptung"* (wild self-assertion)—stems above all from fear, which leads to aggression as well as to resentment (often unconscious) at pleasure denied, which leads to still more aggression. Marcuse calls this cycle the "dialectic of civilization," a term apparently designed to evoke comparison with the dialectic of Enlightenment.[9]

Instrumental reason's ultimate object of domination is not the world but the threat to self-assertive individuality posed by the needs of Dionysus. The Sirens' call comes from within. Probably the Frankfurt School is correct: less repression of inner nature—in other words, the release of Eros and Dionysus—should result in a less aggressive stance toward external nature as well. Aggression represents an effort to subdue aspects of human nature by projecting them onto external nature, as well as resentment at the harshness of nature for having to do so—that is, resentment at having to repress the desire for happiness for the sake of labor. Yet, the limits of this perspective have already been suggested. While the release of eros may reduce human aggression, it is unlikely to lead to a reparative attitude toward nature either. Eros remains fundamentally selfish.

Marcuse answers that while eros may be selfish, it is at the same time a social, life-giving force. While unsublimated eros may seek exclusive possession of another, sublimated eros seeks to win a certain immortality. It thus builds families, creates beauty, or founds and preserves institutions. In its sublimated form, eros is compatible with civilization; indeed, it is the force that builds civilization, standing against the aggression that would destroy it. While all this may be true—even though a Kleinian would see not merely eros behind these phenomena but also the desire to make reparation—it

still finds little place for nature. One sees this in the Frankfurt
School's most elaborate and sophisticated defense of the power of
eros: Marcuse's *Eros and Civilization*. Elsewhere I have argued at
length what can only be asserted here—that in spite of its rhetoric
regarding reconciliation with nature, the liberation of nature, and so
forth, *Eros and Civilization* reflects an attitude that sees nature over-
whelmingly in terms of how it can serve human purposes, albeit
human purposes under the rule of eros. Under an erotic order, nature is expected to cooperate with human needs. This is not an
exploitative attitude toward nature but a narcissistic one. Under the
reign of eros, even nature will wish to cooperate with human purposes.[10] Nowhere else does Marcuse reveal this more clearly than
when he states that a new science and technology, guided by eros,
"could (in a literal sense!) embody, incorporate, the human faculties
and desires to such an extent that they appear as part of the objective
determinism of nature."[11]

Oedipus and Instrumental Reason

It is frequently argued that the Frankfurt School employed a simplis-
tic, one-dimensional interpretation of psychoanalysis, in which eros
and its repression are the sole issues. Christopher Lasch summarizes
Marcuse's argument as follows: repression originates in the subjection of the pleasure principle to the patriarchal compulsion to labor;
thus, if one could abandon labor, repression could be eliminated.[12]
Lasch ignores the fact that Marcuse, like Freud, sees not merely the
repression of eros but also aggression as the source of humanity's
discontent. Yet, in the end this makes little difference, for Marcuse's
solution to the problem of aggression is also based on the release of
eros (nonrepressive desublimation), which might then "bind" aggression without repression.[13] Lasch's criticism is trenchant, its
most powerful aspect being the revelation that, despite Marcuse's
praise of Freud's depth psychology, as well as his criticism of neo-
Freudian revisionism, Marcuse's account is in many respects one-
dimensional, seeing all psychic conflict as centering on the repression of eros. Yet, it should not be overlooked that Horkheimer and
Adorno—as well as Marcuse in later works—develop a more complex argument, in which not merely the repression of eros but also
the societal manipulation of the nascent ego is at stake.

This latter argument has been called by Habermas the "thesis of the end of the individual." Though stated in different ways at different times by Horkheimer, Adorno, and Marcuse, the core of this thesis is the assertion that the subjection of hitherto private sectors of existence (such as child rearing, family planning, and education) to administrative direction and control has led to a generation of individuals no longer able to resist authority. The development of an independent ego is a long, slow process requiring that the child be sheltered for some time from the outside world; but this is precisely what the administrative state's intrusion into family life prohibits—the result being a submissive generation. Yet, as Jessica Benjamin has shown, in the end this argument too sees the issue almost entirely in terms of eros and its repression.[14] Only now the repression of eros is good, or at least better than the alternative, which is the total manipulation of the individual's every need by society. When eros is repressed, Horkheimer and Adorno seem to believe, not only is it less accessible to conscious awareness; it is also less accessible to societal exploitation.

For the Frankfurt School, as for Freud, the key moment in the repression of eros is, of course, the Oedipal conflict. Benjamin has fully explored the irony of Horkheimer's and Adorno's embrace of this conflict. In seeing the Oedipal conflict as the alternative to society's total manipulation of the psyche, they embrace a process—Oedipal internalization—that reproduces instrumental reason. In Horkheimer's words, "When the child respects in his father's strength a moral relationship and thus learns to love what his reason recognizes to be a fact, he is experiencing his first training for the bourgeois authority relationship."[15] Why would Horkheimer and Adorno embrace a process by which the son—in response to the phantasied threat of dismemberment, castration anxiety—internalizes the values of society, values that Horkheimer recognizes are esteemed by the son in large measure simply because they are the values associated with power and authority? That is, why would Horkheimer and Adorno find emancipatory a process that seems to be nothing less than the medium by which instrumental reason is passed from one generation to another? What one learns from the father, says Horkheimer, is that "one travels the paths to power in the bourgeois world not by putting into practice judgments of moral value but by clever adaptation to actual conditions."[16] This *is* instrumental reason.

They support this position in part by recognizing that in the best of circumstances the authority of the bourgeois father was combined with love. It is through this internalization of the values of a feared and loved father that a strong ego was fashioned. As Horkheimer states, "In earlier times a loving imitation of the self-reliant prudent man, devoted to his duty, was the source of moral autonomy in the individual."[17] Similarly, Adorno sees the Oedipal conflict as a source of adult spontaneity and nonconformity, apparently because the resolution of this conflict can take such idiosyncratic forms, among which Adorno seems to include neurotic protest against society, which is better than no protest at all.[18] Horkheimer and Adorno's position seems to be that if the process of building a strong ego via authority and love requires the internalization of society's values, so be it. Such individuals at least have the potential to someday challenge authority—they possess what Horkheimer calls "moral autonomy"—whereas individuals who have failed to internalize the father's authority lack even this potential.

Jessica Benjamin argues that Horkheimer and Adorno have confused the process that produces a strong (primarily in the sense of harsh, demanding, and punitive) superego with the process that produces a strong ego. Internalization produces the former but not the latter. In so doing, internalization actually fosters fearful compliance—cunning but not criticism. Horkheimer and Adorno make this mistake because they confuse the Oedipal conflict, in which the son's sexual identity is consolidated, with an earlier process—separation from mother—in which the basis of individuality and autonomy is laid down.

Benjamin turns to the successors of Melanie Klein, such as W. R. D. Fairbairn and Harry Guntrip, leading representatives of the British Object Relations School, arguing that it is the earliest, pre-Oedipal object relationships, particularly with the mother, that are key to the development of a strong ego.[19] Benjamin's approach clarifies much that is problematic in the Frankfurt School's use of Freud. However, her approach does little to clarify the more fundamental issue addressed here: in turning to eros as the alternative to instrumental reason, did the Frankfurt School adopt an ultimately incoherent strategy? Or did they simply confuse Eros with Oedipus?

What led the Frankfurt School into a cul-de-sac was neither its critique of instrumental reason nor its project of reconciliation with nature, but its overreliance on the concept of eros to explain it. This last point is supported by the preceding analysis, which shows that their psychology and philosophy are operating at cross purposes. For the Frankfurt School to be in the position of praising a psychological process that reproduces instrumental reason, in order to avoid the "end of the individual," is not merely a measure of their desperation. It is also a measure of how poorly their psychological theory supports their philosophical program. This is why turning to Klein is worthwhile. Klein herself did not develop a theory of reason or thinking. Some, as Hinshelwood notes, have regarded Bion's work, particularly as developed in *Attention and Interpretation*, "as a Kleinian theory of thinking."[20] I have not approached Klein through Bion on this issue, instead preferring to develop my own account.

Origins of Instrumental Reason in the Paranoid-Schizoid Position

In her early writings, Klein links the desire for knowledge, the clumsily termed "epistemophilic impulse," with the desire to appropriate the mother's body and its imagined contents, such as babies. In fact, it could be argued that Klein's work began with the study of the "epistemophilic impulse." As Meltzer points out, so much of what is revolutionary in Klein's work stems from her taking seriously, often literally, young children's phantasies about the inside of their own and their mothers' bodies.[21] From the Kleinian perspective, the desire to know and the desire to own and control the contents of the mother's body are virtually identical. "So the epistemophilic instinct and the desire to take possession come quite early to be most intimately connected with one another," she states.[22] Freud linked the desire to know with childhood curiosity about sex, particularly parental intercourse. Intellectual activity is a form of libidinal sublimation, which can be inhibited by castration anxiety, for example. Although Klein's view may seem to be an elaboration of Freud's, it is not. In her early work particularly, the desire to know is an expression not of libido but of sadism.[23] It is sadism, directed against the mother's body, that drives the desire to know. "The early connection between the epistemophilic impulse and sadism is very important for the whole mental development," states Klein.[24]

Actually, it is not clear whether "sadism" is the best term to characterize this orientation. Klein made these remarks a number of years before developing the paranoid-schizoid position. In light of

later developments in her thought, it would probably be more accu-
rate to characterize the early desire to know as motivated by paranoid-schizoid "love," an utterly selfish desire to own, control, and
possess the mother's body and its contents without any regard for
the mother's welfare. Yet, in the end perhaps there is little practical
difference between what Klein called (in 1928) the "anal-sadistic
libido-position, which impels [the child] to wish to appropriate the
contents of the body" and paranoid-schizoid love.[25] Both show utter
disregard for the welfare of the object, seeking only to appropriate it
completely, though only the anal-sadistic position seeks destruction
for its own sake.

This origin of the desire to know in an aggressive, appropriating,
even sadistic orientation towards mother's body connects emotional
and intellectual development. Most important, it makes intellectual
development dependent upon the integration of aggression. All
knowledge of the outside world (including childish theories about
the inside of mother's body) stems from the symbolic equation of a
phantasied internal object with an external one. It is this aspect of
Klein's thought that Meltzer calls Platonic, a term best interpreted as
referring to the doctrine of innate ideas. The symbolic equation originally takes the form of A (an object in the internal world) = B (an
aspect of mother's body).[26] The problem is that too much aggression,
coupled with too much anxiety about this aggression, can inhibit the
desire to know, out of fear that so doing will destroy the mother. In
repressing his sadism, says Klein, the young child also represses his
desire to know:

> The ego's excessive and premature defence against sadism
> checks the establishing of a relation to reality and develop-
> ment of phantasy-life. The further sadistic appropriation and
> exploration of the mother's body and of the outside world
> (the mother's body in an extended sense) are brought to a
> standstill, and this causes the more or less complete suspen-
> sion of the symbolic relation to things and objects represent-
> ing the contents of the mother's body and hence of the rela-
> tion to the subject's environment and to reality.[27]

Lest this all seem particularly unlikely, Klein notes that no less a
Freudian than James Strachey has shown that reading has the unconscious significance of taking knowledge from the mother's body.

Conversely, anxiety and guilt about robbing her are significant factors in inhibitions against reading.[28]

One of Klein's most famous patients, a four-year-old boy named Dick, could barely speak or play, so inhibited was his use of symbolism. One day, while looking at some pencil shavings, Dick said of them, "Poor Mrs. Klein."[29] For Dick, the wood shavings did not merely represent Mrs. Klein, they *were* Mrs. Klein. By expressing his aggression, Dick reduced her from a whole object to pieces and fragments. Yet even this symbolic equation represented progress for the boy. Before the incident he had been unable to make even this terribly rigid and concrete equation because of extreme anxiety about his aggression. Of course, most intellectual inhibitions are not this severe. Nevertheless, what the Frankfurt School calls instrumental reason is characterized by a comparable, albeit less extreme, symbolic rigidity. Like Dick, what Adorno calls identity thinking virtually equates the object with the particular symbol chosen to express it. I shall call this the rigid symbolic equation, in order to suggest its linkage to intellectual inhibitions associated with paranoid-schizoid anxiety.

Identity Thinking and the Symbolic Equation

Normally, as internal phantasies come into contact with reality, they are modified by it. This is the way in which we make contact with reality—and ultimately the way in which we learn all we will ever know about reality. Freud made a similar point, arguing that "everything conscious has a preliminary unconscious stage."[30] For Kleinians, this unconscious stage is unconscious phantasy, and the link to the external world is established through symbolism. As Segal puts it, in finding a symbolic expression for his unconscious phantasy, the child—and the adult too—learns to explore and relate to the world. Originally, as discussed above, the symbolic connection between internal object and external reality is terribly concrete: inner A = outer B. Gradually, as phantasy is modified by contact with external reality, the symbolism is loosened, becoming more abstract. Not only an outer B (mother's body) but also an outer C, D, and so on (that is, other aspects of the world) can represent an inner A, and vice versa. Furthermore, the symbolic equation itself becomes looser. Rather than "inner A = outer B, C, and D," one might write the equation as "inner $A \equiv$ outer B, C, and D," in which $\equiv$, the mathematical symbol for congruence, is interpreted to mean that while the elements of the equation are not identical, they stand in harmonious agreement. One element represents another, because the elements resemble each other in significant ways without being identical. Otherwise expressed, an internal object may come to stand for a number of external objects, and vice versa, in a shifting pattern that changes as we learn more about the world and ourselves. I shall refer to this as the loose symbolic equation. It represents thought becoming less identical with its objects. It does not represent the end of intellectual aggression.

Love plays a key role in this loosening process. It is love and guilt that lead the child to displace his aggressive, appropriative interest in mother's body onto a wider variety of symbolic representatives in the hope that so doing will spare mother from the intrusive character of its researches.[31] Perhaps unconscious reasoning like this lay behind the claim of Francis Bacon, that great popularizer of scientific method, that science must "hound," "vex," and "torture" nature in order to extract her secrets, a process he likens to rape.[32] In turning our appropriative, greedy, aggressive desires toward the outside world, including the often naturelike jungle of economic competition, we protect those we love from our own aggression. At the same time, we further our intellectual development by increasing the number of outer Cs and Ds that may symbolically represent an inner A. This way of thinking, it will readily be seen, is characteristic of paranoid-schizoid morality, in which every act of love and concern is purchased by hatred and aggression directed elsewhere: that is, by splitting and idealization. The same psychological process that explains the behavior of the large group also explains the origins of instrumental reason.

One might also, as some Kleinians have done, express the relationship between the rigid and loose symbolic equation in terms of projective identification (in fact, there seems to be a tendency in recent Kleinian studies to explain as much as possible in terms of this mechanism). In the rigid symbolic equation, there is a projection of emotional states into the symbol. The symbol becomes a container, and because the projective identification is archaic, its relationship to the symbol is one of omnipotence and total control.

Consequently, there is a fusion of symbol with the original emotional state, accounting for the rigidity of the equation.[33] Maturity involves an acceptance of the separation of symbol and the thing symbolized. While projective identification is still involved, it no longer seeks fusion and total control. On the contrary, the loose symbolic equation requires that the subject mourn the loss of identity of symbol and thing.[34] Otherwise expressed, the mature thinker must mourn the loss of a world in which every object is an extension of the mother's body. As we saw in chapter 4, much of art is about precisely this, in which we mourn the loss of objects that have sustained us. Such mourning, it appears, is necessary not just for emotional health. It is also necessary for mature thought.

The problem with paranoid-schizoid epistemology, as it might be called, is its tendency to force reality into prefabricated categories. Otherwise expressed, external C has less opportunity to feed back to and modify internal A, since C is grasped solely in terms of a preconceived identity with A to begin with. As a result, we fail to learn all we could about the world because we force it into a framework determined by our phantasies and needs, giving the world less of an opportunity to modify these phantasies. The Platonic origin of our concepts is never adequately corrected by an Aristotelian respect for experience. According to a certain idealized picture of science, science makes progress in learning about the world because it formulates its theories in such a way that one little fact may disprove a previously accepted theory.[35] Yet, if this is so, then science is surely not an instance of identity thinking but an exception to it, a decisive one, since science is usually conceived as the epitome of instrumental reason.

In fact, this observation about the ideals of science is quite compatible with my account, for the same reason that science does not escape the Frankfurt School's critique of instrumental reason. Paranoid-schizoid epistemology, or instrumental reason, does not exclude all learning (that is, feedback) from nature but only that which does not fit its categories, which are oriented toward prediction, manipulation, and control. Within these categories, falsifiability reigns; we learn about the world by allowing it to correct our theories. I am concerned with the way in which different experiences of nature—experiences not fitting into these categories in the first place—may be excluded. The loosening of the symbolic equation (an achievement of the depressive position) means two things. It refers to the multiplicity of external things, processes, and events that can represent internal reality; and to the way in which this multiplicity is more abstractly linked to the internal world in the first place, so that the external world may show itself more freely, as less constrained by the symbolic equation. It is in this second respect that science is not symbolically loose, for its categories, open to falsification in some respect, exclude those experiences of the world incompatible with its categories of prediction, causal explanation (or association), and control. The experience of nature as beautiful is an obvious example.

In *Languages of Art*, Nelson Goodman seeks to define art. After rejecting various possibilities—for example, that art is representation or art is beauty—he concludes that the work of art is best distinguished from other activities by its "semantic density." In art the relationship among symbols is more important than their denotative function. This, in turn, has to do with the world-making function of art, the way in which it creates another reality.[36] Such a perspective allows us to understand symbolic "looseness" in a slightly different way. In a loose symbolic equation, the relationship among symbols is more important than the denotative relationship between symbol and external reality. In all but the simplest symbolic equation (inner A = external B), both internal and denotative relationships exist. Symbols refer to each other; they also refer to the external world. The balance between these two modes of reference is decisive in defining looseness. From this perspective, art is especially loose, normal science is less so, and accounting still less so. In the accountant's balance sheet, for example, each number denotes something external, even though the internal relationships among the numbers are also important. Conversely, very few of the elements of a modern painting may denote anything external at all; symbolic juxtaposition is everything.

A Kleinian Interpretation of the Dialectic of Enlightenment

Horkheimer and Adorno's account in *Dialectic of Enlightenment* may be interpreted, from a Kleinian perspective, as a phenomenon of intellectual inhibition born of aggression. Nature's scarcity, coupled with anxiety about survival in a hostile and unresponsive world, leads to an aggressive, appropriating attitude toward nature, in which knowledge, possession, and control are, as with the very young child, virtually one. To be sure, the history of instrumental reason is not a case study comparable to that of Dick. It appears, however, that anxiety regarding intellectual aggression may lead to intellectual rigidity, in which the symbolic equation becomes particularly inflexible. An entire world is seen only in terms of how it fits into categories associated with ownership, possession, appropriation, manipulation, and control. In these circumstances, says Klein, stimuli from the external world may be virtually equated with internal stimuli.[37] A realistic perception of the external world as harsh, unremitting, and unresponsive may simply reinforce a perception that one's internal world shares similar characteristics. Otherwise expressed, the defenses associated with splitting and projection become less effective, since what is projected into the external world is (because of the inflexible symbolic equation) equated with the internal world from which these projections have been banned. Human nature becomes a second nature, a virtual copy of what we have projected onto nature. Rather than reinforcing paranoid-schizoid defenses, instrumental reason in the end undermines them.

For this reason the ego frequently resorts to other defenses. The ego, says Klein, sometimes "tries (by means of projection on to the outer world) to demonstrate its independence from . . . [its] imagoes by rebelling against all influences emanating from *real objects*."[38] If it is the interaction of inner world with outer that modifies internal phantasy (thus leading to knowledge of reality), then this rebellion against the influence of reality must also impinge on intellectual development. Expressed in philosophical terms, this rebellion is tantamount to idealism. Adorno labels "idealism as rage" at a world too sparse to be dominated.[39] A Kleinian perspective requires only a slight modification of this insight. Idealism is a *defense* against rage, in which one's dependence upon this world is denied, as though inner phantasy were self-sufficient. "Idealism as narcissism," which Klein defines not in libidinal terms but as a retreat to a world of inner objects (as though they were the whole world), captures this refinement of Adorno's insight.

The dialectic of Enlightenment is the division of reason into a

crass materialism that views the world strictly in terms of instrumental reason and of an irrelevant, impotent idealism. This is, of
course, the process just addressed in Kleinian terms. It is clear how a
crass materialism remains intellectually inhibited because of the rigidity of the symbolic equation involved. Indeed, this is the real
meaning of the mimetic character of instrumental reason. What may
be surprising is how idealism does not really escape this inhibition
either. Or rather, it escapes it only by denying the symbolic equation
altogether. The result is not a looser equation but no equation at all.
Otherwise expressed, the symbolic equation becomes purely self-
referential, having no denotative function at all, as in the most abstract art. Neither materialism nor idealism escapes identity thinking. Materialism identifies inner world with outer; idealism is
merely identical with itself. What is needed is more responsive orientation toward the external world, in which the external world is
given a greater opportunity to modify our preconceptions (internal
phantasies) about it.

Reparative Reason

The connection between reparative reason, understood in terms of
the loose symbolic equation, and love (*caritas*) is apparent. It is
concern for the object qua object that allows us to know it better, by
not forcing it into categories determined by our primitive anxieties
but instead by letting the object in some measure contribute to our
categories. Love lets its love be. In so doing the lover may learn to
know other aspects of his or her beloved, aspects that become apparent only when the beloved is valued in his or her own right, not just
as a satisfier of needs. The preceding considerations suggest that this
is as true of epistemological relations as it is of personal ones.
Whereas paranoid-schizoid (instrumental) reason sees its objects in
terms of the categories of prediction, manipulation, and control,
reparative reason experiences its objects as they are mediated by a
richer, more creative set of phantasies, phantasies concerned with
precisely what Adorno wished art to concern itself with: assisting
the object to become itself. This, ultimately, is what reparation is
about. Anything less—or more—is likely to be merely mock
reparation.

It could be argued that the emphasis on letting the object take the lead in constituting our categories of it (if this is to be anything more than an inchoate romantic impulse) is tantamount to naive realism. This would not, however, be correct. Like Thomas Kuhn in his well-known *Structure of Scientific Revolutions*, Paul Feyerabend argues that theories are never falsified by facts, because theories constitute a conceptual world—thus, they have an opportunity to determine what facts shall count against them. Indeed, says Feyerabend, the better a theory seems to fit the facts, the more suspicious we should be. The fit of theory and facts is probably an indication "that we have failed to transcend an accidental stage of research"—that is, the theory has blinded us to alternative interpretations of the facts or to new facts.[40] What we need are new theories and new concepts that may help us discover new facts, ones that have been overlooked by the prevailing theory. Feyerabend calls his approach "counter-induction."

> Knowledge so conceived is not a series of self-consistent the-
> ories that converges towards an ideal view; it is not a gradual
> approach to the truth. It is rather an ever increasing ocean of
> mutually incompatible (and perhaps even incommensurable)
> alternatives, each single theory, each fairy tale, each myth that
> is part of the collection forcing the others into greater articula-
> tion and all of them contributing, via this process of competi-
> tion, to the development of our consciousness.[41]

This is no naive realism. In fact, Feyerabend characterizes his position as metaphysical instrumentalism, which exploits the loose structure of the world, a structure that allows "practices with differ-ent problematics to have comparable achievements (i.e., to achieve a comparable balance of failure and success)."[42] He notes, however, that the *method* of counterinduction is compatible with the "plural-istic realism" of J. S. Mill, which employs the proliferation of theor-ies and concepts to know the one real structure of the world better. That is, even if one assumes that the world itself is not loosely structured but is only one way, the method of theoretical pluralism (which I use here as a synonym for counterinduction, although they are not truly identical) is the best way to learn about it. In fact, this seems to be the position of Karl Popper as well, at least in his later works.

It is not necessary to decide how loosely structured the world truly is in order to determine whether to employ reparative reason. Whether or not the *world itself* is loosely structured, Feyerabend demonstrates that our *concepts of it* should be—in the Kleinian sense of the loose symbolic equation—in order to learn more about it. Nevertheless, throughout this book I have made a number of assumptions regarding the structure of the world and our relationship to it, as any author who wishes to say something substantive must do. I have assumed that we should want to learn more about the external world, not just internal reality (that is, both are worthy of our study); that the external world is knowable (even if we may never know it for sure); and that the world, even if loosely structured, is not just any way we wish it to be. Expressed thus, it is apparent that "letting the object reveal itself" is not just metaphor, though it is that too. Conceptualizing the world via a multitude of fluid categories, including those that do not even seem to fit very well (counterinduction), is the best way to grasp the way the world really is. In this sense, the loose symbolic equation may indeed be said to assist the object to become itself, as Adorno puts it—that is, to be known by us as it truly is.

Reparative reason is not an expression of naive realism, but neither is it an expression of a passive, waiting-for-being-to-disclose-itself point of view. To the contrary, reparative reason recognizes the need to integrate intellectual aggression, whereas the Frankfurt School, and especially Adorno, would deny it. In fact, this is the fundamental flaw in their epistemology. An interesting case study of intellectual inhibition by Segal sheds light on this claim. A woman writer came to Segal complaining that she had been unable to write for a number of years. Her associations led her to remember an early dislike of using words, a dislike that was still present. Using words, said the writer, made her break "'an endless unity into bits.' It was like 'chopping up', like 'cutting things.'" To this woman, writing was an aggressive, rending act, in which she tore an endless unity into bits. She felt, says Segal, "that using words made her lose the illusion of possessing and being at one with an endless, undivided world: 'when you name a thing you really lose it.'"[43] In using words—symbols for things—the woman had to recognize her own separateness from these things and at the same time confront her own aggressiveness. Because she could do neither, the woman could not write.

The case study illustrates an important point. Words and concepts do involve a certain aggressiveness toward the external world. They do break "an endless unity into bits" and at the same time force us to recognize our own separateness. In her later work, Klein came to recognize that the quest for knowledge stems not merely from sadism and greed but from a desire to know the object in order to repair it. Often this reparative orientation toward knowledge takes the form of discovering, creating, or making something new, in order to replace what we have greedily taken with something better.[44] However, it is important not to let ourselves off the hook too readily with insights such as this. While the motivation or goal may be reparative, the acquisition of knowledge never entirely loses its origins in a certain appropriative attitude that divides up reality in order to intellectually master it. The reason is apparent: whether motivated by greed or love, the intellectual operations are similar, because (pace the Frankfurt School's utopian dreams) the natural world does not change its nature when approached with love. The killer and the surgeon both use a knife, and while the killer is motivated by hate and the surgeon (ideally) by caritas, can it be argued that the surgeon's actions contain not a trace of the killer's aggression? The surgeon must be aggressive, because nature generally neither knows nor cares about our motives. It is the original other.

The Frankfurt School, especially Adorno, fails to integrate aggression. Their alternative to instrumental reason is so incomprehensible primarily because it has no place for aggression. There is a parallel between Segal's patient, who would not name reality lest it be chopped into bits, and Adorno's desire not to force nature into human categories lest we destroy its wholeness and unity. Similarly, the alternative to instrumental reason that one finds in Marcuse, with its idealization of deindividuation, recalls Segal's patient's desire not to recognize her separateness lest she be (in my interpretation) confronted with her own aggression, including her rage at her own mortality.[45]

Adorno characterizes his philosophical ideal as approaching the world "without velleity (Willkuer) or violence, entirely from felt contact with its objects—this alone is the task of thought." Velleity, it will be recalled, is the weakest kind of desire, a thought that does not lead to the slightest action.[46] It is as though Adorno would deny all desire, all willfulness, all self-assertion, in order to protect the world from human aggression. In the long run, however, such an approach cannot work, because it is based on denial, not integration. Indeed, if Klein is correct, Adorno's approach must lead to a certain lack of responsibility, in that we deny what we must do to survive and prosper—that is, categorize the world.

Reparative reason, understood in terms of the loose symbolic equation, is the alternative to instrumental reason. Rather than avoiding the categorization of the external world, it seeks to keep these categories flexible and open to revision, not just by the facts that falsify theories but by new reparative phantasies as well. We must forever chop reality into bits. The trick is to be able to put the bits back together and chop them up in a new way the next day. This is the point of what I called loose symbolism.

Against the tendency of quantitative thought to categorize reality according to the needs of prediction and control, Adorno invokes "qualitative rationality." Qualitative reason was introduced by Plato, he says, "as a corrective for the violence of unleashed quantification. A parable from *Phaedrus* leaves no doubt of it; there, organizing thought and nonviolence strike a balance. The principle, reversing the conceptual motion of synthesis, is that of 'division into species according to the natural formation, where the joints are, not breaking any part as a bad carver might.' "[47] This is not reparative reason either. Sometimes we must break the bones to find out where the joints are (what Feyerabend calls "counterinduction"); and sometimes the location of the joints for us may not be the same as for the object, if in fact there are any objective joints at all. Once again, the trick is not to become so fixated on a particular symbolic equation (a particular model of the joints) as to fail to experiment and play with others. In fact, Adorno's use of this "parable" (when seen in the context of his work as a whole) is itself a rather rigid symbolic equation. To suggest that most intellectual activity is like bone crunching, rending everything it thinks about as though it were a dead body, recalls the sources of intellectual inhibition in the desire to protect the good object from one's own aggression. In reality, thought always leaves its objects untouched. Incomplete in itself, this insight is as true as its bone-crunching opposite.

The analysis of reason is, by its very nature, terribly abstract, and its practical implications are not always clear. In the next two sections I apply the concept of reparative reason developed here to two problems. The first sticks closely to the concerns of the Frankfurt School. In light of the preceding considerations, what remains of the Frankfurt School's program of reconciliation with nature? The second problem moves somewhat further afield. I argue that the model of moral thinking portrayed by Carol Gilligan in *In a Different Voice* exemplifies important principles of reparative reason. Conversely, the model developed by Habermas violates these same principles.

Reconciliation with Nature?

Reconciliation with nature is not a theme that has generated a great deal of excitement in recent years. Successors to the Frankfurt School, such as Habermas, have virtually abandoned this aspect of the school's program. Postmodernist social theory generally seems headed in other directions, perhaps the opposite: not toward the reconciliation of human subjectivity with its natural substratum but toward the disclosure of both subjectivity and a natural substratum as myth. A Kleinian perspective can give new meaning to the ideal of reconciliation with nature. It does so, however, at a cost: the abandonment of the utopian dimension of this project, in which men, women, and nature would abandon their constant struggle for a higher unity. Reconciliation, in the Kleinian tradition, means maintaining a loving connection with those objects, such as nature, that we must also aggressively oppose in order to secure our own humanity.

The Kleinian perspective is compatible with one such as Jacques Derrida's, which seeks to reveal the utter artificiality of any distinction between nature and culture, that "scandalous suture" as he calls it.[48] A Kleinian analysis assumes only that nature is the other; it need not assume that nature constitutes the substratum of human existence. One reason that the Kleinian account is compatible with (though hardly identical to) a perspective such as Derrida's is because Klein roots human nature not in nature at all but in passionate relationships.

Klein seeks to understand why men and women would love nature. After all, in most parts of the world nature gives up her fruits only with great resistance. Indeed, it is this very sparseness of nature, and the rage and anxiety that this provokes, that gives rise to instrumental reason. From this perspective, it seems that Mother

Nature should be generally resented as the bad mother, the frustrating and ungiving mother, as in fact she frequently is. At the same time, many peoples—even, and perhaps especially, in those parts of the world in which nature exacts a harsh toll—feel a deep love and reverence for nature, as well as a desire to make reparation to her. But why? Klein answers that the issue is not so much the generosity of nature, for which we feel gratitude, but rather the fact that we love nature in order to preserve a relationship with her while continuing to aggressively extract her resources.[49]

In order to survive, man must aggressively, even violently, exploit nature's resources. While terms such as this may seem metaphoric (can nature really be the object of violence?), to the unconscious it is not metaphor but reality, because for the unconscious the issue is the phantasies involved, which concern resentment and rage at the harshness of nature, the utterly unresponsive other. In feeling love for nature, in wishing to preserve and make reparation to nature, we seek not merely to assuage our guilt but to maintain a connection with that loved object against which humanity must at the same time fight for its life. The love of nature allows us to do both: attack and exploit what we also love, just as we did with mother. The love of nature allows us to remain close to, and part of, what we must also separate from: Mother Nature. The Frankfurt School never captures this subtle dialectic, largely because its program of reconciliation with nature is based on the denial of aggression (and, in Marcuse's case, the denial of the otherness of nature as well) rather than on its integration with love. As Klein puts it,

> Nature represents . . . a grudging and exacting mother, whose gifts must be forcibly extolled from her. . . . The struggle with nature is therefore partly felt to be a struggle to *preserve nature*, because it expresses also the wish to make reparation to her (mother). People who strive with the severity of nature thus not only take care of themselves, but also serve nature herself. In not severing their connection with her they keep alive the image of the mother of the early days.[50]

While nature must forever be the other, fear and guilt may cause us to render nature strictly as the bad other, a hostile foe. In maintaining loving contact with nature, we allow ourselves to feel ambivalence toward the other and in so doing to keep the door open to the

depressive integration. Otherwise, an aggressive, appropriative attitude toward nature, even when practiced within limits set by genuine human needs, may cause so much guilt, and so much fear about
the survival of nature—and hence ourselves—that we respond with
strictly paranoid-schizoid defenses ("nature is so harsh and bad that
it must be overcome") or manic denial ("nature is so vast and powerful it could never be harmed by mere human actions"). Considered
in this light, the fundamental goal is to become reconciled not with
nature but with our own ambivalence. This reconciliation with our
own love and hate is the foundation of the depressive position—of
gratitude to nature (most fundamentally, gratitude for being alive in
an often beautiful world), and of the ability to make reparation. This
ambivalence is not merely psychological, however, but has roots in
the real material conditions of human existence: we really must
overcome nature while maintaining our connection to it. My argument has concerned why this connection should be one that integrates, rather than denies, aggression.

Reconciliation with nature in the Kleinian spirit recognizes the
fundamental separateness of man and nature, as well as the different
interests of each. At the same time it seeks to maintain their relationship so that nature does not become merely the other (though it is
always this too) but retains something of its primitive meaning as a
source of life as well. In maintaining such a view we strengthen our
belief in the existence of something good that lies beyond ourselves.
That is, we strengthen our belief that this is a world worth living in.
Conversely, we gain confidence in our own ability to take what we
must from nature's goodness without destroying it, or consuming it
utterly, like an angry, greedy child. Far less utopian than the vision
of the Frankfurt School, such a concept of reconciliation nonetheless remains a distant ideal in most cases.

Kohlberg, Habermas, and Gilligan: Who Represents Reparative Reason?

Lawrence Kohlberg's studies of the stages of moral development are
so well known that they will be outlined only briefly. He organizes
moral development into three levels and six stages (two stages per
level). Though Kohlberg came to make a number of caveats regarding the sixth stage especially, these will not be considered here,

since the focus is on Habermas' and Gilligan's critiques of his work.[51] The three levels are:

1. *Preconventional Morality.* While the child at this stage is responsive to cultural definitions of good and bad, this response takes the form of doing good for the expected reward and avoiding bad to escape the expected punishment. The power of others to reward and punish is emphasized. Reciprocity takes the form of "help me and I'll help you."

2. *Conventional Morality.* Meeting the expectations of one's family, school, or nation is central and valuable in its own right. Consequences to self or others are secondary. Not only conformity is central, but so too is genuine loyalty. Maintaining the order that supports these conventions is highly valued. "Law and order" thinking is prevalent, as are precepts such as "my country right or wrong" or "be true to your school."

3. *Postconventional, Principled Morality.* Morality is seen as independent of group or nation. Its validity depends on universal principles that transcend even one's own membership in the group. Principles such as "my country only when it is right" predominate because right is the highest value, independent of group membership. Within this level, a social-contract, legalistic orientation (stage five) ideally gives way to the stage of universal ethical principles (stage six), which are self-chosen, apply to all (including, of course, the self), and exemplify the principles of comprehensiveness, universality, and consistency. The Golden Rule and Kant's "categorical imperative" are exemplary; the Ten Commandments are not.[52]

Kohlberg's stages, it should be emphasized, are not a mere empirical description of moral development. He is arguing that universal forms lie beneath the surface of apparently quite different moral judgments.

Habermas contends that in Kohlberg's sixth stage the conflict between reason and needs is a given. In this respect, Kohlberg expresses a Kantian view of morality, in which happiness is subordinated to universal rational principles. Against such a view, Habermas seeks to uphold the Frankfurt School's traditional commitment to happiness as the highest value. At first, Habermas couched his reply to Kohlberg in terms of a seventh stage of moral development, designed to transcend the hierarchical relationship of universal rational principles and human needs, so that "need interpretations are no longer assumed as given, but are drawn into the discursive formation of will." At this stage, says Habermas, inner nature is no longer regarded as fixed. Rather, needs are "released from their paleosymbolic prelinguisticality" and become subject to discourse themselves. Habermas has come to believe, however, that the idea of stages within the postconventional level is misleading. Stages suggest a naturelike process of development, one incompatible with the reflective character of postconventional morality. However, while Habermas has changed the way in which he thinks about stage seven, he has not changed his view of its content.[53] Thus, I shall continue to refer to stage seven, while keeping in mind this caveat regarding its status.

Habermas' program would seem to represent a significant step toward reparative reason. Universal principles of reason and morality are an expression of identity thinking, in so far as they subject unique individuals to the demands of a symbolic equation, such as Kant's categorical imperative, presumed to be universally valid regardless of individual circumstances. In appreciating the legitimacy of the claim to happiness, Habermas would seem to value the real needs of the concrete individual over the demands of universal principles. Yet, the way in which Habermas seeks to harmonize reason and needs turns out to have little to do with reparative reason. He simply subordinates individual needs to a different set of universal principles, which are in some ways more subversive of the unique individual than Kant's categorical imperative. For Habermas' principles demand not merely the subordination of individual needs but also the subordination of important aspects of individuality itself to the categories of the group.

One sees this most clearly in the relationship of individual and society implicit in stage seven, at which point there is almost no difference between individual and social needs. Whatever individual needs are to be met seems to depend entirely on cultural consensus, and their validity is evaluated solely in terms of "the interpretive possibilities of the cultural tradition," as revealed in discourse.[54] There seems to be no understanding of individual needs as valuable precisely *because* they challenge—by their very privacy and intensity—even a discursively achieved cultural consensus. That is, Habermas shows no appreciation of how the pure individuality of needs and their constant conjunction with unique persons might challenge universal moral principles themselves as being arbitrary and inhumane. Conversely, in "On Hedonism" Marcuse recognizes that happiness has rarely been a moral principle for precisely the reason that its subjective nature renders it resistant to universal formulations. Consequently, Marcuse regards happiness as a revolutionary demand.[55]

To be sure, Habermas would have discourse address such needs as happiness. However, the rules of discourse guarantee that needs can become the basis of new moral principles only after they have been universalized and generalized to all. In the words of Habermas, "Universalization is the only rule under which norms will be taken by each to be legitimate."[56] The moral symbolic equation—universal morality—may be transformed in discourse but only by substituting another equally binding equation for it. In this way, much of the looseness and flexibility of reparative reason, attributes which at first seemed to be recognized in Habermas' appreciation of the claim to happiness, are lost.

If one defines instrumental reason as the subordination of the unique, the particular, and the individual to the universal and general (a definition entirely consonant with the intent of Horkheimer and Adorno), then Habermas' stage seven comes very close to being an instance of instrumental reason. Like instrumental reason, discourse in stage seven conceptualizes the individual and his needs primarily in terms of how they might be rendered universal and general, and thus be transformed into an object of group decision. To be sure, discourse lacks the manipulative, controlling dimension of instrumental reason. Indeed, one could argue that discourse seeks to allow needs to emerge—to speak for themselves, as it were—and so to avoid cultural preformation. As such, discourse would share attributes of reparative reason.

Yet, even this way of expressing it (which surely reveals that discourse is not identical with instrumental reason, even though they overlap) reveals a problem. Needs are not abstract and general; they remain attached to real individuals, as Sandel points out in his criticism of Rawls. Habermas allows needs to emerge, to reveal themselves, only to the degree that they are detached from the hopes, sufferings, and dreams of real people and are rendered utterly transparent in discourse, as though all spoke the same language of needs, words and needs being virtually interchangeable. However, in treating needs in this fashion, Habermas has already gone a long way down the road toward instrumental reason. Only now it is not principles of science but the demands of language, as well as the rules of discourse and group consensus, that transform needs into words for the purpose of subjecting them to the universalizing mediation of discourse.

Others have made similar criticisms. Fred Dallmayr argues that Habermas understands language in a basically instrumental fashion, in which it serves as a vehicle for making individual claims and pursuing individual goals.[57] Dallmayr contrasts conversation and poetry with discourse. Conversation is characterized, as White points out, by an openness to the other and to "strangeness." In a word, conversation embodies the qualities of passivity and noninstrumental thinking that seem missing in discourse.[58] Though Habermas argues that discourse is intended to be open to the claims of the other, my analysis suggests that this is so only after the uniqueness of the other is homogenized in discourse. To be sure, reparative reason is not identical to conversation and poetry, for reparative reason embraces play, accepts aggression, and displays an eagerness to categorize, uncategorize, and recategorize. Dallmayr's account, on the other hand, is influenced by Hans-Georg Gadamer and Martin Heidegger, representatives of a tradition in which openness is defined in terms of passive receptivity rather than play. Nevertheless, as far as Habermas is concerned, reparative reason and Dallmayr's critique converge: Discourse remains more closely bound to instrumental reason than one might have ever imagined.

"A Different Voice"

Does not such a criticism, one might ask, return us to the cul-de-sac of the critique of instrumental reason? If even discourse is an instance of the homogenizing power of reason, are there any alternatives, except perhaps poetry and late-night conversation? Characterizing instrumental reason as a universalizing force that obscures the unique and particular does make instrumental reason more inclusive than is frequently recognized, though surely no more inclusive than Horkheimer and Adorno intended. The perspective of reparative reason, however, allows us to identify alternatives. One of these is the mode of reasoning that Carol Gilligan characterizes as "a different voice," a voice representing what she calls the "care perspective," as opposed to the "justice perspective."[59]

The debate among feminists and others unleashed by Gilligan's *In a Different Voice* is not at issue here. This debate concerns whether women do in fact reason differently than men regarding moral issues. A recent forum on Gilligan's book in *Signs* presented considerable evidence that they do not. And Uwe Gielen's cross-cultural research employing the Defining Issues Test, a version of Kohlberg's test, reveled that women and Asians tend to score highest, challenging also the claim that Kohlberg's scheme is biased in favor of Western values, such as liberal individualism. In light of these considerations, it is apparently premature to conclude that women do in fact score lower than men on Kohlberg's stages.[60] Yet, it can be argued that Gilligan's primary purpose was not to show that women are different from men in their moral reasoning but rather to demonstrate that there are different modes of moral reasoning, and that one—the caring perspective—has not been fully appreciated as distinct and equally valid. It may well be, as Gilligan states, that the association of the caring perspective with women is accidental—that is, dependent on transitory historical and cultural forces. In any case, she recognizes the possibility that intercultural or historical variation in moral reasoning may be more important than sexual variation.[61] It could even be that associating the caring perspective with women is accidental in a more pejorative sense—it may be an artifact of the way Gilligan drew her small samples, as Zella Luria among others has suggested.[62] This would not affect my argument either, which is not about women versus men, but about different ways of reasoning.

Behind the question of whether women do in fact differ from men in their moral reasoning is another issue raised by Gilligan, and questioned by her critics. Gilligan, following Nancy Chodorow (who draws on object relations theory but not on Klein), suggests that girls do not have to separate from mother as completely as do boys in order to establish their own identities. For boys, sexual identity and establishing a firm separation from mother (ego identity) go hand in hand. For girls, sexual identity requires not separation from mother but identification with her.[63] Consequently, girls and women tend to experience the world in a more connected fashion, as though people were bound together in some way, whereas boys and men experience the world as filled with independent actors. This is also an issue that I will not directly address here, except to note that this distinction receives little support from a Kleinian perspective. From a Kleinian perspective, the central developmental task is to enter and remain within the depressive position. Though boys and girls, or men and women, will perform this task in slightly different ways, as Klein recognizes, these differences pale in comparison to the common task faced by every human being: to integrate his love and hate.[64] Indeed, it is because Klein sees the developmental tasks faced by boys and girls as fundamentally similar that some feminists, dissatisfied with Freud's differential account of male and female development under the horizon of the Oedipal conflict, have found Klein's perspective useful.

My discussion of Gilligan's work serves a single purpose: to show that her alternative to universalistic moral reasoning exemplifies reparative reason both in its embodiment of *caritas* and in its rejection of single-principle solutions to complex moral problems, solutions that often fail to respect the complexity and subtlety of the people and facts involved. Gilligan's work shows in a clear and concrete fashion how these two aspects of reparative reason are related. It is because reparative reason cares about the object that it places the needs of the object ahead of the demands of universal principles, the rigid symbolic equation. When forced to choose, reparative reason loves the person more than the idea, the individual more than the principle.

Gilligan's argument is straightforward. Girls and young women seem to score lower than boys and young men of similar age, education, and so forth on Kohlberg's scale of moral development. (In response to criticism, Gilligan has introduced new evidence in support of this claim.)[65] Girls' and women's answers to hypothetical questions—such as whether a poor man should steal a drug to save his wife's life—seem less logical, less principled, less universalistic, and more emotional than boys' and men's answers. In other words, the moral sense of girls and women is never "so inexorable, so impersonal, so independent of its emotional origins as we require it to be in men."[66] These are, of course, the words that Freud used to characterize the incompletely developed superego of women.

Gilligan argues that women's moral reasoning is not less developed but different, so different that it is not adequately captured by Kohlberg's stages, which are premised on the assumption that moral maturity is associated with more abstract and universalistic thinking. Women—or rather, those who reason from the perspective of care—tend to see morality not in terms of universal principles of justice but in terms of concern for particular others, a desire not to cause harm, and above all else care and responsibility for individuals. This comes close indeed to what I have called reparative reason. As Gilligan puts it, women see "the moral problem as a problem of care and responsibility . . . rather than as one of rights and rules. . . . Thus, the logic underlying an ethic of care is a psychological logic of relationships, which contrasts with the formal logic of fairness that informs the justice approach."[67]

In her book she seeks to exemplify this difference by quoting from participants in her study and sometimes from literature. (Since my purpose in using Gilligan is to render more concrete the notion of reparative reason, I shall simply quote from her at length. Internal quotation marks indicate that a participant is speaking. My comments and interpolations are in brackets; page numbers from Gilligan are in parentheses.)

[Reparative reasoning] is "contextual and narrative rather than formal and abstract." (p. 22)

"Considering the moral dilemma to be 'sort of like a math problem with humans,' [Jake] sets it up as an equation and proceeds to work out the solution. Since his solution is rationally derived, he assumes that anyone following reason would arrive at the same conclusion." (pp. 26–27) [This is a perfect example of the rigid symbolic equation. No matter how subtle and sophisticated its application to new experiences, it never really loses its inflexibility. Reality is always subordinated to a particular equation.]

By contrast, Amy sees "in the dilemma not a math problem with humans but a narrative of relationships that extends over time." (p. 28)

"While women [when reasoning reparatively] thus try to change the rules in order to preserve relationships, men [when reasoning universalistically], in abiding by these rules, depict relationships as easily replaced." (p. 44) [Recall how instrumental reason regards its objects, even people, as interchangeable, fungible units.]

Claire "finds in the world no validation of the position she is trying to convey, a position that is neither pro-life nor pro-choice, but based on a recognition of the continuing connection between the life of the mother and the life of the child." (p. 59) [This too is reparative reason, refusing to subordinate individual experience to various preshrunk categories made available by the culture. In so far as is possible, reparative reason lets experience take the lead in formulating the categories by which we apprehend experience.]

For Ned, " 'Morality is a prescription, a thing to follow . . . [it is] a kind of balance, a kind of equilibrium.' " For Sharon, morality is about trying " 'to be as awake as possible, to try to know the range of what you feel, to try to consider all that's involved, to be as aware as you can be of what's going on, as conscious as you can of where you're walking.' " If there are any general principles, they have to do " 'with responsibility, responsibility and caring about yourself and others.' " (pp. 98–99) [Sharon's reasoning is a perfect example of the loose symbolic equation, revealing how this looseness stems from a concern for the object. Yet, Sharon does not abandon herself to the object either; an element of self-assertion remains.]

"The moral imperative that emerges repeatedly in interviews with women is an injunction to care, a responsibility to discern and alleviate the 'real and recognizable trouble' of this world. For men, the moral imperative appears rather as an injunction to respect the rights of others, and thus to protect from interference the rights to life and self-fulfillment." (p. 100)

"The proclivity of women to reconstruct hypothetical dilemmas in terms of the real, to request or to supply missing information about the nature of the people and the places where they live, shifts their judgment away from the hierarchical order of principles and the formal procedures of decision making. This insistence on the particular signifies an orientation to the dilemma and to moral problems in general that differs from any current developmental stage descriptions." (pp. 100–101)

[In these last two paragraphs the difference between universalistic and reparative reasons is captured. Reparative reason is about caring for the concrete suffering of real individuals. Individuals come before general ideas. It is for this reason that the details become so important. Reparative reason is about these details. In order to be rational it must dwell with the particulars.]

"The women's judgments point toward an identification of the violence inherent in the [moral] dilemma itself, which is seen to compromise the justice of any of its possible resolutions." (p. 101) [Adorno makes a similar point in arguing that identity thinking must do violence to its objects. Unlike Adorno, however, these women (and reparative reason) accept that such violence is necessary. It can be mitigated by care and concern for the object, but it cannot be eliminated, at least not without doing violence to oneself, as well as to the ability to think clearly about the world.]

" 'Sometimes these [moral] hierarchies are good . . . but they . . . are not organized somehow to deal with real life decisions, and it doesn't allow much room for responsibility.' " (p. 126) [Appreciating the unique and the particular fosters responsibility. Universal morality avoids it, as if to say, "I'm not really responsible; I'm just following universal principles." Is this really so different from saying, "Don't blame me, I was just following orders"?]

Gilligan concludes by noting that when morality is seen in terms of care and responsibility, then "the underlying epistemology correspondingly shifts from the Greek ideal of knowledge as a correspondence between mind and form to the Biblical conception of knowing as a process of human relationship." (p. 173)

This last remark is cryptic (to say the least), in part because Gilligan never explains what she means by "the Biblical conception." However, it does support an important point addressed earlier: namely, that reparative morality has epistemological implications. Because reparative morality cares for particular others, unique individuals, it does not see moral solutions in terms of the application of universal principles but rather in terms of loosely structured guidelines that put the welfare of the object, and one's relationship to it, first. More generally, if one is truly concerned with the unique and the particular, then the categories by which one conceptualizes the object should be loosely structured, flexible, and revisable, so that the object may have as much opportunity as possible to reveal itself.

Yet, to put it this way is more than a little metaphorical. Though it is useful to think in terms of letting the object reveal itself, it has been shown that the actual intellectual process involved is quite active, even aggressive. It uses a number of categories to apprehend the object, while being willing to change these categories at the behest of the object (when the object is one that can make such a request), all the while being guided by care and concern for the object. While this care and concern fit moral theory especially well, reparative reason is equally relevant to epistemological concerns. Care and concern for the object are expressed epistemologically as a desire to be true to the object, which means capturing its reality as accurately as possible and not imposing our theories (phantasies) on it, at least not without giving the object a chance to reject—that is, falsify—our theories. In science this means that our symbolic equations must be open and flexible when confronted with unexpected facts. Perhaps too it means that the symbolic equations of science must be loose, open, and flexible when confronted with symbolic equations usually associated with other activities, such as art; or at least that we appreciate that the various symbolic equations by which we apprehend reality stand in no universal or hierarchical relationship. In any case, I have shown how even art should be understood as an epistemological undertaking, in which we use our emotions and unconscious phantasies to tell us more about how the world truly is.

Gilligan's research is important because it reveals the presence of reparative reason in everyday moral reasoning. This is especially important because talk about rigid versus loose symbolic equations and the like can be terribly abstract. Gilligan's respondents help bring the concept of reparative reason down to earth. In particular, they connect *caritas* and symbolic looseness, the two key attributes of reparative reason, in a concrete fashion. Yet, surely there are other expressions of reparative reason. I have suggested that in the philosophy of science Paul Feyerabend exemplifies such an approach. However, many cases will be difficult to decide. Take, for example, the deconstructionist movement in literature and social philosophy. Certainly this movement displays remarkable conceptual openness and flexibility. The symbolic equations of texts are almost literally torn apart (to phrase it in a way that is itself an expression of rigid symbolism). But is this deconstruction coupled with a genuine concern for the object? Perhaps the answer depends on whether the object is defined as the author's text or as something else. Apparently the category of reparative reason will itself not be readily defined and applied. But this is the idea.

CHAPTER SIX

Reparation and Civilization

Rather than to write a Kleinian version of *Eros and Civilization* or *Dialectic of Enlightenment*, my goal has been to show that a Kleinian account can successfully address four key problems raised, but not solved, by the Frankfurt School. In chapter 1, I called these problems the four Rs: remembrance of those who suffered; reparation for their loss; the reformation of reason; and reconciliation with nature. The Frankfurt School's inability to solve these problems has to do with an incoherent strategy: that of founding liberation in Freudian instinct theory, especially eros and Oedipus. Eros is ultimately selfish, seeking pleasure wherever it can. Consequently, it would avoid suffering and impose its categories on nature and man. To be sure, these categories concern pleasure rather than domination. Nevertheless, there is a selfish instrumentalism inherent in eros, a point fully appreciated by Plato's Socrates when he emphasizes the poverty, need, and cunning of eros, precisely the same attributes that Horkheimer and Adorno attribute to instrumental reason. Instrumental reason, like eros, stems from human need, greed, and weakness, requiring that humanity become cunning in order to survive. Such an orientation toward the world, quite necessary in some circumstances, is hardly likely to generate a way of life capable of addressing the four Rs. One sees the ultimate incoherence of Horkheimer and Adorno's approach in their embrace of a psychological process—the Oedipus conflict—that can only reproduce instrumental reason, as they themselves recognize.

While seeking to expose and explain this source of incoherence in the Frankfurt School's account of civilization and its discontents, my intent has been to produce not an immanent critique but rather a psychoanalytic account of group life, both in politics and culture, that more adequately accounts for the facts. To be sure, I believe that the tragic view of the individual and group life that is implicit in the Kleinian account ennobles humanity in a way the Frankfurt School's account does not. For the Frankfurt School (most of all for Marcuse, least of all for Adorno), humanity is a victim of its sparse environment. This is as true of *Eros and Civilization* as of Horkheimer's "Authority and the Family." For each author, the scarcity of the natural world—which requires that men and women labor, which in turn requires repression—is the source of humanity's discontent. The Kleinian account, on the other hand, reveals humanity to be the maker of its environment, primarily through the projection of internal phantasy. It is a flaw in humanity—the intensity of our fear, hatred, and aggression, and the need to split it off and project it elsewhere in order to contain it—that renders the environment so inhospitable, or at least helps to make it so. This same phenomenon creates the discrepancy between individual and group morality. We need to belong to bad groups in order to be good individuals. It is this fact that renders human existence tragic, not merely sad.

The purpose of my account is not, however, to dignify humanity but to develop the social-theoretical implications of Kleinian thought, and thus to explain the world we have made more fully. Nevertheless, a Kleinian perspective is not complete. It is a psychoanalytic view of human nature, and hence a worldview.[1] As such it can inform and reinterpret the task faced by moral philosophy, but it cannot replace moral philosophy, a point I discuss in this final chapter. I also seek to show what a Kleinian-inspired political theory would look like, arguing that it challenges, rather than fits into, traditional political categories, such as individualism versus communitarianism. The political implications of Kleinian thought are best captured by the term "reparative individualism," a category that I develop while interpreting John Rawls' *Theory of Justice* from a Kleinian perspective.

I conclude the chapter with a "Critique of Object Relations Revisionism." While the title of this last section is intended to evoke Marcuse's epilogue to *Eros and Civilization*, its inclusion within the chapter is intended to suggest that this issue is central to my argument, which concerns not just Klein or psychoanalysis per se, but the proper way to do psychoanalytic social theory. The proper way, I have suggested all along, is not to flinch from its findings. This does not mean that we should treat its insights as given (and with so many different psychoanalytic views of human nature, one would have to suspend the principle of noncontradiction to do so). It does mean that we take seriously the insights of psychoanalysis regarding human nature. Conversely, we should avoid using these insights to criticize others' social theories, while ignoring these same insights when they seem to set limits to our own.

Reparative Morality: Neither Self-Justifying nor Self-Regarding

There are two moral limits to reparative morality. The first is simple and straightforward: the impossibility of deriving ought from is (naturalistic fallacy). Having the need to make reparation does not necessarily mean that doing so is good and desirable. One could quite consistently argue, somewhat along the lines of Nietzsche, that while the desire to make reparation is natural, it is nonetheless an expression of guilt and compassion. As such it is an instance of human weakness. The naturalness of *caritas* simply reveals the strength of will—and hence nobility of character—of those who are able to overcome it. Such an argument, while logically unassailable, does not, I believe, adequately account for the eudaemonian aspect of Klein's account. If Klein is correct, *caritas* is not only what we owe others but also the way in which we heal ourselves. Through reparation we begin to integrate those parts of the self devoted to love and hate. In so doing, we make ourselves as whole and complete as possible, while gaining confidence in our own goodness. Simply put, it is through caring for others that we make ourselves as *eudaimōn* as humans can be. Like Aristotle's eudaemonian ethic, Klein's psychoanalytic theory may be read as instruction in the pursuit of enlightened self-interest, even if doing so does not fully capture the primacy of concern for the other inherent in her account and absent in Aristotle's.

Wollheim's Freudian Treatment of the Limits of Kleinian Morality

Yet, even if one decides that in this case what is natural (reparative morality) is also good, this does not solve all the difficulties raised by reparative morality. By far the most sophisticated attempt to address the moral implications and limits of the Kleinian account is that of Richard Wollheim in his William James lectures at Harvard. He suggests that what I call reparative morality is incomplete, because it cannot tell us when, how, and toward whom we should direct our reparative impulses. On this point he is absolutely correct. Klein's discussion of how white settlers might make reparation for the destruction of native populations reflects not merely her own moral obtuseness but the unstructured character of the reparative impulse itself. The mere existence of a reparative impulse does not render moral philosophy and institutional reform irrelevant. Quite the contrary. They become not only more important (as they have something decent to work with) but counterparts as well. Both moral philosophy and institutional reform should be concerned with the way in which natural reparative impulses may be fostered and channeled in the right directions, so that they correspond with the deepest moral intuitions of the culture (or contradict them, if the culture is held to be morally bankrupt). A Kleinian account of individual and group life is concerned with the psychological resources that moral philosophy and institutional reform have to draw on. In a word, the Kleinian account is concerned with human nature. It cannot replace moral philosophy or the study of institutions; but it should inform them, because it sets their limits.

Klein appears to appreciate that the reparative impulse is itself morally indeterminate; she recalled a discussion with an anthropologist who told of a culture in which pity and mercy, particularly for an adversary, were regarded strictly as weaknesses. In responding to Klein's questions, however, the anthropologist revealed that this culture did recognize an exception. If the adversary placed himself behind a woman so that he would be covered by her skirt, then it was considered right to spare him. Klein argues, as might be expected, that the skirt is a symbol of the protective mother. Thus, while the rules for showing mercy and pity vary among different cultures, all cultures, she says, recognize the claims of mercy and pity, because these claims stem from virtually universal experiences: the protection we have received from mothers and fathers and the compassion this evokes when it is symbolically recalled. Nevertheless, Klein goes on to characterize as "distortions" the rules under which this culture expressed compassion, suggesting her appreciation of the fact that the reparative impulse is not automatically moral.[2] It becomes moral only when it is applied in the right circumstances to the right people, standards that cannot be derived from the reparative impulse alone.

The problem with Wollheim's account is not, therefore, that he recognizes the incompleteness of reparative morality. This is a given, recognized even by Klein. The problem is that he interprets this incompleteness in terms more appropriate to Freud's account than to Klein's, failing to appreciate the other-directed character of reparative love. Wollheim argues that morality ("which I take . . . to be that which has obligation as its core") and value stem from fundamentally different sources. Unlike value, morality is based not on love of the good but on fear of punishment. Morality is based on the introjection of rules and commands; value is based on the projection of love. A consequence, says Wollheim, is that while the agent will generally use culture and tradition in creative ways to define and realize his values, he will generally follow the morality of obligation in a routine, law-abiding way.[3] My earlier consideration of the difference between reparative morality (based on love) and paranoid-schizoid morality (based on fear) fits nicely with Wollheim's scheme, the primary differences being those of terminology.

Wollheim goes on to argue that contrary to many anthropologists, shame is not a more primitive emotion than guilt but a more sophisticated one. Guilt stems from fear of an alien internal object that says no—what Freud called the superego. Shame, on the other hand, stems not from fear of an internal object but from a failure to live up to the ideals of an internal object with which one has identified: the ego ideal. When Freud introduced the concept of the ego ideal, he did so in the context of a discussion of narcissism. The ego ideal, he said, is the avatar of primary narcissism, a model of what the individual would be were he whole and perfect.[4] We perfect ourselves by living up to, and identifying with, a standard of value that we admire. In this regard, Wollheim too finds the basis of a eudaemonian ethic in Klein.

Like my account of reparative morality, Wollheim's recognizes that the morality of value cannot stand alone. It certainly depends upon a cultural reservoir of decent values, as well as upon appropriate role models (that this term has become banal in recent years need not cause us to reject the psychoanalytic truth behind it). But the morality of value also requires help from the superego, because no matter how great the concern with the interests of others, the morality of value is ultimately self-directed. It will therefore need control and constraint from without, lest what serves the self be too easily identified with what helps others. John Locke's comments, in *Second Treatise of Government*, on why government is necessary even among good men are exemplary. Even with the best will in the world, men tend to see more justice in their own claims than in those of others. Or, as Wollheim puts it, "However liberally the domain of the self-regarding concerns is interpreted, there will always be tasks and problems in life that are purely other-regarding, and in this context the precepts and prohibitions of the superego, softened and attenuated though they may be, will continue to seem appropriate."[5]

Without acknowledging it, Wollheim has subtly transformed Klein's account into a more familiar—and hence less challenging—psychoanalytic one. Wollheim concludes that even the morality of value "is self-directed, though it may be other-regarding. For it expresses itself in a thought that a person has about what he ought to do: though he may well, and appropriately, think that what he ought to do is something for the benefit of others."[6] But this is not Kleinian morality. The morality of reparation is other-directed, as well as other-regarding. We do not love and care for others *in order to* achieve depressive integration. Rather, it is *because* we have achieved this level of integration, and hence this level of consolidation of the self, that we may direct our care and concern toward others. This perspective recognizes that caring for others may enrich the self, but it rejects the view that this is the leading motive. In fact, it seems hardly necessary to argue this point at all, for it is implicit in the very concept of an object-related passion such as love.

Wollheim's position is similar to that of the Socratic lover in the *Phaedrus* (249d–257c). He treats his beloved with care and respect in order to become more whole, perfect, and beautiful himself—to grow his own wings and to soar to meet his ego ideal in another world. This is eros at its most enlightened. The Kleinian lover, on the other hand, cares for the one he loves in order to repair and restore him to wholeness out of love, gratitude, and guilt. One might argue that the goal of reducing guilt is a self-directed action, which it may well be in some circumstances. However, Klein never suggests that we care for others *in order to* reduce our guilt. We feel guilty because we love the other qua other and yet have wished to harm him, not because we feel we have violated an ideal standard of our own, such as "do no harm to whose whom you love." The guilt of the Kleinian lover has nothing to do with violating a categorical imperative. In fact, the psychological reasoning characterized by Wollheim is far more sophisticated and abstract than that of Klein, yet for this reason not necessarily better. The other-directed, other-regarding character of reparative morality stems from our earliest feelings of love and gratitude for those who care for us, who make our life possible. *Caritas* represents an emotional truth even before it becomes the foundation of a moral one.

The psychological legacy of Freud has been to suggest that self-love is primary and that love for others is always secondary, always derivative, always an "investment." Wollheim returns to this familiar idea, and in so doing he abandons the unique contribution of Klein: to show that love and concern for others is as fundamental as self-love. From the Kleinian perspective, it is not self-love, not selfishness, but fear that spoils *caritas*. Wollheim, in spite of his insight into Kleinian moral theory, misses this point, turning to superego morality to constrain the self-regarding character of value morality, a constraint that is necessary in Wollheim's account but not in Klein's. Wollheim subordinates the unique, idiosyncratic character of Klein's thought to more familiar modes of moral reasoning and more familiar psychological assumptions.

What reparative morality requires is not constraint but an opportunity to come into being in the first place. I have shown that it also requires guidance as to the most deserving objects. This guidance is necessary not because we will otherwise make ourselves that object but because reparation is an unschooled impulse or desire. It instructs us to care for others but does not tell us who or how. For this reason we continue to require instruction in ethics. Yet, to put it this way is to put the cart before the horse in that instruction in ethics assumes that this impulse is readily available for social theorists to work with. In fact, as we have seen, the desire to make reparation generally falls victim to fear, at least in the large group. This is probably why the Freudian placement of selfishness at the center of psychic life still seems so compelling. Freud's is certainly an adequate description of most social life, as well as of a great many intimate relationships. The apparent omnipresence of selfishness does not, however, make it primary or more fundamental than *caritas*. It simply reveals the fragility of reparative morality, its extreme vulnerability to fear.

The Political Theory of Reparative Individualism

Before turning directly to my Kleinian interpretation of John Rawls' *Theory of Justice*, it may be useful to note briefly what others have held to be the political implications of Klein's thought. Michael Rustin in "A Socialist Consideration of Kleinian Psychoanalysis" argues that Kleinian object relations theory supports a moderately utopian, socialist vision of man. "A commitment to the values of life, of relationship, of membership in a social community from birth, of creative development, and of a normal care for others, which properly form part of a socialist conception of man."[7]

In so arguing, Rustin claims Klein for the socialist communitarians, albeit with caveats and reservations. These concern the implications of the Kleinian assumption that aggression, hatred, and fear will always be with us, as well as the way in which the Kleinian tradition is sceptical of excessive emphasis on social unity and community. "The value placed on difference in Kleinian theory (difference of generation, life-stage and gender as sources of growth) also casts doubt on ideological commitments to banish differentiation as divisive in some communal utopia. The Kleinian tradition is prone to view hostility to differentiation as mainly a defence against the pains of separation, jealousy and envy, at one level or another."[8]

Though Graham Little turns to Klein for different reasons—and is probably a little more sceptical of the suitability of her work as a foundation for socialism—his interpretation of the political significance of Kleinian thought is similar.[9] A tempered, realistic, socialistic vision, one that recognizes the claims of individuals, not just the group, is for both Rustin and Little the political implication of Kleinian thought.

The conclusions of the Kleinian analyst R. E. Money-Kyrle in "Psycho-Analysis and Ethics" are similar, though he emphasizes socialism less, liberal individualism more. Money-Kyrle argues that paranoid-schizoid morality is essentially relative, since its basic aim is to appease a feared authority by obedience. The content of this authority's commands is morally neutral, or rather, irrelevant.[10] Depressive morality is different. Based on love and concern for the welfare of others, its content is not so culturally variable. Depressive morality will always be opposed to totalitarianism on the one hand and laissez-faire capitalism on the other. The former shows no respect for the integrity and autonomy of others, whereas the latter accepts no obligation and responsibility for others' welfare. The political ideal, says Money-Kyrle, "would be a state that accepted responsibility for welfare without curtailing independence. . . . The effect of increasing [psychoanalytic] insight would be to bring about some convergence in political ideology towards what may still be called, in spite of totalitarian attempts to misappropriate the term, the democratic aim."[11]

My conclusion regarding the political implications of Kleinian thought is similar to Money-Kyrle's, though shaded toward Rustin and Little. But to put it this way is really ideology at its worst, as though the prefabricated ideological category that one's thought falls into actually tells us something important about it. What is important is the reasoning behind the political position. Apparently similar categories may be based on quite different reasoning. Quite different categories may seem similar only because current political thinking is insufficiently subtle and differentiated to make the distinction. The reasoning behind Kleinian individualism ("reparative individualism," I call it) is different from that of liberal individualism. Reparative individualism is a unique political category. It is simply not adequately represented as being somewhere on the continuum between liberal individualism and socialist communitarianism.

The biggest risk associated with Kleinian thought stems ultimately from its uniqueness: we risk coming to understand it only by subordinating it to more familiar categories, be they psychological, moral, or political. Consequently, we fail to learn all we could from Klein. Fortunately, her teachings, as I have interpreted them, include a lesson on how to read her texts (actually, any text): in a spirit of reparation, love, and openness to their uniqueness (not by forcing them into the relatively few categories that we know and are comfortable with). Reparative reason applies also to reading and interpretation.

Rawls: Justice as Fearfulness

It is a cliche, but nonetheless significant, that any comprehensive political theory is founded on assumptions about human nature. Rather than build a Kleinian political theory based on her view of human nature, I shall analyze a familiar one against the grain, so to speak, from the perspective of a Kleinian view of man. The theory is that of Rawls in *A Theory of Justice*, probably the most influential work of Anglo-American social theory since World War II.[12] Rawls' work is frequently credited with almost single-handedly reviving the field of normative political theory. A Kleinian perspective does not diminish this achievement. It does, however, cast it in a new light: as an attempt to mitigate those paranoid-schizoid anxieties that stand in the way of a fuller understanding of justice.

My goal is neither to praise nor to blame Rawls. Rather, I wish to demonstrate the utility of Kleinian thought for social and political analysis, in part by revealing the freshness of its insights. The key Kleinian insight is that greed, avaricious individualism, possessive individualism, and the like are not given; they are responses to fear (ultimately of our own aggression), a fear that stands in the way of *caritas*. It is this, I have argued all along, that makes Klein's view tragic. Our potential to love and care for others is real: it is an expression of a desire whose power is exceeded only by its extreme susceptibility to fear. Here is humanity's tragic flaw, which we nonetheless frequently transcend in personal relations but rarely in the group. In these last four sentences lies the whole of Klein's theory in so far as its relevance to social and political theory is concerned.

In *Politics and Vision* Sheldon Wolin argues that viewing liberalism as an account of the individual's pursuit of pleasure is incorrect. Though Locke grants pleasure and pain equal status as sources of motivation, later liberals return to Hobbes in so far as they make fear and anxiety central. For Hobbes, fear and anxiety are primal, concerned with the preservation of life itself. Liberals such as James Mill, Bentham, and Benjamin Franklin extend this anxiety so that it is equally concerned with the preservation of possessions and status. Wolin states: "Liberal man moved in a world where pain and deprivation threatened him from all sides. His fears were compressed into a single demand: social and political arrangements must ease his anxieties by securing property and status against all threats excepting those posed by the competitive chase itself."[13] From this perspective, possessive individualism, as it has been called, stems ultimately not from selfishness and desire but from fear. We accumulate so much in order to protect ourselves from loss, a loss that sometimes seems tantamount to the loss of life itself. Psychoanalytic studies, such as Klein's, of the origins of greed in fears of loss and emptiness support this insight.[14]

Rawls may be seen as addressing this problem through the founding of a society in which the threatened loss of status and possessions is mitigated, thus reducing the greed and fear that stand in the way of a more benevolent practice of justice. The aspect of Rawls' system to which I am referring is the maximin solution to the bargaining game behind the veil of ignorance, where we know little about ourselves and even less about others. Before preceding further, however, I must address a possible objection to my argument. Rawls' system is so complex and his mode of argumentation so sophisticated that one could object to focusing almost exclusively on this one aspect of *A Theory of Justice*. After all, Rawls takes great care to defend his principles of justice from several perspectives, including the rational reconstruction of everyday moral consciousness. Indeed, reflective equilibrium, as Rawls calls it, claims that the maximin solution is not merely the rational solution of a bargaining game but one that corresponds to our deepest moral intuitions about fairness. Nevertheless, I do not believe that it is misleading to focus on the maximin solution. While an early paper (1951) reveals that this was not Rawls' first solution, it is clearly at the argumentative center of *A Theory of Justice*. All the other arguments are designed to support this solution.[15]

The maximin solution addresses the anxiety that Wolin puts squarely at the center of liberalism. The maximin principle, says Rawls, is based on a situation of "grave risks," in which we must worry about the "worst that can happen." And what is the worst? That a malevolent "enemy is to assign [the individual] his place" in society and so deprive him of the resources necessary for life and self-respect. In such circumstances, individuals are "forced to protect themselves" by assuming that the others with whom they are dealing are this enemy.[16] The language of Rawls is that of severe paranoid anxiety. It is paranoid because one is assuming that the other is hostile and malevolent strictly on the basis of one's own fearful imagination regarding the possibility of one's own greedy and punitive behavior in similar circumstances, since this is almost the only information one has. Rawls' general laws of psychology, which concern how we love those who love us and treat us well, remain operative behind the veil of ignorance but provide no grounds for such anxiety.[17] We must conclude that the self must find its reasons for anxiety elsewhere and the only "elsewhere" left behind the veil is the self itself. Since this anxiety seems to be an attribute of human nature, and not the risk-averse concerns of a few neurotics, it is precisely the type of thing that one could know in the original position, as Rawls calls it.[18] Rawls goes on to note that the "persons in the original position do not, of course, assume that their initial place in society is decided by a malevolent opponent. As I note below, they should not reason from false premises."[19]

However, in defending the maximin solution in this way Rawls is making my point. Of course the individual does not know that his enemy is malevolent. All he knows are his own fears, fears that include how he might act were he to have the tantalizing absolute power to determine the fate of others. In other words, the original position is a screen (like a Kleinian parent), virtually empty of content (like a Rorschach test), and so is a perfectly neutral vehicle by which to capture the needs and anxieties of those behind it. Rawls' original position is the paranoid-schizoid position, in which our greatest fear is that others will respond with a greed and aggression equivalent to our own. Such a position is deeply moral: it is the morality of *lex talionis*, in which the possibility that others will do unto us what we would do unto them frightens us to death.

My point is not that individuals in the original position would behave as Rawls assumes they would. In fact, some clever experiments suggest they would not. My argument is that Rawls' original position is an artistic, literary achievement, whether intended as such or not. Like all great art, it abstracts from distracting particulars to leave us face to face with reality—in this case our own fear, including our fear that we would use any absolute power given to us to exploit others. Furthermore, like so many great works of art, *A Theory of Justice* does so in a way that does not force this insight onto us, an effort that can only intensify denial. Rather, Rawls expresses a challenging and threatening hypothesis—that society is at base an instrument by which we obtain some relief from our paranoid-schizoid anxieties—in the dry and formal language of game theory, even offering reassurance that "of course" people don't really

assume the world is so malevolent. He denies what he has just asserted and thus makes the assertion more persuasive. Here is the
difference between ideology and art.

Viewing the maximin solution as an attempt to address the paranoid anxieties of the liberal self does not deny the importance of
Rawls' other argumentative strategies—those of rational reconstruction and reflective equilibrium. They too are part of the work of art.
My perspective, however, should cause us to reinterpret the role
played by these arguments. Reflective equilibrium suggests that our
confidence in Rawls' game-theoretic solution to the problem of justice is enhanced to the degree that it corresponds to more abstract
and universal solutions, solutions that do not put the needs and
fears of the self first, such as Kant's categorical imperative. My perspective sees this relationship somewhat differently, so that instead
of calling it reflective equilibrium, we might call it causal necessity.
It is not that the maximin solution merely *corresponds* to more abstract thinking about the problem. Rather, the maximin solution *allows* more abstract thinking about the problem by addressing the
fear and greed that stands in the way of such solutions. Otherwise
expressed, by mitigating the intense paranoid fear characteristic of
the liberal self, the fear that it will lose all to its enemies, Rawls
allows this self to begin to think about justice in more abstract,
universal, other-regarding terms. The maximin solution is at the
core of his scheme not merely for the formal, analytic reasons that so
many find attractive (it is clever, brainy, elegant, and so forth) but for
sound psychological reasons as well. Only by mitigating the anxieties of the liberal self can we begin to talk about justice in terms
more abstract, universal, and caring than the self-interest of the
fearful.

My argument is not, of course, that Rawls' solution to the problem of justice partakes of reparative morality. On the contrary, there
is a tit-for-tat dimension to Rawlsian morality, even at its most advanced level (that of reflective equilibrium), that betrays its roots in
the paranoid-schizoid position. One sees this, for example, in
Rawls' account of the general laws of psychology, which operate
even behind the veil of ignorance.[20] These laws are based on a strictly Freudian view of love. Love is an investment, libidinal rather
than capital. We love those who love us first and treat us well, a
phenomenon that unites infancy with the most well-ordered societies. It is this love that transcends maximin thinking to explain the

patriotism and friendship that ideally unites a just society. But, is this really so different from the morality of *lex talionis* that characterizes the paranoid-schizoid position? In this case it is not an eye for an eye, but love for love. Rawls' general laws of psychology are the logic of an advanced stage of paranoid-schizoid development, in which we freely give back what is given to us but rarely give back more.

Rawls' inability to escape paranoid-schizoid thinking is also seen in the way in which he conceptualizes the problem of justice as a problem whose solution is ideally abstract, universal, and categorical, in which everyday moral insight is validated by showing it to be part of a synthetic whole. In chapter 5 I argued that this way of thinking about morality is itself still rooted in the paranoid-schizoid position. Rawls intuits how intense these paranoid-schizoid fears may be, and he designs a system to quell them. It is a brilliant insight and a fine appreciation of our desires. But it is no more than this. Justice as fairness reinforces paranoid-schizoid defenses, creating a more secure space in which reparative impulses may emerge. But Rawls does not even begin to create a society built upon these impulses.

Reparative Individualism

While it is clear how fear threatens justice, the relevance of reparative love to political theory is far less clear, though Meltzer, Little, and Money-Kyrle certainly shed some light on this issue. One of the many reasons for this lack of clarity is that Klein's account of the individual does not readily fit into ways of thinking about the individual implicit in such contemporary political theories as liberalism or communitarianism. Nor does her account fit somewhere in between as though the possible concepts of the individual in social theory were exhausted by the continuum between these poles. Rather than being liberal or communitarian, Klein's account of the individual, in so far as it has political relevance, is better captured by the term reparative individualism.

Reparative individualism sees care and concern for others as stemming from within one's sense of self rather than from one's sense of belonging to others. We ideally treat others with care not because they are part of us but because they are different. Reparative individualism finds grounds for the decent treatment of others that are not, ultimately, a derivative of self-interest. And while it is easily recognized how individualism expresses self-interest, one should not overlook how the communitarian argument, when pushed to the limits of its internal logic (as in "be decent to others for they are part of you") is equally an expression of self-interest. It simply extends the definition of the self. Reparative individualism seeks to extend not the self but the generous emotions that may stem from the self. We care for others best not by identifying with them or belonging to them but by achieving our individuality in such a way that we come to terms with our split-off fear and hatred. It is then that we can best care for others from deep within our selves, so to speak, not merely as extensions of ourselves. In caring for others from within ourselves, we seek not to overcome their separateness but to assert our individuality through an act of *caritas,* an act that reaches outward from my boundaries to another's without denying either.

As Homer's *Odyssey* is the motto of the *Dialectic of Enlightenment,* so Aeschylus' *Oresteia* is the motto of a Kleinian account. Orestes feels depressive guilt at having revenged his father's death by murdering his mother. However, he is only able to make reparation—and thus to care for his kingdom with fairness and gratitude— when he has integrated his furies with his love. In mythology, the king often stands for the highly differentiated individual, the hero (even the tragic hero) who will not be incorporated into the timeless sameness of the mass. As a lesson in reparative individualism, the *Oresteia* tells us that we care for others best not simply by identifying with them, belonging to them, but by achieving our individuality in such a way that we begin to integrate our love and hate. This integration liberates the desire to make reparation, a desire that reaches out to touch another from deep within ourselves. As such, it helps to make us whole, not by obliterating boundaries so that we somehow blend with those we help but by healing the split in ourselves caused by the conflict of love and hate. This is not to say that identification plays no role in reparation. It does, but the identification involved is not primarily with those whom we help but with the goodness of the good parent who once helped us, or whom we wish had helped us more. In identifying with the good parent, we establish our good objects more securely within ourselves, thus increasing our confidence in our own goodness, reinforcing the fact that our goodness is stronger than our hate.[21]

Reparative individualism is not a familiar political category in part because it is so difficult to realize in the large group. Unlike individualism and communitarianism, both of which are quite compatible with paranoid-schizoid morality (community is frequently purchased by projecting all our hatred and aggression into outsiders), reparative individualism as a political category requires that group members qua group members be operating in the depressive position—a rare occurrence. For this reason reparative morality is generally confined to the private sphere. But rare does not mean never. The civil rights legislation of the 1960s as well as aspects of the War on Poverty seem to have been motivated by genuine reparative concerns, in which much of a nation sought to come to terms with its greed and guilt through acts that reached across boundaries of class and race, rather than pretending to obliterate them. More difficult to realize than liberal or communitarian morality, reparative morality is not impossible on a large scale, but just very difficult.

A critic might respond that these last examples reveal reparative individualism to be little more than liberal individualism with a conscience. Such a response would not be wholly mistaken, but only once it is recognized that this conscience stems from neither a social contract nor the internalization of universal values for their own sake; instead it stems from a deep concern with the welfare of others qua others, human beings who deserve our love and concern. There are certainly other visions of the good society, but few preserve so much of what seems valuable about ours while overcoming its central moral limit: its rooting of justice in talion morality, the morality of fear and fair exchange, a limit that Rawls seems also to recognize but cannot overcome.

Critique of Object Relations Revisionism

The integration of Freudian psychoanalysis and social theory is probably the greatest achievement of the Frankfurt School. In this regard, the true successors to Horkheimer, Adorno, and Marcuse are not critical theorists such as Habermas but the so-called psychoanalytic feminists. Nancy Chodorow, Jessica Benjamin, and Dorothy Dinnerstein have employed object relations theory to show that the Oedipal conflict is not the crucible of moral autonomy that Freud held it to be; therefore, female moral development need not be seen as a slightly inferior version of its male counterpart. I have already discussed the way in which Gilligan draws on Chodorow's version of this argument. And I have drawn on Benjamin's version to reveal the incoherence of the Frankfurt School's reliance on Oedipal internalization.

None of the criticism that follows is directed against this aspect of their work, which appears to be essentially correct. My concern is with the epistemic status of psychoanalysis in the projects of these authors: the way in which they use psychoanalysis to criticize prevailing social arrangements, yet turn from psychoanalysis (without acknowledging this departure) to sociology when constructing their alternatives. Taking psychoanalytic theory seriously does not mean sticking to a particular psychoanalytic perspective even when it no longer illuminates the issues. However, it does mean sticking to a psychoanalytic perspective even when the conclusions are troublesome, unless one can show why and how the psychoanalytic perspective is no longer valid at precisely that point where one turns from critique to utopia. These authors do not always do so—and therein lies their revisionism. The authors considered below are not a uniform group; each is a revisionist in a different way. Taking these differences into account, my goal is to show that each abandons psychoanalysis at the same point: when moving from critique to alternative.

The relevance of the following considerations to the issue of the socially-constituted self, as addressed by Sandel and others will be obvious. For it is such a self that these authors are seeking to create, via what Chodorow calls relational individualism.

Chodorow

Chodorow draws not from Klein but from what she calls object relations theory, by which she means the work of Alice and Michael Balint, W. R. D. Fairbairn, Harry Guntrip, and D. W. Winnicott. Though not always mindful of the continuity between these authors and Klein, she realizes that object relations theory is concerned with the way in which external reality is mediated by phantasy, as well as by various psychological defenses, such as projection and splitting.[22] One could argue that whatever "revisionism" one finds in

Chodorow and Benjamin is merely a reflection of the revisionism in their psychoanalytic sources, all of whom depart from Klein in significant respects. This, however, would not be correct. Chodorow and Benjamin are not mere "consumers" of object relations theory. They develop their own social psychologies, and it is this theory that is the object of my concern.

Chodorow defines the "object" with which object relations theory is concerned as follows: "In psychoanalytic parlance 'objects' are people, aspects of people, or symbols of people."[23] Such a definition of objects completely omits the most important aspect of all. Objects are first of all internal objects, the content of our unconscious phantasies. Symbols are not the equivalent of objects but rather their counterpart; they are external representations of internal objects, as shown in the previous chapter. In defining objects as she does, Chodorow would abandon depth psychology before she even begins— except that she does not consistently stick to this definition.

One sees Chodorow's ambivalence toward depth psychology in another interesting place. Addressing the Kleinian account of how the mother's relationship to her child is characterized by a series of complex and multiple identifications (as when the mother identifies with her child and in so doing is able to gain pleasure from being the good parent to herself), Chodorow characterizes this process as the "dynamics of maternal regression." Chodorow apparently regards this process as regressive because it involves "internal object-relationships, defenses and conflicts."[24] Klein, however, never uses the term "regression" or any of its cognates to characterize this process.[25] To be sure, regression is not necessarily a pejorative term within psychoanalysis, and one could argue that Chodorow does not intend it as such. Nevertheless, the tone of Chodorow's entire discussion is that internal object relationships are a less mature alternative to real relationships, albeit an alternative that is natural to such intimate relations as mother and child, becoming pathological only when carried on too long. Yet, while this may sound like the language of a good mental-health professional, it is utterly incompatible with a Kleinian account, which stresses the constant interaction of internal objects (via the unconscious phantasies in which they are embedded) with their external counterparts throughout life. This by itself, however, does not make Chodorow's account nonpsychoanalytic, only non-Kleinian.

In Chodorow's rendering, psychoanalysis is concerned with issues of separation and attachment, autonomy versus connectedness,
and the maintenance of boundaries. That is, psychoanalysis becomes the study of the way in which individuals are either unconsciously part of each other or alone. This is certainly a central issue
in psychoanalysis, but for Chodorow it is really the only issue. Not
only is there no place for the drives (which, in effect, disappear in
Klein's system as well), but there also is no place for, and certainly
very little mention of, the passions: love, hate, envy, rage, greed, fear.
The dance of separation and connection is evidently too civilized
for this. This is why "object relations revisionism" is bad and not
just different. It abandons not just the drives and internal objects but
also the passions—and hence the ways in which these passions
mediate experience, determining (and thus explaining) how humans
connect and separate. It is the passions with which Klein deals that
make the world go around. They are the subject of classical tragedy
and of most great art and literature. This is ultimately why Klein
makes such a profound social theorist. Chodorow's account seems
dry and anemic by comparison. For Chodorow the relationships remain, but the passions that give them their intensity and meaning
are drained.

One reason that Chodorow flattens human nature is to make it
more amenable to sociological explanation. Chodorow states that
"women's mothering as a feature of social structure requires an explanation in terms of social structure."[26] Why? Had Freud thought
this way, we would never have had psychoanalysis. And I have argued that understanding social structure requires a psychological
explanation of how the group becomes the arena in which paranoid-
schizoid anxieties are contained. What one might want to say is that
a complete explanation of mothering requires reference to social
structure, not just psychology. Chodorow, though, does not say this,
but something much more categorical. Why? In the last analysis,
object relations theory becomes a way for Chodorow to substitute
real relationships for the drives. Conversely, what makes Klein so
valuable is that her account of the passions captures the intensity of
human needs and desires once portrayed by the drives—but in a
way that does not carry with it all the conceptual baggage of the
drives. One sees Chodorow's intent in "Beyond Drive Theory," in

which she states that "object-relations theory develops its account of primary sociality by describing the relational construction of the self, both developmentally and in daily life. Because it is clinically rooted, it need not appeal to a vaguely defined, extra-individual, unsubstantiable Eros as a force for unity."[27] The naiveté of such a statement is startling. Do we experience the psychological merger of mother and infant, or the greater connectedness of women than of men, in some sort of direct fashion, unmediated by theory? And if so, how is one to explain that different clinicians, operating with different theories, frequently attribute very different disorders to the same patient?

When confronted with a seemingly incomprehensible statement such as this, made by a person whom we have reason to take seriously, one might well follow the advice of Thomas Kuhn, author of *The Structure of Scientific Revolutions*. Kuhn argues that there is a good chance the author is operating under a different paradigm, one that overlaps ours but yet has differences—differences so subtle that we may not recognize them.[28] This appears to be the case with Chodorow, and her paradigm is simply the normal, everyday perception of how people relate to each other. Though she uses the language of psychoanalysis, she is really talking about relationships as they are perceived by intuitive men and women in everyday life.

One sees this in the very beginning of her account, where she defines an object as something in the external world, not an internal reality. One sees it too in her view of internal-object relationships (whose existence she does not deny) as regressive. This does not mean that Chodorow's account is simply false. *The Reproduction of Mothering* brings an enormous literature to bear on the sociology of gender in a most scholarly fashion. However, it does mean that in the end she too adopts what is in effect a mirror-model psychology—that is, the psychology of everyday life—in which there is little appreciation of how psychic structure might transform experience. For example, Chodorow states that "images of early experiences with primary caretakers and early relationships become part of the self," without conveying any sense of how these relationships are mediated and transformed by psychic structure.[29] This is what I mean by a mirror model. To be sure, Klein too sometimes makes statements such as this, in which the influence of objects seems somehow additive, like filling an empty vase. In Klein's account, however, the patterned dynamics of the passions function as a substitute for psychic structure, as we have seen. What does one get when one abandons both psychic structure and the dynamics of the passions, as Chodorow does? Sociology.

Benjamin

More clearly than anyone before her, Jessica Benjamin shows how the philosophical program of the Frankfurt School is ultimately incompatible with its psychological theory. This is why it is so surprising that she would share the pattern set by Chodorow, abandoning a psychoanalytic perspective in the last pages of two of her essays—the point at which she turns from critique to utopia. Toward the conclusion of "The End of Internalization: Adorno's Social Psychology," Benjamin states that progressive social theory "must recognize that internalization is a defense against unbearable reality, not a natural mode of constituting consciousness."[30] The statement astounds one, even more so than Chodorow's statement on the regressive character of internal object relations. The reasoning behind Benjamin's claim is apparently similar to Chodorow's. Maturity is the realm of real relationships, internalization a regressive defense.

What Benjamin should have said, of course, is that Oedipal internalization, characterized by the boy's identification with father and his authority, is not nearly as fundamental as Freudians believe. It is other, generally pre-Oedipal modes of internalization, such as the child's internalization of the good aspects of mother and its projection of the bad aspects (a process that assumes that the bad aspects were once internalized too), that are central to ego development and morality. While a psychoanalytic approach need not assume the existence of internal objects, it is hard to see how it can get by on the assumption that internalization is strictly a pathological phenomenon.

Toward the conclusion of "Authority and the Family Revisited: or, A World without Fathers?" Benjamin states:

> Had Horkheimer, like others, seeking in the past an image of what the future might hold, sought his image of the anti-authoritarian mother, he would probably have found a lost utopia not of male-female solidarity, but of women's kinship and

friendship networks, of sisterhood. And perhaps he would have seen the logic by which contemporary feminism has articulated an image of revolt based upon identification with others stemming from awareness of one's own suffering and oppression. The knowledge which is based upon paying attention to one's feelings and denied aspirations implies, ultimately, a different view of human nature and the civilizing process as well.[31]

Though the ideal is noble, the reasoning is pure popular psychology, in which awareness of our own feelings ("stay in tune with your feelings," "own your own anger," and so forth) makes us more sensitive to the feelings of others as well. Though this is probably true, it is hardly the basis of an alternative view of human nature and the progress of civilization.

Depth psychology is not sacred, and Benjamin's account is problematic not merely because she abandons it. Abandoning depth psychology is problematic because doing so fails to explain adequately the most obvious fact of all: nice people, nice families, and nice rap groups do not necessarily produce large groups, societies, or nations that are nice. My explanation for this fact has invoked what might be called the return of the repressed. Fairly well-repressed, even fairly well-integrated, paranoid-schizoid anxieties, residing in the deepest level of the psyche, are reactivated in large groups, in part because such groups threaten individual identity. Such anxieties come to dominate group processes, inhibiting the emotional and moral development of the group. This is what connects individual psychology with social structure, and this is why, pace Chodorow, an adequate explanation of this structure cannot remain at the social level. To do so would be to treat this structure as sui generis.

Benjamin's recent volume, entitled The Bonds of Love: Psychoanalysis, Feminism, and the Problem of Domination, only reinforces these conclusions. While continuing to see internalization as pathological ("We have to get beyond internalization theory if we are to break out of the solipsistic omnipotence of the single psyche"),[32] she clearly recognizes the existence and importance of the internal object world with its own dynamics. The problem, says Benjamin, is that while her own intersubjective account clearly owes something to the "intrapsychic" account, as she calls it, the relationship between them is unclear and undeveloped. Thus, she focuses strictly on the intersubjective dimension, appreciating that while these are "complementary approaches," "it is premature to think of synthesizing them."[33] It is hard to imagine a worse assumption on which to build a psychoanalytic social theory! For this assumption abandons from the outset what is most valuable about a psychoanalytic approach: its focus on the connection between the intrapsychic and intersubjective, showing how the former creates the latter, as well as the way in which the intersubjective feeds back to modify the intrapsychic.

The Bonds of Love challenges traditional views of individuation that, according to Benjamin, see maturity as a process of progressive disentanglement from others.[34] Benjamin has a great deal of interest to say on this subject, much of which is supported by a Kleinian perspective, which treats projective identification as a phenomenon of interpsychic commerce, in which individuals are constantly putting aspects of themselves into others, accepting or rejecting the projections of others, reintrojecting their own identifications with others, being enriched or depleted by the response of the other, and so forth. Indeed, this dynamic is the essence of group psychology, a dynamic characterized by that synthesis of the intrapsychic and intersubjective that Benjamin programmatically ignores. To be sure, we do not yet know enough to fully characterize the relationship between these two dimensions; if we did, we would possess a comprehensive theory of the group. However, to use this fact as the reason to focus strictly on the intersubjective dimension is tantamount to substituting social psychology for psychoanalysis until our psychoanalytic knowledge is complete.

There are lots of good intellectual reasons to divide the world into intrapsychic and intersubjective dimensions—or rather (since all the human sciences must make some assumptions about the intrapsychic), to operate on the basis of some very simplified assumptions about the intrapsychic. Economics has done so with considerable success. What makes no sense is to divide psychoanalytic social theory itself along these lines, since it is about the relationship between these dimensions in the first place. Benjamin's approach can only result in the isolation of the intrapsychic from the rest of reality, a tendency psychoanalytic social theory aims at overcoming, not reinforcing. But perhaps this is the point. If it is theoretically isolated, then the phenomena with which intrapsychic psychoanalysis (such a term should, of course, be redundant, but Benjamin has made it necessary) is concerned will not interfere with the construction of humane intersubjective relationships. If only reality followed theory, Benjamin's approach would have much to recommend it.

Dinnerstein

Dinnerstein takes Klein seriously. Consequently, she respects the reality-constitutive character of the passions. Indeed, her ability to convey the nonliteral truth of Kleinian insights in a metaphorical fashion is unsurpassed. Yet, in the end she too abandons (albeit less dramatically than Chodorow or Benjamin) key aspects of psychoanalytic thought. The path of Dinnerstein's argument in *The Mermaid and the Minotaur: Sexual Arrangements and the Human Malaise* is too complex to summarize here. I shall simply state three ways in which her Kleinian-inspired analysis of human sexual arrangements deviates in unacknowledged ways from Kleinian thought. Since Dinnerstein bases much of her argument on Kleinian assumptions, this is a fair criticism.

Dinnerstein argues that mature pleasures and activities allow us to reexperience (sometimes progressively, sometimes regressively) infantile needs and satisfactions. However, she seeks to preserve one realm from this conclusion. Mature mastery of the adult object world (via skills and the ability to plan and carry out various enterprises), she suggests, provides "straightforward" pleasure, uncontaminated by infantile needs.[35] Though on a reduced scale, this way of thinking is similar to that of Chodorow and Benjamin: mature, adult life need not be governed by the same psychoanalytic principles that govern the life of children and neurotics. At least one realm of adult life can be liberated from its infantile origins, and hence rendered immune to psychoanalytic explanation. In response, Christopher Lasch points out that purposeful activity is most satisfying when it reminds "us of the tension that precedes release, the separation that precedes reconciliation, the loss underlying restoration, the unavoidable otherness of the other.[36] Lasch reveals the emotional continuity between our most primitive experiences and our most mature activities. Mastery does not transcend our primitive needs and anxieties. Rather, it helps us deal with them more

effectively by allowing us to better compensate others, and ourselves, for the eternal presence of need and anxiety in our lives. The
mastery that expresses reparation is a good example.

Dinnerstein's revisionism is also seen in her rather literal view of
splitting, which instead of being subtle and fluid along a number of
different planes, as is Klein's, becomes fixed and one-dimensional.
Because mothers do most of the parenting, they become the objects
of all our hatred and love, says Dinnerstein. However, because it is
so difficult to integrate these emotions, we tend to split them along
sexual lines: women, because they resemble mothers physically, become the targets of far more hatred and fear than do men (even as
this hatred and fear is often masked by idealization and denial).
Meltzer, in *The Kleinian Development*, goes into minute detail on
the exegetics of splitting, revealing the way in which the splitting of
good and bad may take place at the part-object level (for example,
between breast and nipple) or on a horizontal plane (between mother's top and bottom), on a vertical plane, and so forth.[37] While I have
not found this level of detail useful, or even terribly convincing, the
basic idea is valid. Splitting is subtle, complex, fluid, and manifold.
To treat it as fundamentally channeled along the male-female axis,
because the first object that we loved and hated was female, the
second male, is too concrete, too literal.

The third aspect of Dinnerstein's revisionism is the counterpart
of the second, and in some ways the most troubling. Dinnerstein
argues that dual parenting would go a long way towards reducing
this tendency to project our most primitive anxieties into woman.
Dinnerstein's argument is not merely that dual parenting would distribute the burden of hatred and aggression more fairly but that it
would force us to integrate our hatred and love by depriving us of a
ready-made external bad object.[38] In a word, dual parenting will
provide the strongest social support possible for the depressive position. "When men start participating as deeply as women in the initi-
ation of infants into the human estate, when both male and female
parents come to carry for all of us the special meanings of early
childhood, the trouble we have reconciling these meanings with
person-ness will finally be faced. The consequence, *of course*, will
be a fuller and more realistic, a kinder and at the same time more
demanding, definition of person-ness."[39]

No doubt dual parenting would carry with it a number of benefits. Certainly it is more fair, and perhaps this is the best argument

for it. However, there is no reason to think that it would force the type of psychic integration that Dinnerstein has in mind. Only if one assumes that the fundamental plane along which splitting occurs is the male-female axis would dual parenting force integration by not giving the splits anywhere else to go, so to speak. This is a far too mechanical and literal reading of splitting. If splitting is as fluid and subtle as Klein and Meltzer suggest, then it will find a million outlets. In fact, Meltzer suggests that there are as many planes of splitting as there are unconscious phantasies. Consider too that it is the child's love and hate for a single person that generates the ambivalence that leads to depressive integration. What reason is there to think that dual parenting, in which the good object is actually two, would lead to greater integration, rather than simply reinforcing paranoid-schizoid defenses associated with splitting and idealization-devaluation, much as the group does?

Dinnerstein's perspective remains psychoanalytic in a way that Chodorow's and Benjamin's do not. In order to make the deepest reaches of the psyche responsive to changes in social structure, Dinnerstein simplifies Kleinian principles (much as Marcuse does with Freudian principles, and for precisely the same reason). Dinnerstein does not, however, abandon these principles for sociology. Nevertheless, there is a significant element of mirror-modeling in her account, in which the actuality of two objects in the external world performing a single function (dual parenting) leads in an unmediated fashion to the integration of the mental representation of these two objects in the psychic world. It is as though we could make the internal object world less fragmented simply by functionally integrating the external counterparts of these objects in real life. This is not truly psychoanalytic thinking. It overemphasizes the external world at the expense of the internal, and it reverses the direction of influence. But neither is Dinnerstein's approach simply social psychology, which remains at the level of relationships among real objects. Rather, Dinnerstein's exhibits the same type of utopian thinking (albeit more toned down) that one finds in Marcuse's *Eros and Civilization*, in which basic principles of mental functioning reflect their social origins with such fidelity that these principles are automatically transformed when society is.[40]

Why do these authors, who clearly take psychoanalytic theory seriously, finally deviate so sharply from it? Juliet Mitchell argues that many who reject Freud actually reject the idea of a dynamic unconscious with its own laws, laws that seem extremely unamenable to reason and unresponsive to social change. However, because it is not considered intellectually fashionable to reject the unconscious per se, they reject Freud.[41] Something similar may be taking place with Chodorow and Benjamin. In turning to object relations theory, they ultimately seek to replace psychoanalysis with relationships, making psychoanalysis an account of emotional pathology, object relations theory—understood as the social psychology of real relationships—an account of emotional health. When society is transformed and repressive social relationships are eliminated, then the necessity of psychoanalytic explanation will also be transcended, as decent and fair external relationships take the place of repressive internal ones. The need for psychoanalytic explanation is itself the mark of a repressive society. Marx's belief that under communism the state would no longer be necessary, that the administration of things would suffice, is analogous. Dinnerstein does not really escape this pattern—except that rather than having social relations take the place of psychological ones, she renders the psyche a virtual mirror of these social relationships.

In their own defense, Chodorow, Benjamin, and Dinnerstein would probably argue that the reason they turn to object relations theory in the first place is because it represents a different psychoanalytic perspective, one that stresses the way in which the self is constituted by actual relationships rather than by internal conflicts generated by the drives. Such a response would not be wholly mistaken or misleading. My argument is that while this is where they begin, they do not end up there. Object relations theory subtly slides over into real relationship theory—that is, social psychology. The reason, I believe, is that the psychoanalytic perspective is for these authors only a means, a ladder that they can kick away once they get to the top. The top is a new society, so thoroughly transformed that the psyche is not merely influenced by the progressive new order but comes to reflect it in an unmediated fashion. Marcuse would have found such an approach familiar. In this respect too, Chodorow, Benjamin, and Dinnerstein are the real legatees of the Frankfurt School's audacious integration of Marx and Freud.

The issues covered in these chapters are difficult and complex, ranging from depth psychology, aesthetic theory, epistemology, and moral theory to the nature of reason. I cannot be certain of having reached the correct conclusion regarding each. I am certain, however, that I have been thorough, in the sense of working out the implications of a single idea as honestly and consistently as possible: that is, if Kleinian psychoanalytic theory is correct, then it must have profound social and political implications, because it is an account of human nature as fundamental and wide-ranging as the accounts with which Hobbes, Locke, Rousseau, Marx, and Freud began. In pursuing these implications, I have sought to work them out to the very end, without turning to a deus ex machina in the last act. Conversely, the mark of object relations revisionism is not so much that it rejects this or that important psychoanalytic principle but that it uses psychoanalysis in the hope, often tacit, of finally being able to transcend it. This has not been my intent.

Notes

CHAPTER 1: MELANIE KLEIN AS A SOCIAL THEORIST?

1. Adorno, "Sociology and Psychology," pt. 2, *New Left Review* 47 (1968): 96.

2. Phyllis Grosskurth, *Melanie Klein: Her World and Her Work* (Cambridge: Harvard University Press, 1987), pp. 153–211.

3. Klein, *The Writings of Melanie Klein*, ed. R. E. Money-Kyrle, 4 vols. (New York: Free Press, 1964–75), vol. 1, pp. 262–89.

4. Sometimes I refer to the Frankfurt School as "they." Though this is not the usual grammatical practice in the United States (it is not uncommon in England), I do so to stress the diversity of the school. Unless otherwise noted, by the Frankfurt School I mean the work of Max Horkheimer, Theodor Adorno, and Herbert Marcuse. That their positions diverge on a number of key issues, making any talk of a "school" at least potentially misleading, will become apparent. For a more precise definition of the Frankfurt School, see Martin Jay, *The Dialectical Imagination* (Boston: Little, Brown and Co., 1973, pp. 3–40.

5. Habermas, "Theodor W. Adorno: Urgeschichte der Subjektivitaet und verwilderte Selbstbehauptung," *Philosophisch-politische Profile* (Frankfurt am Main: Suhrkamp, 1971), pp. 192–96.

6. Marcuse, *Eros and Civilization* (Boston: Beacon Press, 1962), pp. 236–37. Hereafter cited as *Eros*.

7. Freud, *Three Essays on the Theory of Sexuality*, 4th ed., trans. J. Strachey (New York: Basic Books, 1962), p. xviii.

8. Griswold, *Self-Knowledge in Plato's Phaedrus* (New Haven: Yale University Press, 1986), pp. 128–29. Martha Nussbaum, in her otherwise excellent *The Fragility of Goodness: Luck and Ethics in Greek Tragedy and Philosophy* (Cambridge: Cambridge University Press, 1986), does not get this point (pp. 219–21). Nor do I in my *Narcissism: Socrates, The Frankfurt School, and Psychoanalytic Theory* (New Haven: Yale University Press, 1988), pp. 101–02.

9. Donald Meltzer, *The Kleinian Development*, 3 pts. (Perthshire, Scotland: Clunie Press, 1978), pt. 1, p. 84.

10. Jay, *Dialectical Imagination*, p. 103, translation by Jay.

11. Adorno, "Die revidierte Psychoanalyse," *Gesammelte Schriften*, ed. Rolf Tiedemann, 23 vols. (Frankfurt am Main: Suhrkamp, 1970–), vol. 8, p. 40, my translation.

12. Marcuse, *Eros*, pp. 59–60, 131–32.

13. Adorno, "Social Science and Sociological Tendencies in Psychoanalysis" (1946, unpublished), p. 15. Quoted by Jay, *Dialectical Imagination*, p. 105.

14. Adorno, *Minima Moralia: Reflexionen aus dem beschaedigten Leben* (Frankfurt am Main: Suhrkamp, 1951), p. 78. Quoted and translated by Jay, *Dialectical Imagination*, p. 105.

15. Pope is a graduate student in my department.

16. Freud, "Instincts and Their Vicissitudes," in *Collected Papers*, 5 vols., ed. J. Strachey and J. Riviere (London: Hogarth, 1957), vol. 4, pp. 62–67.

17. Nussbaum, *Fragility of Goodness*, pp. 388–90.

18. Freud, *The Standard Edition of the Complete Psychological Works of Sigmund Freud*, ed. James Strachey, 24 vols. (London: Hogarth Press, 1953–74), vol. 12, p. 93.

19. Adolf Grünbaum, *The Foundations of Psychoanalysis: A Philosophical Critique* (Berkeley: University of California Press, 1984). While showing that aspects of the Freudian theory of repression are falsifiable, Grünbaum finds virtually all of Freud's metapsychology nonfalsifiable.

20. Michael Sandel, *Liberalism and the Limits of Justice* (Cambridge: Cambridge University Press, 1982), p. 95.

21. Ibid., p. 80.

22. Nancy Chodorow, "Toward a Relational Individualism," in *Reconstructing Individualism: Autonomy, Individuality, and the Self in Western Thought*, ed. Thomas Heller, Morton Sosna, and David Wellbery (Stanford: Stanford University Press, 1986), 197–207.

23. Jeffrey B. Abramson, *Liberation and Its Limits: The Moral and Political Thought of Freud* (Boston: Beacon Press, 1986).

24. Ibid., p. xi.

25. Ibid., pp. 24–27, 30. Freud, "The Economic Problem of Masochism," *Collected Papers*, vol. 2, p. 256.

26. Abramson, *Liberation and Its Limits*, p. 28.

27. Freud, *Group Psychology and the Analysis of the Ego*, trans. J. Strachey (New York: W. W. Norton, 1961), p. 20.

28. Abramson, *Liberation and Its Limits*, p. 58.

29. Meltzer, *Kleinian Development*, pt. 1, pp. 119–22. Freud, *Group Psychology and the Analysis of the Ego*, pp. 37–56.

30. Meltzer, *Kleinian Development*, pt. 1, p. 122.

31. Abramson, *Liberation and Its Limits*, p. 59.

32. Ibid., p. 60, my emphasis.

33. Reinhold Niebuhr, *Moral Man and Immoral Society* (New York: Scribner's, 1960), esp. pp. xii, xxii.

CHAPTER 2: PSYCHOANALYST OF THE PASSIONS

1. Hermine Hug-Hellmuth had attempted to analyze young children before Klein. However, Hug-Hellmuth's murder (in 1924) by her eighteen-year-old nephew, whom she had brought up and apparently analyzed, not only cut short her promising work in this field but also, as might be imagined, threatened to set back the cause of child analysis. Grosskurth, *Melanie Klein*, p. 123.

2. Peter Gay, *Freud: A Life for Our Time* (New York: W. W. Norton, 1988), pp. 509–10.

3. Jay Greenberg and Stephen Mitchell, *Object Relations in Psychoanalytic Theory* (Cambridge: Harvard University Press, 1983), p. 144 n. I follow Greenberg and Mitchell's treatment of Klein quite closely at several points in this chapter.

4. Hanna Segal, *Melanie Klein* (Harmondsworth, England: Penguin Books, 1981), p. 73. I also follow Segal quite closely at several points.

5. Klein, *Writings*, vol. 1, p. 197.

6. Ibid.

7. Freud, *Beyond the Pleasure Principle*, trans. J. Strachey (New York: W. W. Norton, 1961); "On Narcissism," *The Standard Edition*, vol. 14, pp. 73–74.

8. Greenberg and Mitchell, *Object Relations in Psychoanalytic Theory*, pp. 138–42.

9. Joan Riviere, "On the Genesis of Psychical Conflict in Early Infancy," in *Developments in Psycho-Analysis*, by Klein et al. (London: Hogarth, 1952), p. 50. Quoted in Greenberg and Mitchell, *Object Relations in Psychoanalytic Theory*, p. 140.

10. Klein, "The Origins of Transference," *Writings*, vol. 3, p. 51. Quoted in Greenberg and Mitchell, *Object Relations in Psychoanalytic Theory*, p. 141.

11. Greenberg and Mitchell, *Object Relations in Psychoanalytic Theory*, p. 146.

12. Ibid., p. 142.

13. Freud, *Civilization and Its Discontents*, trans. J. Strachey (New York: W. W. Norton, 1961), p. 96.

14. Klein, "The Importance of Symbol Formation in the Development of the Ego," *Writings*, vol. 1, p. 219. Quoted in Greenberg and Mitchell, *Object Relations in Psychoanalytic Theory*, p. 123.

15. Segal, *Melanie Klein*, p. 12.

16. Freud, *The Standard Edition*, vol. 20, pp. 75–175. Segal, *Melanie Klein*, p. 13.

17. Segal, *Melanie Klein*, pp. 11–15.

18. Ibid., pp. 24–25. Gay's account of Ferenczi's break with Freud over issues such as Ferenczi's attempt to "relativize" the analytic hour, creating an atmosphere that was "mild, passionless" (Ferenczi's terms), certainly supports Klein's objections. (*Freud*, p. 579)

19. Segal, *Melanie Klein*, p. 15. Abraham, "A Short Study of the Development of the Libido, Viewed in the Light of Mental Disorders" (1924), in *Selected Papers of Karl Abraham* (London: Hogarth Press, 1968), pp. 418–501. I follow Segal closely regarding Abraham.

20. Segal, *Melanie Klein*, p. 16.

21. Klein, "Notes on Some Schizoid Mechanisms," *Writings*, vol. 3, pp. 1–24.

22. W. R. D. Fairbairn, *Psychoanalytic Studies of the Personality* (London: Routledge and Kegan Paul, 1952), pp. 28–58. (*An Object-Relations Theory of the Personality* [New York: Basic Books, 1954] is the same book under a different title.) Segal, *Melanie Klein*, p. 115.

23. Segal, *Melanie Klein*, p. 116.

24. Ibid., p. 119.

25. R. D. Hinshelwood, *A Dictionary of Kleinian Thought* (London: Free Association Books, 1989), p. 179. This recent book is a great resource. I follow Hinshelwood's discussion of projective identification closely. Meltzer, *Kleinian Development*, pt. 2, p. 37.

26. Hinshelwood, *Kleinian Dictionary*, p. 182, quoting Spillius, "Some Developments From the Work of Melanie Klein," *International Journal of Psycho-Analysis* 64 (1983): 322.

27. Segal, *Melanie Klein*, p. 117.

28. Meltzer, *Kleinian Development*, pt. 2, p. 64.

29. Segal, *Melanie Klein*, pp. 125–26.

30. Meltzer, *Kleinian Development*, pt. 2, pp. 10–11.

31. Segal, *Melanie Klein*, p. 80.

32. Meltzer, *Kleinian Development*, pt. 2, p. 47.

33. Greenberg and Mitchell, *Object Relations in Psychoanalytic Theory*, p. 126.

34. Ibid.

35. Riviere, "On the Genesis of Psychical Conflict in Early Infancy," p. 60. Quoted in Greenberg and Mitchell, *Object Relations in Psychoanalytic Theory*, p. 127.

36. Klein, "Love, Guilt and Reparation," in *Love, Hate and Reparation*, by Klein and Riviere (New York: W. W. Norton, 1964), p. 65.

37. Ibid.

38. Klein, "The Oedipus Complex in the Light of Early Anxieties," *Writings*, vol. 1, p. 418. Quoted in Greenberg and Mitchell, *Object Relations in Psychoanalytic Theory*, p. 139.

39. Segal, *Melanie Klein*, p. 71. Grosskurth, *Melanie Klein*, pp. 215–16.

40. Klein, "Mourning," *Writings*, vol. 1, p. 369.

41. Klein, "The Oedipus Complex in the Light of Early Anxieties," *Writings*, vol. 1, pp. 370–419. Segal, *Melanie Klein*, p. 84.

42. Klein, "Envy and Gratitude," *Writings*, vol. 3, p. 176.

43. Ibid, p. 192.

44. Greenberg and Mitchell, *Object Relations in Psychoanalytic Theory*, p. 129.

45. Klein, "Envy and Gratitude," *Writings*, vol. 3, p. 189.

46. Segal, *Melanie Klein*, pp. 147–48.

47. Klein, "Envy and Gratitude," *Writings*, vol. 3, pp. 217–21.

48. *Narrative of a Child Analysis* is volume 4 of Klein's *Writings*. Meltzer, *Kleinian Development*, pt. 2, pp. 98–99.

49. Meltzer, *Kleinian Development*, pt. 1, p. 85.

50. Meltzer, "The Kleinian Expansion of Freud's Metapsychology," *International Journal of Psycho-Analysis* 62 (1981): 179.

51. Rustin, "A Socialist Consideration of Kleinian Psychoanalysis," *New Left Review* 131 (1982): 82–83.

52. Habermas, "Psychic Thermidor and the Rebirth of Rebellious Subjectivity," *Berkeley Journal of Sociology* 24–25 (1980): 11–12.

53. Horkheimer, "Materialism and Morality," *Telos* 69 (Fall 1986): 107. John Torpey, "Ethics and Critical Theory: From Horkheimer to Habermas," *Telos* 69 (Fall 1986): 72–73.

54. Jean-Jacques Rousseau, *Emile*, trans. A. Bloom (New York: Basic Books, 1979), p. 222.

55. Freud, *Civilization and Its Discontents*, pp. 79–82.

56. Greenberg and Mitchell, *Object Relations in Psychoanalytic Theory*, pp. 132–33.

57. Money-Kyrle, "Psycho-Analysis and Ethics," *New Directions in Psycho-Analysis*, ed. M. Klein, P. Heimann, and R. Money-Kyrle (London: Tavistock Publications, 1955), pp. 421–39.

58. Klein, "Love, Guilt and Reparation," in *Love, Hate and Reparation*, pp. 108–09.

59. Segal, *Melanie Klein*, pp. 96–101.

60. Isaacs, "The Nature and Function of Phantasy," *Developments in Psycho-Analysis*, by Klein et al. (London: Hogarth Press, 1952), pp. 81–87. Segal, *Melanie Klein*, p. 101.

61. Meltzer, *Kleinian Development*, pt. 2, p. 31, his emphasis.

62. Isaacs, "Nature and Function of Phantasy," p. 82. Segal, *Melanie Klein*, p. 100.

63. Segal, *Melanie Klein*, p. 101. Hinshelwood, *Kleinian Dictionary*, pp. 37–44.

64. Meltzer, *Kleinian Development*, pt. 1, pp. 139–40.

65. Meltzer, "The Kleinian Expansion of Freud's Metapsychology," p. 179.

66. Meltzer, *Kleinian Development*, pt. 2, p. 115. From Klein's *Narrative*, 15th week, sessions 84–89.

67. Klein, "Love, Guilt, and Reparation," in *Love, Hate and Reparation*, pp. 104–05.

68. Ibid., p. 111.

69. Meltzer, *Kleinian Development*, pt. 2, p. 115.

70. Greenberg and Mitchell, *Object Relations in Psychoanalytic Theory*, pp. 148–49.

71. Following standard practice in object relations theory, I treat the ego and the self as virtual synonyms here. Although potentially misleading, this practice (like so many others in psychoanalysis) emerged in order to preserve a continuity with Freud.

72. Meltzer, *Kleinian Development*, pt. 2, p. 86. First italics are mine.

73. Richard Wollheim, *The Thread of Life* (Cambridge: Harvard University Press, 1984), pp. 125–26.

74. Ibid., pp. 126–27.

75. Compare Klein's "Psychogenesis of Manic-Depressive States," *Writings*, vol. 1, pp. 267–69, where objects seem to live a life of their own, with "Notes on Some Schizoid Mechanisms," *Writings*, vol. 3, pp. 11–12, where the autonomy of objects is a sign of emotional illness. Eleven years separate these works (1935–1946), but this shift cannot be adequately explained in terms of the development of Klein's thought, for it occurs even within works. Cf. Klein, "Mourning and its Relationship to Manic-Depressive States" (1940), *Writings*, vol. 1, pp. 362–63, 368–69.

76. Hinshelwood, *Kleinian Dictionary*, p. 72.

77. Ibid., p. 42, citing an unpublished paper (1943) by Edward Glover.

78. Ibid., p. 68.

79. Wollheim, *Thread of Life*, p. 129.

CHAPTER 3: A PSYCHOANALYTIC THEORY OF THE LARGE GROUP

1. Money-Kyrle, *Psycho-Analysis and Politics* (London: Duckworth, 1951), p. 98.

2. May Brodbeck, "Methodological Individualisms: Definition and Reduction," in *Readings in the Philosophy of the Social Sciences*, ed. M. Brodbeck (New York: Macmillan, 1968), pp. 280–303. Ernest Nagel, *The Structure of Science* (New York: Harcourt, Brace and World, 1961), chap. 11.

3. Wilfred R. Bion, *Experiences in Groups* (New York: Basic Books, 1961), p. 134.

4. George Devereux, *Basic Problems of Ethnopsychiatry*, trans. B. M. Gulati and G. Devereux (Chicago: University of Chicago Press, 1980), p. 6.

5. Ibid., p. 18.

6. Donald W. Winnicott, *The Maturational Processes and the Facilitating Environment* (New York: International Universities Press, 1965), p. 60; see also pp. 44–48, 113.

7. Winnicott, *Holding and Interpretation* (New York: Grove Press, 1986), p. 16.

8. Ibid., p. 18.

9. Bion, *Attention and Interpretation* (New York: Basic Books, 1970), pp. 8–9.

10. Turquet, "Threats to Identity in the Large Group," in *The Large*

Group: Dynamics and Therapy, ed. L. Kreeger (London: Maresfield Reprints, 1975), pp. 100–101.

11. Freud, Group Psychology and the Analysis of the Ego, pp. 9–12.

12. Turquet, "Threats to Identity in the Large Group," pp. 106, 113.

13. Ibid., pp. 104–05.

14. Tom Main, "Some Psychodynamics of Large Groups," in The Large Group: Dynamics and Therapy, ed. L. Kreeger, pp. 64–65.

15. Otto Kernberg, Internal World and External Reality: Object Relations Theory Applied (Northvale, N.J.: Jason Aronson, 1985), pp. 215–16.

16. Ibid., p. 217.

17. Graham Little, Political Ensembles (Oxford: Oxford University Press, 1985), p. 79.

18. Ibid., p. 164.

19. Bion, Experiences in Groups, p. 131. Quoted by Little, Political Ensembles, p. 78, his emphasis.

20. Patrick de Maré, "The Politics of Large Groups," in The Large Group: Dynamics and Therapy, ed. L. Kreeger, p. 153.

21. Bion, Experiences in Groups, p. 163.

22. Ibid., p. 89.

23. Ibid., p. 189.

24. Ibid., p. 122.

25. Ibid., p. 177.

26. Kohut, The Restoration of the Self (New York: International Universities Press, 1977), p. 77.

27. Money-Kyrle, Psycho-Analysis and Politics, p. 158. Manic denial defends against both paranoid-schizoid and depressive anxiety, though it tends to be more closely associated with the latter, as it is a slightly more sophisticated defense mechanism than splitting and projection.

28. Grosskurth, Melanie Klein, p. 271.

29. Meltzer, Kleinian Development, pt. 2, p. 64.

30. Klein, Writings, vol. 3, pp. 38–40.

31. Louis Zurcher, Social Roles: Conformity Conflict and Creativity (Beverly Hills, Calif.: Sage, 1983), p. 14.

32. Erving Goffman, The Presentation of Self in Everyday Life (Garden City, N.Y.: Doubleday, 1959).

33. Ralph Turner, "The Role and the Person," American Journal of Sociology 84 (July): 1–23. Zurcher, Social Roles, pp. 223–38.

34. Bernard Meltzer and J. Petras, "The Chicago and Iowa Schools of Symbolic Interactionism," in Symbolic Interaction, 2d ed., J. Manis and B. Meltzer (Boston: Allyn and Bacon, 1972), pp. 43–57.

35. Freud, "The Dissolution of the Oedipus Complex," The Standard Edition, vol. 19, pp. 176–77.

36. Jaques, "Social Systems as Defence Against Persecutory and Depressive Anxiety," New Directions in Psycho-Analysis, ed. M. Klein, P. Heimann, and R. Money-Kyrle, p. 479.

37. Ibid.

38. Ibid., pp. 490–91.

39. Ibid., pp. 492–93.

40. Ibid., p. 487.

41. Coles, *Children of Crisis*, 5 vols. (Boston: Atlantic-Little, Brown and Co., 1967–78), vol. 5, *Privileged Ones*, pp. 391–92 and passim.

42. Klein, "Love, Guilt and Reparation," pp. 108–09.

43. Meltzer, "The Kleinian Expansion of Freud's Metapsychology," *International Journal of Psycho-Analysis*, p. 184.

44. Klein, "Love, Guilt and Reparation," p. 93.

45. Freud, *Civilization and Its Discontents*, p. 55.

46. Jaques, "Social Systems as Defence," p. 487. In his later (1970) *Attention and Interpretation*, pp. 123–24, Bion makes a systematic, but very brief, attempt to relate his account to Klein's paranoid-schizoid and depressive positions. Here Bion argues that not only analysis but also much of world history can be interpreted in terms of the relationship between the contained and the container. Examples of the former category would be the ineffable anxieties of the analysand, the insights of the mystic, and the desires of Dionysus. Examples of the latter category would be the insight of the analyst, the constraints of institutions, and the reason of Apollo. It is a fascinating hypothesis, but Bion's attempt to reinterpret it in terms of Klein's categories requires, as the reader will surely appreciate by this point, a great deal of imagination.

47. Klein, "Envy and Gratitude," *Writings*, vol. 3, pp. 192–93.

48. Money-Kyrle, "Psycho-Analysis and Ethics," pp. 430–33.

49. Freud, *Civilization and Its Discontents*, p. 104.

50. Marcuse, *Five Lectures*, trans. Jeremy Shapiro and Shierry Weber (Boston: Beacon Press, 1970), p. 59.

51. Volkan, "Narcissistic Personality Organization and 'Reparative' Leadership," *International Journal of Group Psychotherapy* 30 (1980): 131–52. Volkan's recent volume, *The Need to Have Enemies and Allies* (Northvale, N.J.: Jason Aronson, 1988), though not explicitly based on a Kleinian account, sees group processes in terms not terribly different from my own, in which the projection of disintegrative anxiety into enemies is central.

52. Freud, *Group Psychology and the Analysis of the Ego*, pp. 18–19.

53. Angus Campbell et al., *The American Voter* (New York: Wiley, 1960); D. R. Kinder and R. P. Abelson, "Appraising Presidential Candidates: Personality and Affect in the 1980 Campaign," paper presented at the 1981 annual meeting of the American Political Science Association, New York; G. B. Markus, "Political Attitudes During an Election Year: A Report on the 1980 NES Panel Study," *American Political Science Review* 76 (1982): 538–60.

54. Warren Miller and J. Merril Shanks, "Policy Directions and Presidential Leadership: Alternative Interpretations of the 1980 Presidential Election," *British Journal of Political Science* 12 (1982): pp. 346–51.

55. D. O. Sears and R. R. Lau, "Inducing Apparently Self-Interested Political Preferences," *American Journal of Political Science* 27: (1983): 223–52.

56. D. R. Kinder and S. T. Fiske, "Presidents in the Public Mind," in *Political Psychology*, ed. M. Hermann (San Francisco: Jossey-Bass, 1986), p. 210.

57. Ronald Reagan and Richard Hubler, *Where's the Rest of Me?* (New York: Karz Publishers, 1981) [originally published 1965], pp. 66–67.

58. Garry Wills, *Reagan's America: Innocents at Home* (Garden City, N.Y.: Doubleday, 1987), p. 119.

59. Freud, *The Future of an Illusion*, trans. J. Strachey (New York: W. W. Norton, 1961), pp. 16–17, 24, 43.

60. *Public Opinion* 8, no. 2 (1985): 28–34. *Public Opinion* 8, no. 4 (1985): 21–25. *Public Opinion* 8, no. 6 (1986): 30–34. *Public Opinion* 9, no. 4 (1986): 21–28.

61. Michael Rogin's *Ronald Reagan, The Movie* (Berkeley: University of California Press, 1987) comes close to the theme of my case study, arguing that Reagan "embodies national fears of helplessness and dependence in order to overcome them by punishing enemies responsible for American weakness." (p. 35) However, Robert Dallek's *Ronald Reagan: The Politics of Symbolism* (Cambridge: Harvard University Press, 1984) comes even closer to my theme (pp. 6–10), viewing Reagan as an "idol of consumption." Unlike the "idol of production," the idol of consumption sells illusion, not substance. Unlike the hard-working figure admired for his Promethean effort and productivity, the idol of consumption is just like us, only luckier. As such, the idol of consumption demands less of us. Though such an idol may praise the values of production (hard work, independence), we all know that he really doesn't mean it. If our idol could succeed by luck and illusion, why can't we? That there is a connection between the appeal of such an idol and what Christopher Lasch calls the "culture of narcissism" may be apparent.

62. Wills, *Reagan's America*, p. 280.

63. Ibid., p. 381.

64. Lou Cannon, *Reagan* (New York: Putnam, 1982), p. 73.

65. George H. Smith, *Who Is Ronald Reagan?* (New York: Pyramid Books, 1968), p. 95. Lloyd de Mause, *Reagan's America* (New York: Creative Roots, 1984), p. 44.

66. Betty Glad, "Black-and-White Thinking: Ronald Reagan's Approach to Foreign Policy," *Political Psychology* 4 (1983): 33–76.

67. Janine Chasseguet-Smirgel, *The Ego Ideal*, trans. Paul Barrows (New York: W. W. Norton, 1984), pp. 218–19.

68. Meltzer, *The Kleinian Development*, pt. 2, p. 64.

69. Donald Regan, *For the Record: From Wall Street to Washington* (New York: Harcourt Brace Jovanovich, 1988), as well as other recent "kiss and tell" books.

70. Meltzer, *Kleinian Development*, pt. 2, p. 85; Klein, *Narrative*, 11th week, sessions 60–65.

CHAPTER 4: ART AND REPARATION

1. Albert Hofstadter and Richard Kuhns, eds., *Philosophies of Art and Beauty* (Chicago: University of Chicago Press, Phoenix edition, 1976), p. 240. Their overview of the history of aesthetics was helpful.

2. Nietzsche, *The Birth of Tragedy*, trans. W. Kaufmann, in *Basic Writings of Nietzsche*, ed. Kaufmann (New York: Modern Library, 1968), sect. 12, pp. 83–84.

3. Heidegger, "The Origin of the Work of Art," in *Poetry, Language, Thought*, trans. Albert Hofstadter (New York: Harper and Row, 1971). Benedetto Croce, *Encyclopaedia Britannica*, 14th ed., s. v. "Aesthetics"; Susanne Langer, *Problems of Art: Ten Philosophical Lectures* (New York: Scribner's, 1957). Hofstadter and Kuhns on Langer, *Philosophies of Art and Beauty*, pp. 555–56.

4. "To write poetry after Auschwitz is barbaric"; Adorno, *Prisms*, trans. S. and S. Weber (Cambridge: MIT Press, 1981), p. 34.

5. Adorno, "Commitment," in *The Essential Frankfurt School Reader*, ed. A. Arato and E. Gebhardt (New York: Urizen Books, 1978), pp. 312–13.

6. Ibid.

7. Adorno, "Looking Back on Surrealism," in *The Idea of the Modern in Literature and the Arts*, ed. I. Howe (New York, 1967), p. 223; Martin Jay, *Adorno* (Cambridge: Harvard University Press, 1984), p. 129.

8. Adorno, *Prisms*, p. 31.

9. Adorno, *Philosophy of Modern Music*, trans. A. G. Mitchell and W. V. Blomster (New York: Seabury Press, 1973), p. 133; Adorno, "Zur gesellschaftlichen Lage der Musik," *Zeitschrift fuer Sozialforschung* 1, no. 3 (1932), p. 359; Jay, *Adorno*, pp. 27, 150–54. Jay, *The Dialectical Imagination*, p. 183.

10. Adorno, *Aesthetic Theory*, trans. C. Lenhardt (London: Routledge and Kegan Paul, 1984), pp. 12–15, 338. (The original, *Aesthetische Theorie*, is vol. 7 of Adorno's *Gesammelte Schriften*, 23 vols., ed. R. Tiedemann [Frankfurt am Main: Suhrkamp, 1970].)

11. Marcuse, *Aesthetic Dimension*, p. 69.

12. Adorno, *Aesthetic Theory*, p. 369.

13. Adorno, *Aesthetic Theory*, p. 15; Marcuse, *Counterrevolution and Revolt* (Boston: Beacon Press, 1972), p. 81; Marcuse, *Aesthetic Dimension*, p. 8.

14. Marcuse, *Counterrevolution and Revolt*, p. 101.

15. Marcuse, *Aesthetic Dimension*, p. 59; cf. pp. 10, 55. When referring to Marcuse's concept of catharsis as purgation, I retain his spelling with a *c*. Otherwise I spell the term, as Nussbaum does, with a *k* to connote clarification.

16. Adorno, *Aesthetic Theory*, pp. 338–39.

17. Marcuse, *Eros and Civilization*, p. 144.

18. Marcuse, *An Essay on Liberation* (Boston: Beacon Press, 1969), p. 43.

19. Marcuse, *Counterrevolution and Revolt*, p. 99.

20. Marcuse, *Aesthetic Dimension*, p. 66. Internal quote from Adorno.

21. Ibid., pp. 55–61.

22. Richard Wollheim, "Freud and the Understanding of Art," *British Journal of Aesthetics* 10, no. 3 (1970): 224. Freud, "Leonardo da Vinci and a Memory of His Childhood," *The Standard Edition*, vol. 11, pp. 59–137.

23. Adrian Stokes, *Three Essays on The Painting of Our Time* (London: Tavistock, 1961); Stokes, *The Invitation in Art* (New York: Chilmark Press, 1965).

24. Hanna Segal, "A Psycho-Analytical Approach to Aesthetics," in *New Directions in Psycho-Analysis*, ed. Klein et al. See also the two pieces on aesthetics in this collection by Joan Riviere: "The Unconscious Phantasy of an Inner World Reflected in Examples from Literature" and "The Inner World in Ibsen's *Master-Builder*."

25. Segal, "A Psycho-Analytical Approach to Aesthetics," pp. 389–90. Segal cites no page numbers. Presumably she is referring to Proust's description of an afternoon party at the Princesse de Guermantes. *Remembrance of Things Past*, trans. C. K. S. Moncrieff et al. (New York: Vintage, 1982), vol. 3, pp. 957–1088.

26. Segal, "A Psycho-Analytical Approach to Aesthetics," p. 390.

27. Freud, "Mourning and Melancholia," *Standard Edition*, vol. 14, pp. 237–60.

28. Segal, "A Psycho-Analytical Approach to Aesthetics," p. 400.

29. Ernst Gombrich, "Norm und Form," in *Theorien der Kunst*, ed. Dieter Henrich and Wolfgang Iser (Frankfurt am Main: Suhrkamp, 1984), p. 171.

30. Rilke, *Duineser Elegien*, trans. Lieshman and Spender; quoted in Segal, "A Psycho-Analytical Approach to Aesthetics," p. 384.

31. C. Fred Alford, *Science and the Revenge of Nature: Marcuse and Habermas* (Gainesville: University Presses of Florida, 1985), chap. 3; Alford, *Narcissism: Socrates, the Frankfurt School, and Psychoanalytic Theory* (New Haven: Yale University Press, 1988), chap. 4; Alford, "Eros and Civilization After Thirty Years: A Reconsideration in Light of Recent Theories of Narcissism," *Theory and Society* 16 (1987): 869–90.

32. Jay, *Adorno*, p. 68. Adorno, "Subject and Object," pp. 497–511.

33. Marcuse, *Aesthetic Dimension*, p. 73.

34. Adorno, *Negative Dialectics*, trans. E. B. Ashton (New York: Seabury Press, 1973), p. 23: "Rage is the mark of each and every idealism."

35. Klein, "Love, Guilt and Reparation," p. 105.

36. Adorno, *Aesthetic Theory*, pp. 68–75.

37. Nelson Goodman, *Languages of Art* (Indianapolis and New York: Bobbs-Merrill, 1967), p. 242.

38. See my *Narcissism*, pp. 112–15, for Adorno's concept of mimesis as an active, creative process.

39. Adorno, *Aesthetic Theory*, p. 80.

40. Goodman, *Languages of Art*, pp. 255–62.

41. Turquet, "Threats to Identity in the Large Group," p. 106.

42. Freud, "The 'Uncanny,'" *The Standard Edition*, vol. 17, p. 245.

43. Marcuse, *Aesthetic Dimension*, p. 59.

44. Martha Nussbaum, *The Fragility of Goodness* (Cambridge: Cambridge University Press, 1986), pp. 388–91.

45. Ibid., p. 389.

46. Ibid, pp. 389–90.

47. Arianna S. Huffington, *Picasso: Creator and Destroyer* (New York: Simon and Schuster, 1988).

48. Marcuse, "Ueber die philosophischen Grundlagen des wirtschaftswissenschaftslichen Arbeitsbegriffs," in *Kultur und Gesellschaft* (Frankfurt am Main: Suhrkamp, 1965), vol. 2, pp. 7–48.

49. Adorno, *Aesthetic Theory*, p. 439.

50. Adorno, *Negative Dialectics*, p. 14.

51. Brigitte Baer, in a brochure for the exhibit at the Metropolitan Museum of Art, New York City, Spring 1988.

52. Adorno, "Erpresste Versoehnung," in *Theorien der Kunst*, ed. Henrich and Iser (Frankfurt am Main: Suhrkamp, 1984), pp. 313–42.

53. I refer to the larger of the two paintings with the same title, painted in the same year, in the collection of the Kunsthalle, Mannheim.

54. Rilke, *Letters on Cézanne*, trans. Joel Agee (New York: Fromm International, 1985), p. 67.

55. Ibid., p. 4.

56. Klein, "Envy and Gratitude," *Writings*, vol. 3, p. 225.

57. Abramson, *Liberation and its Limits*, p. 120, quoting Paul Roazen, *Freud: Social and Political Thought* (New York: Vintage Books, 1968), p. 292.

58. Freud, *The Standard Edition*, vol. 16, p. 434; Abramson, *Liberation and its Limits*, p. 121.

59. Abramson, *Liberation and its Limits*, p. 121.

60. Money-Kyrle, "Psycho-Analysis and Ethics," p. 433.

61. Rilke, *Letters on Cézanne*, p. 4.

62. Adorno, *Negative Dialectics*, pp. 404–05; quoted in Jay, *Adorno*, p. 53, who alters the translation slightly.

63. Adorno, *Aesthetic Theory*, p. 6.

64. Peter Uwe Hohendahl, "Autonomy of Art: Looking Back at Adorno's *Aesthetische Theorie*," in *Foundations of the Frankfurt School of Social Research*, ed. J. Marcus and Z. Tar (New Brunswick, N.J.: Transaction Books, 1984), p. 219.

65. Adorno, *Aesthetic Theory*, p. 190.

66. Russell Berman, "Adorno, Marxism and Art," *Telos* 34 (Winter 1977–78): 158.

67. Adorno, *Dissonanzen* (Goettingen: Vandenhoek, 1972), p. 140; quoted and translated by Hohendahl, "Autonomy of Art," p. 222. See Adorno, *Aesthetic Theory*, p. 338, for a similar claim.

68. Adorno, "Lyric Poetry and Society," trans. Bruce Mayo, *Telos* 20 (1974), p. 65.

69. Lucien Goldmann, *Colloque international sur la sociologie de la littérature* (Bruxelles: Institut de la Sociologie, 1974), p. 40; quoted in Marcuse, *Aesthetic Dimension*, p. 13.

70. Richard Wolin, "The De-Aestheticization of Art: On Adorno's *Aesthetische Theorie*," *Telos* 41 (Fall 1979): 124.

71. Adorno, "Commitment," p. 312.

72. Adorno, *Aesthetic Theory*, p. 369.

73. G. W. F. Hegel, *The Philosophy of Fine Art*, 4 vols., trans. F. P. B. Osmaston (London: G. Bell and Sons, 1920), vol. 1, pp. 272–313; vol. 2, pp. 213–15; vol. 4, pp. 295–342. Murray Krieger, *The Tragic Vision* (Chicago: University of Chicago Press, 1966), pp. 5–7.

74. Nietzsche, *The Birth of Tragedy*, trans. Walter Kaufmann, in *Basic Writings of Nietzsche*, ed. W. Kaufmann (New York: Modern Library, 1968), pp. 3–146.

75. Richard Sewall, *The Vision of Tragedy* (New Haven: Yale University Press, 1959), p. 5.

76. Klein, *Writings*, vol. 3, pp. 280–82.

77. Ibid., pp. 283–84.

78. Ibid., p. 298.

79. Joel Kovel, *The Age of Desire* (New York: Pantheon Books, 1981), pp. 197–98.

80. Ibid., p. 104.

81. Wolfgang Fritz Haug, "Das Ganze und das ganz Andere: Zur Kritik der reinen revolutionaeren Transzendenz," in *Antworten auf Herbert Marcuse*, ed. J. Habermas (Frankfurt am Main: Suhrkamp, 1968), pp. 60–61.

CHAPTER 5: REASON AND REPARATION

1. Horkheimer and Adorno, *Dialectic of Enlightenment*, trans. J. Cumming (New York: Herder and Herder, 1972), pp. 43–81.

2. David Held, *Introduction to Critical Theory: Horkheimer to Habermas* (Berkeley: University of California Press, 1980), p. 404.

3. Adorno, *Negative Dialectics*, p. 5.

4. Ibid., p. 10.

5. Horkheimer, *Eclipse of Reason* (New York: Seabury Press, 1974), pp. 63–71.

6. Habermas, *The Theory of Communicative Action*, trans. T. McCarthy (Boston: Beacon Press, 1984), vol. 1, pp. 382–83. German terms are taken from the original, *Theorie des kommunikativen Handelns*, 2 vols. (Frankfurt am Main: Suhrkamp, 1981), vol. 1, p. 512.

7. Habermas, "The Entwinement of Myth and Enlightenment: Rereading *Dialectic of Enlightenment*," trans. T. Levin. *New German Critique* 26 (1982): 29.

8. Adorno, "Subject and Object," p. 499.

9. Marcuse, *Eros and Civilization*, chapter 4.

10. Alford, *Science and the Revenge of Nature*, chap. 3; Alford, *Narcissism*, chap. 5.

11. Marcuse, *An Essay on Liberation* (Boston: Beacon Press, 1969), p. 31.

12. Christopher Lasch, *The Minimal Self* (New York: Norton, 1984), pp. 233–34.

13. Marcuse, *Eros and Civilization*, pp. 197–213. See my discussion of "binding," and why it makes no sense as Marcuse employs it, in *Narcissism*, pp. 145–47.

14. Jessica Benjamin, "Authority and the Family Revisited: or, A World without Fathers?" *New German Critique* 13 (Winter 1978): 35–57. Benjamin, "The End of Internalization: Adorno's Social Psychology," *Telos* 32 (Summer 1977): 42–64.

15. Horkheimer, "Authority and the Family," in *Critical Theory*, trans. M. O'Connell et al. (New York: Seabury Press, 1972), p. 101.

16. Ibid., p. 107.

17. Horkheimer, "Authority and the Family Today," in *The Family: Its Function and Destiny*, ed. R. Anshen (New York: Harper, 1949), p. 365.

18. Adorno, "Sociology and Psychology," pt. 2, p. 85.

19. Benjamin, "End of Internalization," pp. 47–50.

20. Hinshelwood, *Dictionary*, p. 442.

21. Klein, "Early Stages of the Oedipus Conflict," *Writings*, vol. 1, p. 188; and "The Importance of Symbol Formation in the Development of the Ego," *Writings*, vol. 1, p. 222. Meltzer, "Kleinian Expansion of Freud's Metapsychology," p. 178.

22. Klein, *Writings*, vol. 1, p. 188.

23. Money-Kyrle, in Klein, *Writings*, vol. 1, p. 429.

24. Klein, *Writings*, vol. 1, p. 188.

25. Ibid.

26. Ibid., pp. 220–21.

27. Ibid., p. 232.

28. Ibid., p. 241. James Strachey, "Some Unconscious Factors in Reading," *International Journal of Psycho-Analysis* 11 (1930): 322–31.

29. Klein, *Writings*, vol. 1, p. 137.

30. Quoted in Isaacs, "The Nature and Function of Phantasy," p. 82.

31. Segal, *Melanie Klein*, p. 110; Klein, *Writings*, vol. 1, p. 188.

32. Francis Bacon, *Advancement of Learning*, in *The Works of Francis Bacon*, 7 vols., ed. J. Spedding (London: Longman, 1870), vol. 4, p. 296 and passim (many editions have the same volume and page numbers); William Leiss, *The Domination of Nature* (Boston: Beacon Press, 1974), pp. 59–60, 224.

33. Hinshelwood, *Dictionary*, pp. 428–40, esp. 436.

34. Ibid., pp. 437–38.

35. The fallibilism of Karl Popper best exemplifies this ideal. Popper

introduced his doctrine of fallibilism in *The Logic of Scientific Discovery* (New York: Harper and Row, 1968).

36. Goodman, *Languages of Art*, pp. 226–30, 252–55.

37. Klein, *Writings*, vol. 1, p. 245.

38. Ibid.

39. Adorno, *Negative Dialectics*, pp. 22–24.

40. Paul Feyerabend, "Two Models of Epistemic Change: Mill and Hegel," in his *Philosophical Papers*, 2 vols. (Cambridge: Cambridge University Press, 1981), vol. 2, p. 73.

41. Feyerabend, *Against Method* (London: NLB, 1975), p. 30.

42. Feyerabend, *Science in a Free Society* (London: NLB, 1978), p. 169.

43. Segal, "A Psycho-Analytical Approach to Aesthetics," p. 395.

44. Klein, "Love, Guilt and Reparation," pp. 103–10.

45. For a discussion of Marcuse's idealization of deindividuation see my *Narcissism*, pp. 138–43.

46. Adorno, *Minima Moralia*, trans. E. F. N. Jephcott (London: NLB, 1974), p. 247. Willkuer covers an enormous range of possibilities, from free will to arbitrary action. With such a wide range of dictionary meanings available, the translator must obviously choose according to the context.

47. Adorno, *Negative Dialectics*, p. 43. The material from *Phaedrus* is found at 265e.

48. Jacques Derrida, *Of Grammatology*, trans. G. Spivak (Baltimore: Johns Hopkins University Press, 1976), pp. 104–05.

49. Klein, "Love, Guilt and Reparation," pp. 107–10.

50. Ibid., p. 110.

51. Lawrence Kohlberg, "A Reply to Owen Flanagan and Some Comments on the Puka-Goodpaster Exchange," *Ethics* 92 (April 1982): 513.

52. Kohlberg, "From Is to Ought," in *Cognitive Development and Epistemology*, ed. T. Mischel (New York: Academic Press, 1971).

53. Stephen White, *The Recent Work of Juergen Habermas: Reason, Justice and Modernity* (Cambridge: Cambridge University Press, 1988), p. 63; Habermas, *Communication and the Evolution of Society*, trans. T. McCarthy (Boston: Beacon Press, 1979), p. 78, for the status of stages. That Habermas has not changed his view regarding the content of stage seven is apparent from his discussion of the ideal of transparency, in "A Reply to my Critics," in *Habermas: Critical Debates*, ed. J. B. Thompson and D. Held (Cambridge: MIT Press, 1982), p. 235. See *Communication and the Evolution of Society*, p. 93, for the essential similarity with Habermas' "older" view.

54. Habermas, *Communication and the Evolution of Society*, pp. 93–94.

55. Marcuse, "On Hedonism," in *Negations*, trans. J. Shapiro (Boston: Beacon Press, 1968). pp. 159–64.

56. Habermas, *Moralbeweusstsein und kommunikatives Handeln* (Frankfurt am Main: Suhrkamp, 1983), p. 103; translated and quoted by White, *Recent Work of Habermas*, p. 57.

57. Fred Dallmayr, *Polis and Praxis: Exercises in Contemporary Politi-*

cal Theory (Cambridge: MIT Press, 1984), pp. 239–40. I follow White's discussion of Dallmayr closely here, in Recent Work of Habermas, pp. 46–47.

58. White, Recent Work of Habermas, p. 46.

59. Linda Kerber et al., "On In a Different Voice: An Interdisciplinary Forum," Signs 11 (1986): 329–30. Hereafter cited as Signs forum.

60. Ibid., pp. 312, 318, contributions by Kerber and Luria. Gielen, "Cross-Cultural Research on Moral Reasoning Employing the Defining Issues Test," paper presented at the Annual Meeting of the International Society for Political Psychology, New York, July 1–5, 1988.

61. Carol Gilligan, In a Different Voice: Psychological Theory and Women's Development (Cambridge: Harvard University Press, 1982), p. 2. Kerber et al., Signs forum, pp. 327–28.

62. Kerber et al., Signs forum, pp. 316–20.

63. Gilligan, A Different Voice, pp. 7–8. Nancy Chodorow, The Reproduction of Mothering (Berkeley: University of California Press, 1978).

64. Klein, "Love, Guilt and Reparation," pp. 76–82, on some male-female developmental differences. However, A Dictionary of Kleinian Thought notes that Klein's discussion of the "femininity phase" (a concern of hers in the 1920s and 1930s, when Freud's inadequate understanding of female psychology was becoming increasingly apparent) should not be seen strictly as a discussion of female sexuality. "Both boys and girls turn away from the first object (mother) to the father and his penis. In this sense they adopt a position of femininity." (p. 84) Once again, Klein emphasizes the problems boys and girls share—in this case, separation from the first object—more than she does the problems unique to each.

65. Kerber et al., Signs forum, p. 329.

66. Freud, "Some Psychical Consequences of the Anatomical Distinction Between the Sexes," The Standard Edition, vol. 19, pp. 257–58. Gilligan, A Different Voice, p. 7.

67. Gilligan, A Different Voice, p. 73.

CHAPTER 6: REPARATION AND CIVILIZATION

1. While recognizing that Klein's references to human nature ("constitutional" is a favorite term of hers) are often not references to nature at all but to passions, I have not hesitated to use the term "human nature." To make a claim about human nature is simply to state a hypothesis that may be false. If such a hypothesis is falsified, this does not, of course, falsify the very existence of human nature, but only the particular hypothesis. One risk in writing about human nature, a risk to which Klein frequently succumbs, is the tendency to employ it as a residual category along the lines of "I know that A causes B, and B causes C, but I don't know what causes A, so I'll call it human nature." Another risk is that contingent aspects of human behavior will be reified as given in nature. I have tried to be sensitive to both risks. The epistemological objection popular with Juergen Habermas and others, that we can only know what is called human nature through what is

not nature—the self as mediated by culture—does not eliminate the existence of human nature but only makes it impossible that we could know it in some sort of direct, unmediated fashion. But this is true of all knowledge. Despite these difficulties, I can see little virtue in such euphemisms as Joel Kovel's "transhistorical" human attributes (*The Age of Desire*, pp. 62–63). Either one talks about human nature or one does not. Not talking about human nature avoids some risks but invites others, such as viewing the self as little more than a mirror of its culture.

2. Klein, *Writings*, vol. 3, pp. 262–63.

3. Wollheim, *The Thread of Life*, pp. 216–18.

4. Freud, "On Narcissism," *The Standard Edition*, vol. 14, pp. 93–94. See my discussion of the complexity of the concept of the ego ideal in *Narcissism*, pp. 59–60, 210 n. 101.

5. Wollheim, *The Thread of Life*, p. 221.

6. Ibid., p. 224.

7. Rustin, "A Socialist Consideration of Kleinian Psychoanalysis," p. 96.

8. Ibid.

9. Little, *Political Ensembles*, pp. 50–55, 67.

10. Money-Kyrle, "Psycho-Analysis and Ethics," pp. 429–31. Money-Kryle's claim that paranoid-schizoid morality is essentially without content seems mistaken. Because paranoid-schizoid morality is based upon the projection of persecutors into the word, it leads to a worldview characterized by an "us versus them" mentality, in which the "them" becomes the evil other. Such a worldview must affect one's morality, even though it need not lead to a morality of hatred and revenge, as the Christian doctrine of "love thy enemy"—often (but not always) associated with a paranoid-schizoid worldview—reveals. Excessive idealization and black-and-white thinking are just as characteristic of paranoid-schizoid morality as overt hatred and aggression, and it is hard to see how a morality based upon fear of authority could avoid all of the above.

11. Ibid., p. 439

12. Rawls, *A Theory of Justice* (Cambridge: The Belknap Press of Harvard University Press, 1971).

13. Sheldon Wolin, *Politics and Vision* (Boston: Little, Brown and Co., 1960), p. 329.

14. Klein, "Envy and Gratitude," in *Writings*, vol. 3, pp. 176–235.

15. Robert Paul Wolff, *Understanding Rawls: A Reconstruction and Critique of A Theory of Justice* (Princeton: Princeton University Press, 1977), p. 80.

16. Rawls, *A Theory of Justice*, pp. 152–53.

17. Ibid., p. 490. More on these general laws shortly.

18. Wolff, *Understanding Rawls*, pp. 129–32, argues that in principle one cannot know the general laws of psychology behind the veil, in that knowledge of even general laws of psychology requires intimate knowledge

of oneself, such as that gained in the psychoanalytic transference. An insightful objection, it assumes that knowledge gained outside the original position cannot then be rendered abstract and objective, and so made available to those behind the veil, an assumption that Wolff does not defend. In any case, Wolff's objection does not apply to the psychological knowledge that fear of loss is the dominant motivation, since Rawls assumes that this fear operates unreflectively in all human beings—that is, it is not so much knowledge as nature.

19. Rawls, *A Theory of Justice*, p. 153.

20. Ibid., p. 490.

21. Klein, "Love, Guilt and Reparation," pp. 66–67.

22. Chodorow, *The Reproduction of Mothering*, pp. 50–52.

23. Ibid., p. 42.

24. Ibid., pp. 89–90.

25. Chodorow, p. 89, cites Klein's "Love, Guilt and Reparation," in support of her claim, but gives no page numbers.

26. Chodorow, *Reproduction of Mothering*, p. 205.

27. Chodorow, "Beyond Drive Theory," *Theory and Society* 14, no. 3 (1985): 307.

28. Thomas Kuhn, *The Essential Tension* (Chicago: University of Chicago Press, 1977), pp. xii–xiii.

29. Chodorow, "Beyond Drive Theory," p. 307.

30. Benjamin, "End of Internalization: Adorno," p. 63.

31. Benjamin, "Authority and the Family Revisited," p. 56.

32. Benjamin, *The Bonds of Love* (New York: Pantheon Books, 1988), p. 46.

33. Ibid., pp. 20–21; 251 n. 18.

34. Ibid., p. 49.

35. Dorothy Dinnerstein, *The Mermaid and the Minotaur* (New York: Harper Colophon Books, 1976), p. 141.

36. Lasch, *The Minimal Self*, p. 247.

37. Meltzer, *The Kleinian Development*, pt. 2, p. 64.

38. Dinnerstein, *The Mermaid and the Minotaur*, pp. 69, 93–94.

39. Ibid., p. 94, my emphasis.

40. Ibid., pp. 93–94, 113. Note Dinnerstein's surprisingly utopian tone—surprising because her assessment of the present is generally so glum.

41. Juliet Mitchell, *Psychoanalysis and Feminism* (New York: Random House, Vintage Books, 1974), pp. 8–9, passim.

References

Note: Classical sources given in the text in the form that is usual in classical studies are not repeated here.

Abraham, Karl. "A Short Study of the Development of the Libido, Viewed in the Light of Mental Disorders." In *Selected Papers of Karl Abraham.* London: Hogarth Press, 1968.

Abramson, Jeffrey B. *Liberation and Its Limits: The Moral and Political Thought of Freud.* Boston: Beacon Press, 1986.

Adorno, Theodor. *Aesthetic Theory.* Translated by C. Lenhardt. London: Routledge and Kegan Paul, 1984.

———. "Commitment." In *The Essential Frankfurt School Reader,* edited by A. Arato and E. Gebhardt. New York: Urizen Books, 1978.

———. *Dissonanzen.* Goettingen: Vandenhoek, 1972.

———. "Erpresste Versoehnung. Zu Georg Lukács: *Wider den missverstandenen Realismus.*" In *Theorien der Kunst,* edited by D. Henrich and W. Iser. Frankfurt am Main: Suhrkamp, 1984.

———. "Looking Back on Surrealism." In *The Idea of the Modern in Literature and the Arts,* edited by I. Howe. New York: Horizon Press, 1967.

———. "Lyric Poetry and Society." Translated by B. Mayo. *Telos* 20 (1974): 56–71.

———. *Minima Moralia: Reflexionen aus dem beschaedigten Leben.* Frankfurt am Main: Suhrkamp, 1951. Translated by E. F. N. Jephcott, under the title *Minima Moralia: Reflections from Damaged Life.*

———. *Negative Dialectics.* Translated by E. B. Ashton. New York: Seabury Press, 1973.

———. *Philosophy of Modern Music.* Translated by A. G. Mitchell and W. V. Blomster. New York: Seabury Press, 1973.

———. *Prisms.* Translated by S. and S. Weber. Cambridge: MIT Press, 1981.

———. "Die revidierte Psychoanalyse." In *Gesammelte Schriften,* 23 vols., edited by Rolf Tiedemann, vol. 8: pp. 3–42. Frankfurt am Main: Suhrkamp. 1970–.

———. "Social Science and Sociological Tendencies in Psychoanalysis." Unpublished (quoted in Martin Jay, *The Dialectical Imagination*, p. 105).

———. "Sociology and Psychology," part 2. *New Left Review* 47 (1968): 79–97.

———. "Subject and Object." In *The Essential Frankfurt School Reader*, edited by A. Arato and E. Gebhardt. New York: Urizen Books, 1978.

———. "Zur gesellschaftlichen Lage der Musik." *Zeitschrift fuer Sozialforschung* 1, no. 3 (1932): 349–63.

Adorno, Theodor, et al. *The Authoritarian Personality*. New York: Harper, 1950.

Alford, C. Fred. "*Eros and Civilization* After Thirty Years: A Reconsideration in Light of Recent Theories of Narcissism." *Theory and Society* 16 (1987): 869–90.

———. *Narcissism: Socrates, the Frankfurt School, and Psychoanalytic Theory*. New Haven: Yale University Press, 1988.

———. *Science and the Revenge of Nature: Marcuse and Habermas*. Gainesville: University Presses of Florida, 1985.

Bacon, Francis. *Advancement of Learning*. In *The Works of Francis Bacon*, 7 vols., edited by J. Spedding. London: Longman, 1870.

Baer, Brigitte. Brochure for the exhibit of Donald Sultan's *Black Lemons* at the Metropolitan Museum of Art. New York, Spring 1988.

Benjamin, Jessica. "Authority and the Family Revisited: Or, A World without Fathers?" *New German Critique* 13 (Winter 1978): 35–57.

———. *The Bonds of Love: Psychoanalysis, Feminism, and the Problem of Domination*. New York: Pantheon Books, 1988.

———. "The End of Internalization: Adorno's Social Psychology." *Telos* 32 (Summer 1977): 42–64.

Berman, Russell. "Adorno, Marxism and Art." *Telos* 34 (Winter 1977–78): 157–66.

Bion, Wilfred R. *Attention and Interpretation: A Scientific Approach to Insight in Psycho-Analysis and Groups*. New York: Basic Books, 1970.

———. *Experiences in Groups*. New York: Basic Books, 1961.

Brodbeck, May. "Methodological Individualisms: Definition and Reduction." In *Readings in the Philosophy of the Social Sciences*, edited by M. Brodbeck. New York: Macmillan, 1968.

Campbell, Angus, et al. *The American Voter*. New York: Wiley, 1960.

Cannon, Lou. *Reagan*. New York: Putnam, 1982.

Chasseguet-Smirgel, Janine. *The Ego Ideal*. Translated by P. Barrows. New York: W. W. Norton, 1984.

Chodorow, Nancy. "Beyond Drive Theory." *Theory and Society* 14, no. 3 (1985): 271–319.

———. *The Reproduction of Mothering: Psychoanalysis and the Sociology of Gender*. Berkeley: University of California Press, 1978.

———. "Toward a Relational Individualism: The Mediation of Self Through Psychoanalysis." In *Reconstructing Individualism*, edited by T. Heller,

Morton Sosna, and David Wellbery. Stanford: Stanford University Press, 1986.

Coles, Robert: *Privileged Ones.* Vol. 5 of *Children of Crisis.* Boston: Atlantic-Little, Brown and Co., 1967–78.

Croce, Benedetto. *Encyclopaedia Britannica,* 14th ed., s. v. "Aesthetics."

Dallek, Robert. *Ronald Reagan: The Politics of Symbolism.* Cambridge: Harvard University Press, 1984.

Dallmayr, Fred. *Polis and Praxis: Exercises in Contemporary Political Theory.* Cambridge: MIT Press, 1984.

de Maré, Patrick. "The Politics of Large Groups." In *The Large Group: Dynamics and Therapy,* edited by L. Kreeger. London: Maresfield Reprints, 1975.

deMause, Lloyd. *Reagan's America.* New York: Creative Roots, 1984.

Derrida, Jacques. *Of Grammatology.* Translated by G. Spivak. Baltimore: Johns Hopkins University Press, 1976.

Devereux, George. *Basic Problems of Ethnopsychiatry.* Translated by B. Miller Gulati and G. Devereux. Chicago: University of Chicago Press, 1980.

Dinnerstein, Dorothy. *The Mermaid and the Minotaur: Sexual Arrangements and Human Malaise.* New York: Harper Colophon Books, 1976.

Fairbairn, W. R. D. *Psychoanalytic Studies of the Personality.* London: Routledge and Kegan Paul, 1952.

Feyerabend, Paul. *Against Method.* London: NLB, 1975.

———. *Science in a Free Society.* London: NLB, 1978.

———. "Two Models of Epistemic Change: Mill and Hegel." In his *Philosophical Papers,* vol. 2: pp. 65–79. Cambridge: Cambridge University Press, 1981.

Freud, Sigmund. *Beyond the Pleasure Principle.* Translated by J. Strachey. New York: W. W. Norton, 1961.

———. *Civilization and Its Discontents.* Translated by J. Strachey. New York: W. W. Norton, 1961.

———. "The Dissolution of the Oedipus Complex," *The Standard Edition,* vol. 19: pp. 173–79.

———. "The Economic Problem of Masochism." In *Collected Papers,* 5 vols., edited by J. Strachey and J. Riviere, vol. 2: pp. 255–68. London: Hogarth Press, 1957.

———. *The Future of an Illusion.* Translated by J. Strachey. New York: W. W. Norton, 1961.

———. *Group Psychology and the Analysis of the Ego.* Translated by J. Strachey. New York: W. W. Norton, 1959.

———. "Inhibitions, Symptoms and Anxiety," *The Standard Edition,* vol. 20: pp. 75–175.

———. "Instincts and Their Vicissitudes." In *Collected Papers,* 5 vols., edited by J. Strachey and J. Riviere. vol. 4: pp. 60–83. London: Hogarth Press, 1957.

———. "Leonardo da Vinci and a Memory of his Childhood," *The Standard Edition,* vol. 11: pp. 59–137.

———. "On Narcissism," *The Standard Edition*, vol. 14: pp. 73–107.

———. "Some Psychical Consequences of the Anatomical Distinction Between the Sexes," *The Standard Edition*, vol. 19: pp. 243–58.

———. *The Standard Edition of the Complete Psychological Works of Sigmund Freud*, 24 vols., edited by J. Strachey. London: Hogarth Press, 1953–74.

———. *Three Essays on the Theory of Sexuality*. 4th ed. Translated by J. Strachey. New York: Basic Books, 1962.

———. "The 'Uncanny,' " *The Standard Edition*, vol. 17: pp. 217–52.

Gay, Peter. *Freud: A Life for Our Time*. New York: W. W. Norton, 1988.

Gielen, Uwe. "Cross-Cultural Research on Moral Reasoning Employing the Defining Issues Test," paper presented at the Annual Meeting of the International Society for Political Psychology, New York, July 1–5, 1988.

Gilligan, Carol. *In a Different Voice: Psychological Theory and Women's Development*. Cambridge: Harvard University Press, 1982.

Glad, Betty. "Black-and-White Thinking: Ronald Reagan's Approach to Foreign Policy." *Political Psychology* 4 (1983): 33–76.

Goffman, Erving. *The Presentation of Self in Everyday Life*. Garden City, N.Y.: Doubleday, 1959.

Goldmann, Lucien. *Colloque international sur la sociologie de la littérature*. Bruxelles: Institut de la Sociologie, 1974.

Gombrich, Ernst. "Norm und Form." In *Theorien der Kunst*, edited by D. Henrich and W. Iser. Frankfurt am Main: Suhrkamp, 1984.

Goodman, Nelson. *Languages of Art*. Indianapolis and New York: Bobbs-Merrill, 1967.

Greenberg, Jay, and Stephen Mitchell. *Object Relations in Psychoanalytic Theory*. Cambridge: Harvard University Press, 1983.

Griswold, Charles. *Self-Knowledge in Plato's Phaedrus*. New Haven: Yale University Press, 1986.

Grosskurth, Phyllis. *Melanie Klein: Her World and Her Work*. Cambridge: Harvard University Press, 1987.

Grünbaum, Adolf. *The Foundations of Psychoanalysis: A Philosophical Critique*. Berkeley: University of California Press, 1984.

Habermas, Juergen. *Communication and the Evolution of Society*. Translated by T. McCarthy. Boston: Beacon Press, 1979.

———. "The Entwinement of Myth and Enlightenment: Rereading *Dialectic of Enlightenment*." Translated by T. Levin. *New German Critique* 26 (1982): 13–30.

———. *Moralbeweusstsein und kommunikatives Handeln*. Frankfurt am Main: Suhrkamp, 1983. [*Communication and the Evolution of Society* is a translation of some of these essays.]

———. "Psychic Thermidor and the Rebirth of Rebellious Subjectivity." *Berkeley Journal of Sociology* 24–25 (1980): 1–12.

———. "A Reply to my Critics." In *Habermas: Critical Debates*, edited by J. B. Thompson and D. Held. Cambridge: MIT Press, 1982.

———. "Theodor W. Adorno: Urgeschichte der Subjektivitaet und verwilderte Selbstbehauptung." In *Philosophisch-politische Profile*, 184–99. Frankfurt am Main: Suhrkamp, 1971.

———. *The Theory of Communicative Action*. Vol. 1, *Reason and the Rationalization of Society*. Translated by T. McCarthy. Boston: Beacon Press, 1984. Originally published as *Theorie des kommunikativen Handelns*, 2 vols. (Frankfurt am Main: Suhrkamp, 1981).

Haug, Wolfgang Fritz. "Das Ganze und das ganz Andere: Zur Kritik der reinen revolutionaeren Transzendenz." In *Antworten auf Herbert Marcuse*, edited by J. Habermas. Frankfurt am Main: Suhrkamp, 1968.

Hegel, G. W. F. *The Philosophy of Fine Art*, 4 vols. Translated by F. P. B. Osmaston. London: G. Bell and Sons, 1920.

Heidegger, Martin. "The Origin of the Work of Art." In *Poetry, Language, Thought*. Translated by A. Hofstadter. New York: Harper and Row, 1971.

Held, David. *Introduction to Critical Theory: Horkheimer to Habermas*. Berkeley: University of California Press, 1980.

Hinshelwood, R. D. *A Dictionary of Kleinian Thought*. London: Free Association Books, 1989.

Hofstadter, Albert, and Richard Kuhns, eds. *Philosophies of Art and Beauty*. Chicago: University of Chicago Press, Phoenix edition, 1976.

Hohendahl, Peter Uwe. "Autonomy of Art: Looking Back at Adorno's *Aesthetische Theorie*." In *Foundations of the Frankfurt School of Social Research*, edited by J. Marcus and Z. Tar. New Brunswick, N. J.: Transaction Books, 1984.

Horkheimer, Max. "Authority and the Family." In *Critical Theory*, translated by M. O'Connell et al. New York: Seabury Press, 1972.

———. "Authority and the Family Today." In *The Family: Its Function and Destiny*, edited by R. Anshen. New Yorker: Harper, 1949.

———. *Eclipse of Reason*. New York: Seabury Press, 1974.

———. "Materialism and Morality." *Telos* 69 (Fall 1986): 85–118.

Horkheimer, Max, and Theodor Adorno. *Dialectic of Enlightenment*. Translated by J. Cumming. New York: Herder and Herder, 1972.

Huffington, Arianna S. *Picasso: Creator and Destroyer*. New York: Simon and Schuster, 1988.

Isaacs, Susan. "The Nature and Function of Phantasy." In *Developments in Psycho-Analysis*, by M. Klein et al. London: Hogarth Press, 1952.

Jaques, Elliott. "Social Systems as Defence Against Persecutory and Depressive Anxiety." In *New Directions in Psycho-Analysis*, edited by M. Klein, P. Heimann, and R. Money-Kyrle. London: Tavistock, 1955.

Jay, Martin. *Adorno*. Cambridge: Harvard University Press, 1984.

———. *The Dialectical Imagination*. Boston: Little, Brown and Co., 1973.

Kerber, Linda, et al. "On *In a Different Voice*: An Interdisciplinary Forum." *Signs* 11 (1986): 304–33. (This issue contains articles by Kerber, Catherine Greeno and Eleanor Maccoby, Zella Luria, Carol Stack, and Gilligan.)

Kernberg, Otto. *Internal World and External Reality: Object Relations Theory Applied*. Northvale, N. J.: Jason Aronson, 1985.

Kinder, D. R., and R. P. Abelson. "Appraising Presidential Candidates:

Personality and Affect in the 1980 Campaign." Paper presented at the 1981 meeting of the American Political Science Association, New York.

Kinder, D. R., and S. T. Fiske. "Presidents in the Public Mind." In *Political Psychology*, edited by M. Hermann. San Francisco: Jossey-Bass, 1986.

Klein, Melanie. "Envy and Gratitude." In *Writings*, vol. 3, pp. 176–235.

———. "The Importance of Symbol Formation in the Development of the Ego." In *Writings*, vol. 1, pp. 219–32.

———. "Love, Guilt and Reparation." In *Love, Hate and Reparation*, by Klein and J. Riviere. New York: W. W. Norton, 1964.

———. "Mourning and Its Relation to Manic-Depressive States." In *Writings*, vol. 1, pp. 344–69.

———. "Notes on Some Schizoid Mechanisms." In *Writings*, vol. 3, pp. 1-24.

———. "The Oedipus Complex in the Light of Early Anxieties." In *Writings*, vol. 1, pp. 370–419.

———. "On the Theory of Anxiety and Guilt." In *Writings*, vol. 3, pp. 25–42.

———. "The Origins of Transference." In *Writings*, vol. 3, pp. 48–56.

———. *The Writings of Melanie Klein*, 4 vols., edited by R. E. Money-Kyrle. New York: Free Press, 1964–75.

Kohlberg, Lawrence. "From Is to Ought." In *Cognitive Development and Epistemology*, edited by T. Mischel. New York: Academic Press, 1971.

———. "A Reply to Owen Flanagan and Some Comments on the Puka-Goodpaster Exchange." *Ethics* 92 (April 1982): 513–28.

Kohut, Heinz. *The Restoration of the Self*. New York: International Universities Press, 1977.

Kovel, Joel. *The Age of Desire: Reflections of a Radical Psychoanalyst*. New York: Pantheon Books, 1981.

Krieger, Murray. *The Tragic Vision*. Chicago: University of Chicago Press, 1966.

Kuhn, Thomas. *The Essential Tension*. Chicago: University of Chicago Press, 1977.

Langer, Susanne. *Problems of Art: Ten Philosophical Lectures*. New York: Scribner's, 1957.

Lasch, Christopher. *The Minimal Self*. New York: W. W. Norton, 1984.

Leiss, William. *The Domination of Nature*. Boston: Beacon Press, 1974.

Little, Graham. *Political Ensembles: A Psychosocial Approach to Politics and Leadership*. Oxford: Oxford University Press, 1985.

Main, Tom. "Some Psychodynamics of Large Groups." In *The Large Group: Dynamics and Therapy*, edited by L. Kreeger. London: Maresfield Reprints, 1975.

Marcuse, Herbert. *The Aesthetic Dimension*. Boston: Beacon Press, 1978.

———. *Counterrevolution and Revolt*. Boston: Beacon Press, 1972.

———. *Eros and Civilization*. Boston: Beacon Press, 1966.

———. *An Essay on Liberation*. Boston: Beacon Press, 1969.

———. *Five Lectures: Psychoanalysis, Politics, and Utopia*. Translated by Jeremy Shapiro and Shierry Weber. Boston: Beacon Press, 1970.

————. "On Hedonism." In *Negations*, translated by J. Shapiro. Boston: Beacon Press, 1968.

————. *One-Dimensional Man*. Boston: Beacon Press, 1964.

————. "Ueber die philosophischen Grundlagen des wirtschaftswissenschaftslichen Arbeitsbegriffs." In *Kultur und Gesellschaft*, by Marcuse, vol. 2, pp. 7–48. Frankfurt am Main: Suhrkamp, 1965.

Markus, G. B. "Political Attitudes During an Election Year: A Report on the 1980 NES Panel Study." *American Political Science Review* 76 (1982): 538–60.

Meltzer, Bernard, and J. Petras. "The Chicago and Iowa Schools of Symbolic Interactionism." In *Symbolic Interaction*, 2d ed., edited by J. Manis and B. Meltzer. Boston: Allyn and Bacon, 1972.

Meltzer, Donald. *The Kleinian Development*, 3 pts. in 1 vol. Perthshire, Scotland: Clunie Press, 1978.

————. "The Kleinian Expansion of Freud's Metapsychology." *International Journal of Psycho-Analysis* 62 (1981): 177–84.

Miller, Warren, and J. Merril Shanks. "Policy Directions and Presidential Leadership: Alternative Interpretations of the 1980 Presidential Election." *British Journal of Political Science* 12 (1982): 299–356.

Mitchell, Juliet. *Psychoanalysis and Feminism*. New York: Random House, Vintage Books, 1974.

Money-Kyrle, Roger E. "Psycho-Analysis and Ethics." In *New Directions in Psycho-Analysis*, edited by M. Klein, P. Heimann, and R. Money-Kyrle. London: Tavistock, 1955.

————. *Psycho-Analysis and Politics*. London: Duckworth, 1951.

Nagel, Ernest. *The Structure of Science*. New York: Harcourt, Brace and World, 1961.

Niebuhr, Reinhold. *Moral Man and Immoral Society*. New York: Scribner's, 1960.

Nietzsche, Friedrich W. *The Birth of Tragedy*. In *Basic Writings of Nietzsche*, edited and translated by W. Kaufmann. New York: Modern Library, 1968.

Nussbaum, Martha. *The Fragility of Goodness: Luck and Ethics in Greek Tragedy and Philosophy*. Cambridge: Cambridge University Press, 1966.

Popper, Karl. *The Logic of Scientific Discovery*. New York: Harper and Row, 1968.

Proust, Marcel. *Remembrance of Things Past*, vol. 3. Translated by C. K. S. Moncrieff et al. New York: Vintage Press, 1982.

Public Opinion 8, no. 2 (1985).

Public Opinion 8, no. 4 (1985).

Public Opinion 8, no. 6 (1986).

Public Opinion 9, no. 4 (1986).

Rawls, John. *A Theory of Justice*. Cambridge: The Belknap Press of Harvard University Press, 1971.

Reagan, Ronald, and Richard Hubler. *Where's the Rest of Me?* 1965. Reprint. New York: Karz Publishers, 1981.

Rilke, Rainer Maria. *Letters on Cézanne.* Translated by Joel Agee. New York: Fromm International, 1985.

Riviere, Joan. "The Inner World in Ibsen's *Master-Builder.*" In *New Directions in Psycho-Analysis,* edited by M. Klein, P. Heimann, and R. Money-Kyrle. London: Tavistock, 1955.

———. "On the Genesis of Psychical Conflict in Early Infancy." In *Developments in Psycho-Analysis,* by M. Klein, Paula Heimann, Susan Isaacs, and Joan Riviere. London: Hogarth Press, 1952.

———. "The Unconscious Phantasy of an Inner World Reflected in Examples from Literature." In *New Directions in Psycho-Analysis,* edited by M. Klein, P. Heimann, and R. Money-Kyrle. London: Tavistock, 1955.

Roazen, Paul. *Freud: Political and Social Thought.* New York: Vintage Books, 1968.

Rogin, Michael. *Ronald Reagan, The Movie.* Berkeley: University of California Press, 1987.

Rousseau, Jean-Jacques. *Emile.* Translated by A. Bloom. New York: Basic Books, 1979.

Rustin, Michael. "A Socialist Consideration of Kleinian Psychoanalysis." *New Left Review* 131 (1982): 71–96.

Sandel, Michael. *Liberalism and the Limits of Justice.* Cambridge: Cambridge University Press, 1982.

Sears, D. O. and R. R. Lau. "Inducing Apparently Self-Interested Political Preferences." *American Journal of Political Science* 27 (1988): 223–52.

Segal, Hanna. *Melanie Klein.* Harmondsworth, England: Penguin Books, 1981.

———. "A Psycho-Analytical Approach to Aesthetics." In *New Directions in Psycho-Analysis,* edited by M. Klein, P. Heimann, and R. Money-Kyrle. London: Tavistock, 1955.

Sewall, Richard. *The Vision of Tragedy.* New Haven: Yale University Press, 1959.

Smith, George H. *Who Is Ronald Reagan?* New York: Pyramid Books, 1968.

Spillius, Elizabeth. "Some Developments from the Work of Melanie Klein." *International Journal of Psycho-Analysis* 64 (1983): 321–32.

Stokes, Adrian. *The Invitation in Art.* New York: Chilmark Press, 1965.

———. *Three Essays on the Painting of Our Time.* London: Tavistock, 1961.

Strachey, James. "Some Unconscious Factors in Reading." *International Journal of Psycho-Analysis* 11 (1930): 322–31.

Torpey, John. "Ethics and Critical Theory: From Horkheimer to Habermas." *Telos* 69 (Fall 1986): 68–83.

Turner, Ralph. "The Role and the Person." *American Journal of Sociology* 84 (July): 1–23.

Turquet, Pierre. "Threats to Identity in the Large Group." In *The Large Group: Dynamics and Therapy,* edited by L. Kreeger. London: Maresfield Reprints, 1975.

Volkan, Vamik D. "Narcissistic Personality Organization and 'Reparative'

Leadership." *International Journal of Group Psychotherapy* 30 (1980): 131–52.

———. *The Need to Have Enemies and Allies: From Clinical Practice to International Relationships.* Northvale, N. J.: Jason Aronson, 1988.

White, Stephen. *The Recent Work of Juergen Habermas: Reason, Justice and Modernity.* Cambridge: Cambridge University Press, 1988.

Wills, Garry. *Reagan's America: Innocents at Home.* Garden City, N.Y.: Doubleday, 1987.

Winnicott, Donald W. *Holding and Interpretation.* New York: Grove Press, 1986.

———. *The Maturational Processes and the Facilitating Environment.* New York: International Universities Press, 1965.

Wolff, Robert Paul. *Understanding Rawls: A Reconstruction and Critique of A Theory of Justice.* Princeton: Princeton University Press, 1977.

Wolin, Richard. "The De-Aestheticization of Art: On Adorno's *Aesthetische Theorie.*" *Telos* 41 (Fall 1979): 105–27.

Wolin, Sheldon. *Politics and Vision: Continuity and Innovation in Western Political Thought.* Boston: Little, Brown and Co., 1960.

Wollheim, Richard. "Freud and the Understanding of Art." *British Journal of Aesthetics* 10 (1970): 211–24.

———. *The Thread of Life.* Cambridge: Harvard University Press, 1984.

Zurcher, Louis. *Social Roles: Conformity Conflict and Creativity.* Beverly Hills, Calif.: Sage, 1983.

Index